Patronage in Early Christianity

Princeton Theological Monograph Series

K. C. Hanson, Charles M. Collier, D. Christopher Spinks,
and Robin Parry, Series Editors

Recent volumes in the series:

Linda Hogan
Religion and Politics of Peace and Conflict

Chris Budden
Following Jesus in Invaded Space

Ryan Neal
Theology as Hope

David Hein
Geoffrey Fisher

Catherine L. Kelsey
Schleiermacher's Preaching, Dogmatics, and Biblical Criticism

Christian Collins-Winn
"Jesus Is Victor!"

Abraham Kunnuthara
Schleiermacher on Christian Consciousness of God's Work in History

Paul S. Chung
Martin Luther and Buddhism

Philip Ruge-Jones
Cross in Tensions

Jedediah Mannis
Joseph Tuckerman and the Outdoor Church

Jerry Root
C. S. Lewis and the Problem of Evil

Pérez-Álvarez , Eliseo
A Vexing Gadfly

Patronage in Early Christianity

Its Use and Transformation from Jesus to Paul of Samosata

Alan B. Wheatley

☙PICKWICK *Publications* · Eugene, Oregon

PATRONAGE IN EARLY CHRISTIANITY
Its Use and Transformation from Jesus to Paul of Samosata

Princeton Theological Monograph Series 160

Copyright © 2011 Alan B. Wheatley. All rights reserved. Except for brief quotations in critical publications or reviews, no part of this book may be reproduced in any manner without prior written permission from the publisher. Write: Permissions, Wipf and Stock Publishers, 199 W. 8th Ave., Suite 3, Eugene, OR 97401.

Pickwick Publications
An Imprint of Wipf and Stock Publishers
199 W. 8th Ave., Suite 3
Eugene, OR 97401

www.wipfandstock.com

ISBN 13: 978-1-59752-587-9

Cataloging-in-Publication data:

Wheatley, Alan B.

    Patronage in early christianity : its use and transformation from Jesus to Paul of Samosata / Alan B. Wheatley.

    Princeton Theological Monograph Series 160

    viii + 204 p. ; 23 cm. Includes bibliographical references.

    ISBN 13: 978-1-59752-587-9

    1. Patronage. 2. Church history—Primitive and early church, 30–600—Social aspects. I. Title.

BR166 W45 2011

Manufactured in the U.S.A.

Contents

List of Abbreviations / vii

1. Patronage: The Heart of Roman Life / 1
2. The Challenge to Traditional Patronage in the New Testament / 9
3. Early Church Order Documents / 43
4. The Christian Communities at Rome / 52
5. The Work of Irenaeus of Lyons / 78
6. The Christian Communities around the Aegean / 85
7. The Christian Communities of Syria and Osrhoene / 101
8. The Christian Communities in Alexandria and Southern Palestine / 129
9. The Christian Communities of Northwest Africa / 155
10. Conclusion: An Overview of the Patristic Project / 178

Appendix 1 / 189
Appendix 2 / 191
Bibliography / 195

Abbreviations

Ancient

Ad Auto.	Theophilus, *Ad Autolycum*
Adv. Haer.	Irenaeus, *Adversus Haereses*
Adv. Marc.	*Adversus Marcion*
Apol.	Aristides, *Apology*
Apol.	Tertullian, *Apologeticum*
1 Apol.	Justin, *First Apology*
2 Apol.	Justin, *Second Apology*
Ap. Tr.	Hippolytus, *Apostolic Tradition*
Banq.	Methodius, *The Banquet*
Barn.	*Epistle of Barnabas*
1 Clem.	*1 Clement*
Cont. Marc.	Tertullian, *Contra Marcion*
De Ben.	Seneca, *De Beneficia*
Dem.	Cyprian, *To Demetrian*
Dial.	Justin, *Dialogue with Trypho*
Did.	*Didache*
Domin.	Cyprian, *De Dominica Oratatione*
Don.	Cyprian, *Ad Donatum*
Eccl.	Cyprian, *De Catholicae Ecclesiae Unitate*
Eph.	Ignatius, *To the Ephesians*
Hab.	Cyprian, *De Habitu Virginum*
H.E.	Eusebius, *Historia ecclesiasticus*
Laps.	Cyprian, *De Lapsis*
Magn.	Ignatius, *To the Magnesians*
Man.	*Shepherd of Hermas, Mandates*
Marc.	Tertullian, *Adversus Marcionem*
Mart. Pol.	*Martyrdom of Polycarp*
Mort.	Cyprian, *De Mortalitate*
Opere	Cyprian, *De Opere et Eleemosynis*
Pan.	Epiphanius, *Panarion*
Pasc. Hom.	Melito of Sardis, *Pascal Homily*

Pat.	Tertullian, *De Patientia*
Paen.	Tertullian, *De Paenitentia*
Phil.	Polycarp, *Letter to the Philippians*
Philad.	Ignatius, *To the Philadelphians*
Poly.	Ignatius, *To Polycarp*
Praes.	Tertullian, *De Praescriptione hereticorum*
Ref. Haer.	Hippolytus, *Refutatio Omnium Haeresium*
Rom.	Ignatius, *To the Romans*
Sim.	*Shepherd of Hermas, Similitudes*
Smyr.	Ignatius, *To the Smyrneans*
Spect.	Tertullian, *Spectaculis*
Trall.	Ignatius, *To the Trallians*
Virg.	Tertullian, *De Virginibus Valandis*
Zelo	Cyprian, *De Zelo et Livore*

Modern

ACW	Ancient Christian Writers
ANF	Ante Nicene Fathers
ANL	Ante Nicene Library
CSEL	Corpus Scriptorum Christianorum Latinorum
CSCO	Corpus Scriptorum Christianorum Orientalium
ET	English Translation
FOC	Fathers of the Church
GCS	Die griechischen christlicher Schriftstellar
JECS	*Journal of Early Christian Studies*
JSNT	*Journal for the Study of the New Testament*
JSNTSup	Journal for the Study of the New Testament Supplement Series
LCL	Loeb Classical Library
New Docs.	*New Documents Illustrating Early Christianity: A Review of the Greek Inscriptions and Papyri*
NovT	*Novum Testamentum*
OECT	Oxford Early Christian Texts
PMS	Patristic Monograph Series
SBL	Society of Biblical Literature
SC	Sources Chretiennes
TDNT	*Theological Dictionary of the New Testament*

Patronage
The Heart of Roman Life

THE STUDY OF EARLY CHRISTIANITY HAS OFTEN FOCUSED UPON THE theological, the moral and the institutional. As valuable as these studies have been, important aspects of social relationships in the early Christian community, indeed the social shape of that community, have been less examined. The purpose of this volume is to give clearer focus upon the dynamics of the early Christian community by a thorough examination of the use and transformation of a primary social practice, patronage. That which Seneca stated "binds society together" cannot have been either ignored or unchanged in a religion in which the Kingdom of God was to modify or replace the current form of society.

In this chapter I will outline the functions of patronage in different areas of Roman society. In chapter two, I will use this outline as background for examining the function of patron/client relation among members of the early Christian community, and for attention to and critique of the practices that are presented in the New Testament. These two chapters will serve, in turn, as the basis for examination of successive periods in early Christian history and in various areas in which it occurred, from about 90 to 290 CE, though the last major figure is Paul of Samosata.

The Setting in Roman Society

In its various forms, patronage consisted of long term relationships, bonded by a reciprocal exchange of resources between partners of unequal position. Within Roman society, reciprocity functioned in three primary ways. Generalized reciprocity was the pattern that typified family relations, where gifts were given because of the bond and honor of the family, without expecting equivalent repayment. Negative reciprocity was the refusal to honor a gift or repay it, deliberately conveying an assessment of the value of the giver. Balanced or mutual reciprocity was the practice of giving or accepting a gift with the understanding that a response of gratitude and obligation was expected. In this last arena, when the parties were of decisively different rank, resources or status, the result was a patron/client relation, or patronage.

All forms of reciprocity functioned within an honor and shame framework, where every male was expected to maintain or increase honor every day. Honor consisted of a perception of worth for oneself and one's family that was accepted and affirmed by the community in perceptible ways.

Generalized reciprocity was testimony to the coherence of the family. Negative reciprocity attempted to reduce the honor of another, while balanced reciprocity increased the honor of both parties, though not necessarily in the same manner or with the same measure.

An Overview of Patron/Client Relations

Patronage brought protection, assistance or sponsorship from individuals to both individuals and communities, in an informal and extralegal manner, with the exception of the legally regulated one between freedmen and their former owners. Evidence for the function and prevalence of these relationships has been found in personal letters and letters of commendation, in the formal literature of the Roman period, in works which are specifically dedicated to the ideal, in papyri and in inscriptions. The resources that the benefactor brought to the reciprocal ethic included such obvious factors as wealth, power, and influence. It could, however include other less obvious and associative matters, such as noble birth, education and its effects, and moral stature or holiness. Some figures with perceived connection to divine or quasi-divine powers were able to be patrons in the field of religion. Patrons were able to change the circumstances of the clients either by using a resource on their behalf, or using it to widen their horizon. Thus even those who were justifiably viewed as "the great ones" could and did stand in need of those holding resources of a religious nature, as evidenced by their ambivalent relationships to shrines, oracles, and soothsayers. By accessing the connection of such entities to power or knowledge beyond the and support, and the point was never to balance the equation, but to continue the bond and maintain honor. As Hands notes: "it is not the isolated 'gift' which is significant, but the whole sequence of relationship which it establishes or confirms." In a most interesting letter, Pliny indicated that the Baetici have asked for his services as a prosecutor, based on their need and upon his prior service to them, which he affirmed as "ties of hospitality." Pliny further noted: "I felt I ought to maintain my credit with them for my former service by adding a new one. It is generally agreed that past benefits cease to count unless confirmed by later ones; for if a single thing is denied people who have every reason to be grateful, the denial is all they remember" (*Letters* III,4). Though this illustrates the relationship of a patron to a corporate group, it is clear that the long-term relationship involved new *beneficia*. Pliny also affirmed, in sometimes moving language, his gratitude to former patrons Corellius Rufus (I,12) and Vergilius Rufus (II,1). This gratitude was the basis for further favors on behalf of the remaining families of these patrons. This exchange and brokering of resources has been effectively documented from the higher estates. Very clear lines of decorum were involved, and the language is quite clear in epistolary material. The great or good man also acted on behalf of groups, from a *collegium* to a province, and these benefits and the responses are well documented in inscriptions throughout the Empire. Substantive benefits, such as either building or provisioning a public bath, were celebrated along with actions such as representation to higher authorities. Long-term endowments proved difficult to manage, since civic machinery did not provide well for guarding them, so various provisions were made. Pliny related how he arranged a carefully constructed trust for the support of freeborn children, by dedicating the proceeds of a piece of land which was rented for much less than it could yield, thereby assuring that it would never lack a tenant (VII,18). Frederick Danker catalogued the language used in numerous inscriptions in which tasks done and responsibilities assumed by benefactors were remembered with honorifics and descriptions of the attitudes which were demonstrated by the same.

In addition to answering the good works (*euergesiai*) of their patrons, the stimulation of others to imitation was an underlying goal, as shown by an inscription which includes the following language: "So that all people may know that the people of Histaia understand how to honor their benefactors and that more may be responsive to the best more mundane, they were able to function in light of or in connection with powers or gods beyond their immediate control.

Those who received *beneficia* from their patrons answered with support publicly given. Among the upper classes, cooperation for widely varied purposes of advancement was exchanged, from formal nomination for offices to recommendations to others with influence. Between the upper and lower classes, the support took the form of the *salutatio*, a spoken acknowledgment of the patron's importance, accolades by the more gifted, and small favors. The perceived value for the upper classes included social coherence or stability, as well as establishing and enhancing honor. Value for the lower classes ranged from survival to some measure of advancement. Though voluntary on both parts, such relations lasted for long periods. Exploration of the range of such relations will show their variety and commonality.

Patronage was frequent in relations between members of the higher estates, under the general rubric of "friendship" (*amicitia* or *philia*), for the terms *patronus* and *cliens* were avoided as indicating strong social difference. The term of choice was "friend" (*amicus* and *philos*), with such adjectives such as *maior* or *inferior* added to indicate a dependence that often was temporary, though the bond was permanent. Various resources could be given for career advancement (the *cursus honorum*), either by direct request or by request of another friend with a prior bond, which we will call "brokering," following the suggestion of Bruce J. Malina. As Seneca said: "help one man with money, another with credit, another with influence, another with advice, another with sound precepts" (*De Ben.* I,2,4). In evidence from the letters of Pliny, fellow townsman Romatius Firmus received 300,000 sesterces so that he could enter into the equestrian ranks (*Epistles* I,19), and a mutual friend was challenged to make sure that Suetonius was able to buy a particular property for a good price (*Letters* I,24). Suetonius' gratitude to Pliny was shown by the tone in which he made a request to Pliny on behalf of one of his relatives (*Letters* III, 8). In one of his letters, Dio Chrysostom commends one friend to another in these words: "But though you do me many favors in many matters, it would favor me especially if you would also consider Herrenius a friend of yours."

The expected response was gratitude, both that which was expressed and that which remained as a bond that could be called upon later in time of need. Many favors could granted, including hospitality

interests of the city, as they see worthy people in receipt of honors..."
At this point a talented and trained orator could fill a "broker" role by speaking eloquently of the worth and greatness of a patron, then asking favors on behalf of his community. Plutarch recommended that one who has the favor of great men should seek the benefit of one's own community (*Precepts of Statecraft* 18).

Relations between patrons and communities could appear to be disadvantageous to the patron. The wealthy benefactors often even paid for the inscription or statue with which the community honored them, "being content with the honor alone." Titles were sometimes given in graded proportion to the size of a gift or favor. The communities could be demanding, even somewhat threatening, as Dio Chrysostom's defense of his actions and abilities to his detractors in Prusa demonstrated. Nevertheless, it would seem that the relations between communities and their benefactors were often equable. On some occasions the attachment could be ferocious, as in the example Syme cites, when the citizens of Cales refused to surrender their patron, Sittius, to the proscriptions of the Triumvirate, and backed their refusal with arms.

It is of significant interest to our project that the members of higher estates also functioned as benefactors to the communities by facilitating the practice of religion. Among the inscriptions are those that thank the leading citizens for building and maintaining the temples, providing resources for periodic festivals, and serving as the priests in some cases. Since the practice of traditional religion was understood to be essential to the wellbeing of the whole community, these gifts by those of higher status were both expected and honored. To a significant extent, those who were benefactors in other more mundane areas also acted as brokers in the area of public religion. Both the Jewish and Christian communities can be seen as claiming to be brokers of divine benefits on a much larger scale. On a smaller scale, itinerant teachers and healers could function as brokers of divine power, and be sought as such by persons of any rank or status.

Another area of benefaction combined public and private, the patronage of literary and artistic figures. These figures offered well-developed gifts, and could enhance the prestige of the patron simply by association, or to extol his excellence by written or spoken word, or in visual art. In a larger sense, however, the productions often became available to the society, increasing and enhancing the culture. As such, the patronage could extend through several levels. Some patrons also provided instruction for a community through paying the living expenses of gifted individuals, or provided the artist's expenses by appointments either to their own staff or to other posts in the imperial administration.

Resources were also extended to those who were properly called *cliens*. Those with resources and influence provided protection and assistance of various kinds for the less fortunate. Paul Millett documents that the patron (*prostatēs*) acted as a mediator for non-citizens needing access to civic institutions. Connections and positions as well as financial or legal assistance were all available to those in client relationship to a patron. Recipients far below the status of the "good man" were often required to show their gratitude and dependence by regular, even daily, attendance as well as the morning *salutatio*. The retinue thus seen at the gate, in a procession or as applauders in court, constituted an essential part of the public image of those aspiring for office, or simply enhanced their honor publicly. The client was also available for various tasks and could receive, in addition to the possibility of larger favors, an "allowance" called the *sportula*, which has been estimated to be about 7 sesterces daily. One need not assume that the rather gritty picture of this common patronage painted by Juvenal and Martial was universal in order to conclude that for some, at least, it approached slavery. There is little doubt that the warmth and courtliness visible in *amicitia* among the higher estates were much less available to the *cliens*, and that the gratitude more often was felt and expressed as obligation. Seneca and others give us insight into the varied ways in which the ideal might function and be perceived.

In terms of corporate understanding of the practice, two quotes may frame the question. Polybius acidly stated: "no one ever gives anything of his own willingly to anybody." Seneca balanced that sentiment with one of his own: "even were I deprived of the hope of finding a grateful man, I should prefer not recovering benefits to not giving them ... He who does not return a benefit, sins more; he who does not give one, sins earlier" (*De Ben.* I,1, 13). This statement can be confirmed by Cicero (*De Amicitia* 9,31). Yet Seneca's *De Beneficia*, in its chiding of his peers, provides evidence that partially confirms Polybius' suspicions. Finding it necessary to insist that his peers continue to provide benefits, Seneca provided a brief catalog of unworthy attitudes and actions which he had observed in those in patron roles (I,2, 4; I,1,4–8). Similarly, Pliny found it necessary and appropriate to correct one of his peers, who was absenting himself from Rome. Pliny, speaking quite bluntly, accused his friend of neglecting "your honors and official duties, your influential friendships and your clients' attention" (*Letters* VII,3). Plutarch said "the masses are more hostile to a rich man who does not give them a share of his private possessions than to a poor man who steals from the public funds . . ." (*Precepts of Statecraft* 30), pointing also to the problem of persons capable of patronage who do not extend themselves to be benevolent. Yet we have much more evidence that many did so and with apparent good will. What were their motives, and what was the underlying social theory, or ideology?

In addition to the aspect of social bonding, which is mentioned often enough to be well accepted by the higher estates (and probably by some of the lower, for whom the arrangement worked effectively and/or pleasantly), a primary motive was *philotimia* or the *cursus honorum*. Ambition was not considered inappropriate, but rather was expected and praised. The *amici* and benefactors cooperated in public honor and ambition, for the same was applauded as a worthy motive by the clients or friends. Chrysippus happily termed it "a most honorable competition."[1] Yet part of being the "great man" was an attitude toward giving that did not seek profit, did not demand a return, and which did recognize the common good involved in benevolent relationships. Seneca, in expounding the theory of patronage, argued for a more spiritual nature. Note the following: "a benefit cannot possibly be touched by the hand, its province is the mind . . ." (*De Ben.* I,5,2); "There is a great difference between the matter (*materiam*) of a benefit and the benefit itself, and so it is neither gold nor silver nor any of the gifts which are held to be most valuable that constitutes a benefit, but merely the goodwill of him who bestows it (I,5,2). In keeping with this ideal, Seneca placed great emphasis upon the attitude of the "good man" who is appropriately grateful, for in making his gratitude clear, he returns benefit (I,1,3). Again, though it is the privilege of the benefactor to seek for the "good man" and even to prioritize gifts in the direction of such individuals, the activity of the benefactor is not limited to them, for the value of benefaction is greater than the sum of individual actions (I,10,5; I,1,12).

---

1. Hands, *Charities*, 31.

It would seem, then, that the ideology accepted by higher and lower estates is that those capable of patronage were expected to extend their resources in a variety of ways, expected to be honored and answered by the recipients, of whatever rank or nature, and that these reciprocal relations constituted a primary bonding of the community as well as significant energy for movement upward or forward. That the conventions as accepted did not always function as expected can be assumed, yet we can say with confidence that the variety of relationships sketched above did constitute elements of typical social structure.

Questions for the Study of the New Testament

From the brief exposition of the practice and vitality of patronage in Graeco-Roman society, the following questions should be posed to New Testament writings:

1. Were the practices of patronage to be abolished, transformed in some way, or used with minor modifications?

2. What was the received position of those who normally functioned as patrons? Were they excluded, received with reservations, welcomed with open arms? Indeed, was there an accepted pattern?

3. How were the commonly extended resources viewed? Were there new resources that are available, thus defining patrons differently? If so, what were the perceived relative values?

4. How was the process of honor-giving viewed? Were the same honorifics appropriate? Were some excluded and why? Were some redefined, and how? Were new honorifics created? Were positions within the community granted on the basis of favors granted? Was the whole pattern refined, inverted or simply abolished?

5. What difficulties are visible in the New Testament with the dynamic and definition of a community, and in the application of the critique or reconstruction?

2

The Challenge to Traditional Patronage in the New Testament

When attention is turned to the New Testament, considerable use of and reference to the practice of patronage can be found. In this chapter, I will present select evidence[1] found there, giving both my own findings and those of scholars who are working in this area. I will demonstrate the following in successive sections:

1. The practice of patronage is clearly visible in New Testament material, both in the social world there portrayed and in the operations of the early Christian community.

2. In usage and instruction regarding patron/client relations, early Christian leaders substantially redirected the form and dynamic of the practice. This redirection was initiated by Jesus of Nazareth, and was followed by the primary leaders, as far as can be detected.

3. Early leaders experienced significant difficulties in applying the new paradigm of patronage, both in unconscious assumptions and in conscious rejection, among new members.

Glimpsing the Traditional Paradigm

Patronage among the elite, as outlined in chapter one, can be glimpsed in Acts 24:27 and 25:9, where it is stated that the Roman governors Antonius Felix and Porcius Festus were intent on doing the Jews a favor

---

1. The material of this chapter is in no sense exhaustive, for that would be a dissertation in itself. A sampling of material is used to show orientation and direction. Luke's use of the language of patronage is especially crisp and clear.

(*charis*). In 25:3, it is said that the high priests and the "first men" (*hoi prōtoi*) asked a favor of Festus, to keep Paul in custody. In a similar pattern, the attempt by Festus to send Paul to Jerusalem was requested by those whom he calls "the influential men" (*hoi dunatoi*, 25:5). In both cases, the governors intended to maintain terms of peace in Judea by favors, to be reciprocated by the Jewish elite, on behalf of their people. Reciprocity was useful to both parties.

An accusatory speech made against Paul and presented in Acts 24:1–8 demonstrates the pattern as well. Given by Tertullus, an orator (*rhētor*) employed by the high priest, the speech emphasized in florid terms the benefits of Felix's rule (*ēirenē, diorthōma*), his foresight and care (*pronoia*),[2] and the gratitude of the party of the high priest (*apodechometha, pantē, pantachou, pasēs eucharistias*). This honor-giving, which functioned to affirm and enlist the procurator, began with the honorific "most excellent" (*kratistos*)[3] and continued with flattery about competence as a judge. It concluded with an appeal to Felix's kindness, seeking a hearing. If it was successful, the flattery aimed at Felix reinforced the relationship with the high priest by adding to the governor's honor, and prepared the latter to grant a new favor. In the secular arena, then, the strands of patron/client or friendship bonds are clearly seen, among members of the ruling elite, in the New Testament.[4]

Two centurions, whose actions as patrons were remembered, show the pattern at a lower stratum of Roman society.[5] Cornelius, of the Italian division, was stationed at Caesarea Maritima, where he was remembered as a profoundly religious person who used his resources for charitable purposes (*poiōn eleēmosunas pollas tō laō*). He was "remembered" by God (Acts 10:4),[6] as well as by the Jewish people in general. These works combined a religious motive with the practical effect of promoting peace, salutary for his position. The form of the narrative implies that his piety underlay God's invitation to participate in the new

---

2. See Danker, *Benefactor*, 359–60, on *pronoia* as an honorific term used in inscriptions.

3. This term is also used by the chiliarch Claudias Lysias to address Felix (23:26).

4. Pontius Pilate's relations with Herod Antipas well illustrate the friendship ideal (Luke 23:12), while his connection with the Jewish elite, more standard patron/client relations.

5. For this section and several others, which I will note parenthetically, I am reflecting and building on the work of Moxnes, "Patron-Client Relations."

6. See Danker, *Benefactor*, 436, on *mnēmoneuō* as an honorific verb.

community. His good works made him a pivotal figure in the extension of Christianity to the nations, since he had valuable bonds to friends (v. 24) who were brought into his home and ultimately into the Christian community. He did not subsequently receive an exalted position in the coastal Christian community. One might ask why.

Jesus' encounter with the centurion at Capernaum clearly demonstrates, both in language and in interpersonal dynamics, how his work could intersect with patterns of obligation and favor (Luke 7:1–10). The centurion had a slave near death, described as precious (*entimos*) to him. Being aware of Jesus' reputation as a healer, he "sent" the elders of Capernaum to ask for a healing. The grounds for the favor were multifaceted: "he built the synagogue for us"; "he loves our people"; and "he is worthy" (vv. 4–5).[7] These same reasons were stated to Jesus as justifying their request. Jesus was thus a potential benefactor and the benefaction was understood to accrue to the askers and to their patron. It would, however, also create new lines of favor, between Jesus and both requesting parties, as well as between the Jewish leaders and their patron. A line of favor did also accrue to the God whose power was mediated through the agency of Jesus. When the centurion affirmed the authority of Jesus and his spiritual superiority (*ou hikanos; oude emauton ēxiōsa*), Jesus added a public commendation of the centurion to the healing of the servant. Thus the entire exchange was executed within the framework of reciprocity, obligation and favor. Each party provided benefits from their resources, and bonds of favor were strengthened in all relationships. In section 2, I will show more precisely how the career of Jesus relates to the practice of patronage.[8]

The parable of the unrighteous steward (Luke 16:1–13) illustrates the practice of patronage in an even lower social stratum. The steward (*oikonomos*), who is about to lose his position, utilizes the authority that he still has to grant favors to his master's creditors,[9] thus creating obligations that would open the creditors' doors to him later. The size of the

---

7. "Worthy" (*axios*) in Jewish perspective may imply moral stature as well as status.

8. That Jesus would accept a grateful response in the form of material support for his mission is clear by the brief mention of women, some of higher rank, who provided such support after their healing at his hand (Luke 8:1–3). Note the feminine *heterai pollai*, thus *many* female patronesses.

9. I insist that Jesus here reflects contemporary practice and is not just creating a literary figure, as Beavis seems to assert in "Ancient Slavery," 37–54.

debts (1,000–2,500 denarii) points the probable social location of the recipients toward the level of a decurion. In the telling and interpreting of the story, Jesus does not approve the morality of the action, but the wisdom of using existing resources to create bonds of favor, valuable for the future. The word "receive" (*dechomai*) is used both for the intent of the steward (v. 4) and in the application given by Jesus (v. 9), thus linking the two. *Dechomai* and its derivatives were used to refer to hospitality, a common favor granted to "friends," and to the receiving of clients. Strikingly, Jesus commanded his disciples to "make friends" in a manner analogous to the action of the unrighteous steward, but with a more long range goal, "being received into eternal dwellings." Thus, Jesus at least partially endorsed the method of balanced reciprocity.

To conclude this section, we clearly see the operation of patron/client relationships in Palestinian society at various levels, and how the patronage pattern shaped sample interchanges in the ministry of Jesus and his followers. Did Jesus' approval of participation in the patron/client relation as a method in the parable just discussed indicate that he would "do business as usual"? How did Jesus use or direct the use of this social pattern? Did the other leaders of early Christianity follow his example?

Use and Revision of the Traditional Paradigm

In the Mission of Jesus of Nazareth

In the broadest terms, the work of Jesus must be seen as acting on behalf of the God of Israel. Both in a Jewish matrix and even more explicitly in the Christian, the God of Israel was seen as a benefactor of the first order. In addition to discrete and intermittent benefits, a generalized benevolence was predicated, from resources that were understood to be unlimited (Matt 5:45). In the context of Greco-Roman religion, similar regard was given to Jupiter Optimus Maximus, whose celestial influence could benefit, or harm, all within its path. The deification of emperors may also be seen as an answer to very large-scale benevolence,[10] which

---

10. Consider the decree of the Asian League, responding to generalized benevolence through Augustus, endowed by *Pronoia*: "*enenkamenē ton Sebaston, hon eis euergesian anthrōpōn eplērōsen aretēs, hōsper emein kai tois meth' hēmas sōtēra charisamene ton pausanta men polemon, kosmēsonta de eirēnē. . . .*"

could effectively be "remembered" only by something as far-reaching as apotheosis.[11]

Though some of the later theologizing of the followers of Jesus predicate this type of nearly universal and generalized benevolence for his sphere of influence,[12] Jesus was originally understood to function as a "broker." His brokering operated with regard to an emerging moment in the favor of God, a sphere of contingent sovereignty, announced as the Kingdom of God. Jesus and his followers were seen to provide access to benefits within the favor of God, and so to fulfill the promises made by the latter through prior servants, the prophets. Luke assists our perception within the patron/client model by using the word family based on *charis*, "favor," to frame the mission.[13] The approach to Mary in Luke 1 employs a perfect participle of *charitoō* ("one who has been favored," v. 28), and quickly assured her that she has found favor (*charis*) with God.

The breadth of God's favor is shown in the endowment to be given to Jesus (vv. 32-33), in the title *Sōtēr* (2:11)[14] and in the prophecy of Simeon (2:29ff.). The peoples, the nations, Israel and the poor were specifically mentioned for benefaction. Mary's song excluded from the benefits those who are hostile to God and three classes in particular: the proud (*huperēphanous*); the rulers (*dunastas*); and the rich (*ploutountas*, 1:51ff.). By excluding the social classes which would be most involved in patronage, the song thus indicates an inversion of normal expectations about favor, who has it and who gives it.

11. So Hands, *Charities*, 55.

12. Col 1:17—"in Him all things stand together" (*sunestēken*); Heb 1:3—"bearing all things by the word of his power"; cf. 1 John 1:3. At least by inference, all beneficent natural benefits are included in these formulae.

13. Familiarly translated "grace" and given a somewhat restricted theological meaning, the *charis* word family denoted favor in the Hellenistic world: favor given, expressed, received or answered (Conzelmann, "*chairō, ktl.*," 9:373ff.). *Charis* could even refer to favorable perception (Acts 2:47). That this is an integral aspect of the "credit" of a benefactor has been creatively explored by Malina, "Patron and Client." See Luke 6:32-33, where Jesus speaks of *charis* as the credit which accrues to those who love enemies, etc. Jesus' high impact teaching was called "words of grace" (*logois tēs charitos*, Luke 4:22). *Charizomai* is used in the descriptions of healing (7:21) and the forgiveness of debt (7:42). In Lukan and Pauline material, this family of words is used frequently. To avoid the later ecclesiastical overlay and retain the historical context, I will focus on the meanings of favor, gift, thanks, and gratitude throughout this chapter.

14. "Savior." Both is title and its derivitive *sōtērian*, used in 2:30, were common honorific terms.

Though it is true that Jesus and the Father are called some of the same titles, especially Savior and Lord, it is clear that Jesus functioned as a broker of God's favor, in a framework of extensive trust, yet subordinate.[15] In the famous passage, "Come unto me ..." (Matt 11:28), Jesus preceded the invitation by stating: "All things were handed over to me by my Father."[16] Jesus then made a relationship of favor with the Father available to those to whom he wished to provide access (Matt 11:27). The connection to a greater benefactor was a standard benefit provided by a patron.

The specific conditions of Jesus' brokering were quite surprising, beginning with the declaration that the Father had kept the things of the kingdom from the "wise and intelligent" (*sophōn kai sunetōn*) and had revealed them to children (*nēpiois*). These were terms of honor and lack of honor, respectively. This statement also indicates that we may expect an inversion in the actions of God's broker with regard to those honored.

Given the breadth of authority and benefaction in his brokering, the invitation of Jesus continued to surprise in the intended effects and qualities of his leadership: rest, gentleness and humility in heart, kindness, and lightness (*anapausō; praus kai tapeinos tē kardia; chrēstos; elaphron*). Out of this list, only *chrēstos* might have conformed to the typical description of a patron. The behavior and attitudes that characterized Jesus' model also then expressed an inversion in the patronage process with regard to his brokering role. As will be seen, these qualities and attitudes were an important part of continuing benefaction by the followers of Jesus.

By connection to the Father, benefits to be mediated by Jesus included forgiveness of wrongs done to God and others, healing for various disorders, restoration of social dynamics, teaching/guidance in life, and a future life in a world made right.[17] However, how would one know that he was authorized to mediate in the name of God? Both in Jesus' own day and in Acts, first the miracles and then the Resurrection were

---

15. Jesus refusal to accept the adjective *agathos* (Mark 10:18 and parallels), in light of patronage honorifics, may be seen as asserting subordination to God, to whom the credit is due.

16. *Paradidōmi* here means to "hand over" in the sense of giving access and authority in a defined area or matter.

17. Matt 7:29; Mark 1:41ff.; 2:9ff.; Luke 4:18–19.

considered divine confirmation of Jesus' mediatory position, as shown by Acts 2:22 and 37.[18] Luke mentions the social institution and employs the language of patronage.

Jesus was, of course, not the only one who was perceived to function as a broker of divine benefits. Others who presented themselves as brokers of divine favor made their opposition known. A primary question for the contemporaries was to sort out why and how a party could be trusted to act as the broker of God. The priestly party had high public recognition as those who were the representatives of God in sacrifice and ritual, and they were understood to be qualified for this role by heredity, public reputation and connection to the Temple. So, attacks were made upon Jesus' pedigree (John 8:41), his right to teach and the correctness of his Torah observance. Perhaps most appropriate for the present discussion, he behaved in ways inappropriate for such a broker, acting as "the friend of tax gatherers and sinners" (Matt 11:19). As Malina has noted, this attack aimed to reduce Jesus' "credit" in public perception,[19] thereby reducing the bond between Jesus and those who might trust in him for divine benefits and access to God.

Those who specialized in the Torah offered yet another avenue for benefit. Jesus specifically addressed their model of acting as patrons in the spiritual sphere. The Pharisees are described in Matthew's gospel as having "seated themselves in the chair of Moses," offering approval by the God of Israel through rigorous examination and observances, in which process they acted as guides. Jesus challenged them (Matt 23:13) describing their brokering as dysfunctional, because they "locked off" (*kleiō*) the Kingdom of Heaven both for themselves and for those who were inclined to go in. One could say that Jesus identified them as antibenefactors.[20] Earlier in the passage, Jesus described the behavior of the

---

18. He was a man "attested (*apodedeigmenon*) to you by God" (22); "God has made him both Lord and Christ" (37), referring to the Resurrection. See Danker, *Benefactor*, 442ff., regarding attestation as an essential element in answering and confirming benefaction. He speaks primarily of the *martureō* ("witness") word family, but these expressions function in precisely the same manner. See Acts 14:3 for the use of "witness" as attestation of Paul's mission by the power of God.

19. Malina and Neyrey, "Patron and Client," 16; and Malina and Neyrey, "Conflict in Luke-Acts."

20. Saldarini, "Delegitimation," seems oblivious to the issues with regard to honorifics, though clear about the conflict. Compare the language of Paul in 1 Thess 2:15–16, which could be seen as identifying some opponents as antibenefactors.

Pharisees as being calculated to attract attention from the common folks, precisely because they were perceived as advanced in spirituality. The external accoutrement that symbolized their piety was also mentioned: phylacteries and tassels. While not unusual or inappropriate, they were exaggerated in size according to Jesus. They expected to receive public salutations, the title of Rabbi and places of honor at dinners (vss.5ff.), as answers to their role as brokers of God. Jesus delivered an instruction to his disciples that inverted the critique, aimed first at the use of honorifics: rabbi, father, and leader (*kathēgetai*). The first and third of these three were not to be received from others, while the second was not to be given to anyone except the Father in Heaven. Jesus thus denied the pattern of honor-giving in the arena of spiritual brokering, with regard to these titles.

Jesus then indicated an alternative behavior, found in vss. 11–12: to be a servant (*diakonos*) constituted being "greater." Note that "servant" is not identified as an honorific, but rather refers to the function or actions of one who follows Jesus. A governing principle was added in the saying that follows, which spoke to intent of action, clearly alluding to the actions that accompanied the dysfunctional brokering of the scribes and Pharisees. The attempt to lift oneself high in public attention and honor will be answered by lowering, while to lower oneself by design will be answered by being lifted. In the context of his teaching, this would be the action of God.

It is clear that in this complex of teaching, Jesus identified and rejected a pattern of accepted religious patronage, while he pointed to a radical alternative.[21] I have shown, however, that Jesus affirmed patron relations both in both in practice and in teaching. How then were patron's relations to be conducted in the Kingdom being introduced? To state the question in the framework we are investigating, how did Jesus identify the requirements of the Supreme Patron? How were the benefits of the Kingdom of God to be distributed? How did the Father's *charis* function? How and to whom is His honor given?

---

21 Some characteristic terms should be noted. The inversion uses terms like *diakonos* = servant with responsibility but not status, *doulos* = slave or bondservant with servile status, *tapeinos* = low or humble in estimation, and the opposite *hupsēlos* = exalted or proud. With their cognates and synonyms, these terms formed a characteristic rhetorical group for the redirection of patronage. Jesus' washing of the disciples' feet in John 13 demonstrated this attitude, in stark contrast to the titles and privileges there acknowledged to belong to Jesus.

The compendium of teaching called the "Sermon on the Mount" (Matthew 5–7) provides significant insight into the inversion of perspective and behavior that is normative for participants in this Kingdom of God. The opening of the compendium is the eight lapidary statements called the Beatitudes, each beginning with the nominative plural of *makarios*, often translated "blessed." However, classical writers used the term in reference to the gods, who were free from care and worry.[22] In the Hellenistic period, *makarios* denoted also those who because of great wealth were considered in popular thinking to live like the gods. Thus *makarios* was in Jesus' day a term readily applied to the class who most commonly functioned as patrons and were regularly honored as such.[23] This denotation of honor is in view when Jesus employs the term in his programmatic sayings. Imagine then the shock when Jesus associated *ptōchos* with *makarios*, in the first saying. The *ptōchoi* were those who have no resources and whose lack is apparent both personally and publicly.[24] They had no reason to be proud or honored. This awareness of being destitute and dependent was to be the attitude ("spirit") even of those in this Kingdom who have existing resources and status, as well as all who have now special resources from their new Patron. Those who show mercy (*eleēmones*) and those who mourn were also considered *makarioi*. The first of these would be associated with public patrons, but not the mourning. Nor would the attitudes and behavior implied by "meek" (*praeis*) and "persecuted" or "maligned," which would have run counter to the usual honor gathering flow of the *cursus honorum*. The issue of persecution is extended in the longer macarism of v. 11, which emphasized the heritage and the inversion of typical social dynamics. As a conclusion for the set, the point was "a reversal of custom-

---

22. Many thanks to Professor Scott Bartchy, who pushed me to rethink the denotation of *makarios*, and to K. C. Hanson, whose clear argument sets this understanding against a much larger context in "How Honorable!" Betz, *Sermon*, 94–95, sees the function of these makarisms both as indicating the final judgment of God and a reality already existing. The former will confirm the latter. Further, the evaluations of God have become those of the community. Compare Matt 25:31–46, in which a parallel term, *eulogēmenoi* is used to denote approval of disciples in the end, *connected with their favor to those who are insignificant* (*elachistos*).

23. Hauck, "*makarios*," 362–63.

24. The root of *ptōchos* was "begging," implying that one was dependent, miserable, impotent.

ary evaluation."[25] Note that only this last saying is in the second person plural, making clear that the principles had specific and current application. Honor given was implicit to the meaning of *makarios*, and in some following segments of the Sermon, Jesus made clear what he intended.

In Matthew 6, three related pericopae illustrate the principle enunciated in v. 1, previewing the concerns that Jesus addressed in the criticisms of chapter 23. The works of his followers were not to be directed toward public honor, or one would not have a reward with the Father. The first pericope (vv. 2–4) forbade the public and showy giving of mercy, so that one received glory from the public. The mention of "trumpets" may have been hyperbole, but something performing the function of a trumpet was denoted. Charity was rather to be given privately and the reward was a matter between the disciple and the Father. When that reward would be given was not stated.

Similar constraints applied to public prayer (vv. 5–6) and fasting (vv. 16–18). Thus the search for or expectation of honor from humanity was negated, while activities that benefit others or answer to the Patron were essentially private. Honor given by the Father defined the meaning of *makarios* and should be associated with the second half of each macarism. Present approval, as given through the members of the community and reflecting the values of God, and future reward replace the search for public honor. This is one of the standard structures of patronage as redirected by Jesus.[26]

Other sections of the Sermon also add focus to the inversion of investment and motive. Jesus compared the quality of life and behavior characteristic of the members of this community to salt and light, which were great and universal goods (5:13–14). Good works were to be done in such a manner that the credit ("glory") was to be given to the Father (5:16). Response by those benefited was directed through the disciples to the Patron.

Again, the command to "love your enemies and pray for those who persecute you" contradicted the pursuit of *philotimia*, by which one

---

25. Hauck, "*makarios*," 368.

26. Pertinent in this regard is the double teaching complex presented in Luke 14:7–14. The parable intends to use the banquet as model of the Kingdom, promising honor to those who deliberately choose the lower place, reinforcing that thought by the logion that closes. The direct instruction following shows that a deliberate inversion is honored by God (*makarios*) and finds future reward. Those who cannot repay are top priority for the community in the granting of favor.

seeks "friends" and cultivates them for mutual advantage. This balanced reciprocity was worthy of no "reward" and was contrasted strongly with the activity and character of the Father (vv. 45, 48) who is the model of universal benefaction.

Before moving to the examination of the continuation of the new paradigm in Acts and the Epistles, a summary of the redirection of Jesus regarding benefaction is in order.

1. The practice of patronage was not forbidden; in fact, it can be seen to underlie the mission of Jesus and to be practiced by him, both as patron and as friend. The God called Father is the Supreme Patron. The benefaction of the Kingdom flows from him in both substance and method.

2. The way in which patronage operates is redefined in a radical way. The intentional pursuit of honor, either as *cursus honorum* or as *philotimia*, is not a part of the new Kingdom. Neither public recognition nor the granting of honorifics is in order. Rather, the deliberate humbling of oneself was taught, with the servant or child as paradigms of identity.

3. A deliberated inversion of honor-giving is connected with perception of importance and greatness. Both in the Lukan framing and in the instruction of Jesus, those usually assumed to be honored are not in the primary focus of the Father or of his followers, who are to honored by God by approval in the present and reward in the future. Their brokering reflects that of the Patron, who gives regularly and with conscious joy to those considered insignificant, and to those who cannot repay.

4. Finally, the attitude of the benefaction extended to others has a consistent theme: kindness, consideration, and humility.

In Other New Testament Writings[27]

In this section, I will show that the redirection of the patronage ideal traced in the previous section did continue in the early community. It was reinforced by early Christian leaders both in their example, as

---

27. This section presents the evidence from Peter, John, James and their associates. That which comes from Paul, much more extensive, will be in part 3 below.

portrayed in Acts, and in the teaching of the epistles that bear their names.

Note first the direction that Jesus gave to the early leaders in Acts 1. A necessary part of the Kingdom of God (v. 3) is the gift of the Holy Spirit, by which the disciples should have the power to function as witnesses (v. 8). Here again we see the theme of the attestation that was given to benefactors. The power given, like that of Jesus, would be able to effect change in circumstances, and thus attract attention, requiring explanation. Who then would be honored primarily in the explanation of great acts?

As noted above, Peter gave the primary witness to the actions of God that confirmed Jesus as the broker of divine benefits. This witness continued in the operation of the new community, since Jesus was understood to be alive. In answering the question of those who observed the miracle of languages which led to the glory of God, Peter then indicated that the expected favor had been granted: the members of this community without regard to rank or sex, would receive the life and power promised by one of the prophets, the continuing presence of God's spirit.[28]

In Luke's description of community dynamics (Acts 2),[29] the effects of this climactic favor granted were seen to have extensive results: miracles performed, a broad scale benevolence in which property is converted into to meet the needs of others, the praise of God and "credit" (*charis*) with all the people. The language used by Luke to describe the function of the community is drawn from the ideal of friendship,[30] but the reality stretches that ideal and finally transcends it. This was a large group including multiple classes, following an agenda not set in advance, but understood to be by the Patron's wishes and leading.

---

28. Note that in the Hebrew text of Joel 2:29, the connective (*vegam*) indicates surprise that the slaves would be included in this favor. The discomfort of Septuagint translators is often noted, adding *mou* to both nouns so that they could be taken metaphorically, but for our purposes we note the translation to *doulos*, highly significant in Jesus' redirection, and that the emphasis continued in the Greek (*kai ge*).

29. Bartchy, "Credibility Factor" 151–81, cogently argues the importance of the integration of community function and broad scale benevolence with the public declaration that this is indeed the work of God.

30. Marshall, *Enmity*, 258. Marshall points out that this language would have made sense specifically to the more affluent members of the congregation, encouraging them to rethink the reciprocity ethic (259) and "to use their normal 'powerbrokering' technique to care for the poor in their midst" (264).

Robert Grant notes that the phrase "one heart and soul" was known and used in Pythagorean circles to describe the ethos of their communities, including common goods. It is not clear, however, that they are similar phenomena.[31]

What then could have been happening for there to be "no needy among them"? Would it have been likely for a very few to have met all the needs of such a large and growing group? While some individuals of significant resources are known, the activity behind such results was probably the giving of many members, led by the example and teaching of the principal disciples of Jesus, and demonstrated by a few such as Barnabas.

Only Joseph Barnabas was mentioned by name, and there is no evidence, even in his case, that benefactors received special places or titles in the Jerusalem community. Rather the reason and motivation for such benevolence is the operation of a circle of favor, which was extended by God to the various members, was answered by the extension of favor to others and was completed by a joint return of honor to God. The atmosphere of joy and praise permeating Acts 2–4 was inherent to the circle.

At least one couple in this early community missed the point. In Acts 5:1ff., an attempt to subvert this pattern was conducted by Ananias and Sapphira. After selling a piece of property, they brought a portion of the proceeds to the leaders, ostensibly following the new paradigm. Peter was quite severe with them, denoting their deceit as "lying to the Holy Spirit." If it is true that the Holy Spirit is the director of this dynamic community, the attempt to appear as benefactors in whole heart, but actually acting in a rather calculating manner would in fact falsify the governing "spirit" of the community.

Luke continued to use the *charis* word family to frame the mission as it expanded. The description of Stephen in Acts 6:8 calls him "full of favor and power," doing great wonders for the people. Barnabas evalu-

---

31. Grant, *Early Christianity*, 100. Walter Burkert's discussion of the evidence and dynamic of the Pythagoreans would seem to show that while the community of goods was practiced, the purposes were not comparable, nor indeed the purpose of the community itself. Also, the date of sources in Iamblichus' compilation of Pythagoran material is much controverted. See his "Craft versus Sect." See also Bartchy, "Community of Goods," and Capper, "Palestinian Cultural Context," 323–56. Both argue that the community of goods in Acts was not only social reality but distinct in nature, though some parallel in other contexts can be demonstrated.

ated the work of the gospel in Antioch, "seeing the favor of God" (Acts 11: 23). What precisely did Barnabas see? By what standard would he have approached the phenomena in Antioch, if not that of the Jerusalem community? Some convincing evidence persuaded him of authenticity, concluding that the favor of God was working among the disciples. At the end of the chapter, the members of this community were described as each gathering some money, "as they had prospered" (*euporeito*), some money to send to the community in Jerusalem for relief from a famine. I would argue that this action was simply an extension of the normal action of the new community, a community of broad-scale benevolence. This collection does not seem to have been compelled, nor to have come from a few. Participation by the more wealthy was not, of course, precluded.

In two further pericopae, Luke used the concept of favor to summarize major aspects of the Christian mission. Paul and Barnabas are spoken of as having been committed (*paradedomenoi*) to the favor of God unto the work which they had fulfilled (14:26). Those who reported on the mission attributed the results to God's work and initiative. Similarly, Peter's summary of the extension of the gospel to non-Jews dwelt upon the gift of God (11:17–18; 15:8) and concluded the matter with reference to the favor of Jesus Christ (15:11), as directly analogous to God's dealings with the original disciples.

Before we consider the teaching of Peter relevant to the issue, we should examine the extended narrative concerning Peter and John after the healing of the paralytic (Acts 3–4). The length cannot be an accident; Luke was giving extended treatment to an important event. Peter's interpretation of the event was critical, first to the crowd that had gathered, then to the Sanhedrin, which had to respond to the problem.

Within the model of patronage, the healing of the man brought attention to the two disciples who had acted as second level brokers for the power of God. Glory was expected to accrue to their account and to be accepted as their due. Peter's response addressed precisely that issue (3:12, 13, 16). He denied that he or John had the power or piety to accomplish the act being celebrated. Credit was given to "the God of Abraham, Isaac and Jacob," whose power had been mediated through "the name of Jesus." God was identified as the first order Patron, Jesus as the broker. The occasion then served as an opportunity to invite those impressed to participate in the benefits of the God whose power was just seen (vv. 19, 21, 26). In the following chapter, Peter gave a similar ascription of honor and called the act a benefit (*euergesia*, 4:9–12). This event then serves, among other things, as a cameo of the redirected paradigm of benefaction.

In 1 Peter, the principles are clearly in place among his pastoral concerns. Gifts and gratitude are elaborated in what Danker has called a "contrapuntal structure."[32] The complex of benefits granted to God's people was outlined in 1:3ff., with reference both to present and future gifts. Gratitude was indicated as the appropriate response, while several references to the favor of God punctuated the rest of the epistle.[33] In addition, there was a final gift to be granted "at the revelation of Jesus Christ" (1:13). Some glory or reward was indicated, and is more clearly indicated in time than in the Sermon.

Gratitude is expressed, first of all, by imitation of God (1:15), echoing both Jesus in the Sermon (Matt 5:45, 48) and the Torah of his people (Lev 19:1–18). Immediately Peter alluded to an aspect of God's impartial way of dealing with humanity (1:17), seen already in the redirection by Jesus and in the manner in which the promised favor of God is given without regard to gender or status in Acts 2.

Gratitude is expressed, secondly, by a pattern of behavior outlined in chapter 2, following a florid expression of the identity of the favored people in vv. 9 and 10. Good works (*kalōn ergōn*) were to be characteristic of this pattern of behavior (v. 12), which again may be summarized as noble or honorable (*kalēn*). Three verses later, practicing excellence (*agathopoiountas*) was declared to be the will of God. Was Peter simply encouraging his readers to continue patterns of accepted benefaction?[34]

The use of *agathopoieō* in 1 Peter is connected with honoring God by behaving in ways which are surprising to observers: the slave who gains favor (*charis*) with God by maintaining a good attitude toward an unreasonable master (2:19–20), the wife who acts with a consistent pattern toward her husband without fear (3:6) and those citizens who suffer rejection at the hands of others while continuing to practice good works

---

32. Danker, *Benefactor*, 452.

33. 1 Pet 1:18–19; 2:10, 24–25; 3:18–19; 5:10.

34. So Winter *Seek the Welfare* 21. Winter sees this passage, especially vv. 14–15, as encouragement to Christians of substance to continue to be benefactors in the traditional sense and so to attract official attention. It is not clear, however, why this should eventuate in "bad-mouthing" (v. 12) or suffering (3:17). Nor is it clear that Christians of substance are particularly in view in v. 15.

(3:16–17). Several related purposes are defined for these behaviors. In 3:16, those who "bad-mouth" will be put to shame by the behavior of the disciple. In 2:12, those who "bad-mouth" may finally glorify God. In 2:15, the purpose is to silence the ignorance of the foolish. In short, a salutary effect upon others is a goal of defined behavior that honors God. This is seen most clearly in the extended passage addressed to the house slave (*oiketai*) in 2:18ff. There the operation of the *charis* of God is connected with the example of Jesus, who suffered unjustly for the purpose of a good effect on others. John Elliot summarizes this matter: "*Agathopoiia*, therefore, is the expression of Christian holiness following the Divine call, because God himself is holy. It is the positive aspect of the holy life, a doing good for the benefit of the 'outsider' as well as the fellow Christian."[35] Peter sees the grateful answering of the privileged people as effective for both insiders and outsiders. This is made clear by the four imperatives of 2:17, especially the first two. "Honor everyone" is a startling statement in its cultural context.[36] It redirects the honor-game by refusing to limit honor to particular groups and by extending it to groups that were not usually to be honored. This redirection was grounded in the agenda of the Patron.

In 4:10–11, Peter spoke about the internal relations of the community. He stated that each member of the community had received a gift which bears the favor of God (*charisma*), and that the expression of such gifts is in serving one another as stewards (*oikonomoi*) of the multi-faceted favor of God. Holders of two classes of gifts in v. 11, they are bearers of a continued divine favor. The purpose of their exercise is the honor that accrues to God, with Jesus as the mediator of all. We should notice in particular that no privileged classes are evident at any phase in the process, either before or after the *charismata* are given, but rather that a quite extensive circle of favor and gratitude is indicated. One should also note that the term "serving" (*diakonountes*), so prominent in Jesus' redirection, is the term of choice here as well.

Last in the consideration of Peter's instruction is a passage directed to those who emerged as leaders, or were appointed as such (5:1–5). These "elders" were instructed to exercise their leadership in terms that arise from and yet redirect their mediatory role. In v. 2, the adverbs

---

35. Elliott, *Elect and the Holy*, 182.

36. I am translating *pantas* here as gender inclusive, since the neuter would include impersonal matters.

"voluntarily" and "eagerly" (*ekousiōs; prothumōs*) belong to the language of patronal inscriptions.[37] Verses 3 and 5, however, confirm the new paradigm with regard to the manner in which benefit is conveyed. Elders were forbidden to "lord it over" (*katakurieuō*) their charges, but to lead by example, and along with the disciples, to conduct business in a consciously humble manner. Divine support for such a pattern is given in the form of a promise of future reward as well as a citation from Proverbs that indicates that God favors the humble.

We have seen that Peter, in his interaction with the Sanhedrin and the council of elders in Jerusalem, confirms the new paradigm, and that the instruction of 1 Peter adds further confirmation to the manner in which leadership is to be humble, while outlining a broad scale benevolence both within his community and the larger human community. An emphasis upon future reward is also congruent with Jesus' instruction, especially in the Sermon. Like Luke, Peter used some traditional benefaction language, but articulated substantial changes in the operation of the ideal. As such, he confirmed the redirection of the paradigm given by Jesus of Nazareth.

Before examining the work of Paul, we must evaluate the slender evidence with regard to James, brother of Jesus and revered leader of the Jewish Christian community in Jerusalem. Eusebius indicates that the immediate blood relatives of Jesus received a group title, the *desposunoi*.[38] James exercised considerable influence within the church as a whole, as is shown by Paul's reference to him as a "pillar" (Gal 2:9), by the place he held at the council of Acts 15 and even by the reference to him in the epistle of Jude (vs. 1). Did James ascend to the position of leader because of his blood relation to Jesus; was Harnack correct in seeing here an attempt to establish a "caliphate" in Jerusalem, consisting of a bloodline of Jesus' family? Perhaps, but two facts must immediately be faced. First, such an attempt did not succeed.[39] Second, James possessed other qualifications that seemed to weigh heavily both in the nascent Christian community and in other observers, related to us by Hegesippus. He was a man who impressed others by his austerity and

37. Danker, *Benefactor*, 320–21.

38. Eusebius, *H.E.* I,7,15.

39. Von Harnack, *Entstehung*, 26. See Eusebius, *H.E.* III,20,5–6, for the story of two grandsons of Jude who were revered as of Jesus' family, but even more because they were also *martures,* interrogated during the time of Domitian.

sincerity with regard to a most rigorous Jewish Christian community.[40] Though it is clear by the actions of Paul that James was a force with whom one must reckon, there is no evidence that he deliberately fostered the fame that he received. What instruction did he give to the church?

Within the epistle of James, three passages address our concerns either directly or indirectly. The first is in 2:1–5. James outlined a hypothetical situation, yet one that must have been quite pertinent. The acceptance of an obviously well-to-do person both in evaluation and action, while rejecting a poor one both in look and action was vehemently rejected. No prior involvement with the congregation is indicated, only the appearance of one who is capable of being a patron for the community and its members. That action is regarded as evil judgment with regard to the evaluation (*diekrithete*) as well as the motives behind such an action ("considering evil things" *dialogismōn ponērōn*).[41] The issue is introduced (v. 1) by forbidding the exercise of faith in an attitude of personal favoritism,[42] and the statement of v. 6a shows that this situation is not hypothetical. The poor have been dishonored, and it is they who have been chosen by God to be rich in their connection with divine things (v. 5). James was attempting to deal with an evasion of the redirection that Jesus had indicated.[43]

In two related passages, James reiterated an injunction that directly confirms the attitude with which Jesus acted and which he had emphasized. James 1:9–10 enunciated clearly the reversal of position that was characteristic of the new community. The humble brother should boast in the high place (*hupsei*) which is his, while the rich should boast

---

40. Eusebius, *H.E.* II,23.

41. Note that the poor are referred to by the term we have already encountered in Jesus' Sermon (*ptōchos*), while here and in 4:13, those with more resources are not called rich (*plousios*). The clothing and seated position are significant indications of status and honor.

42. *Prosōpolēmpsiais* (and *prosōpolēmpteite* v.9). The term is not used in classical or Hellenistic Greek, but may be derived from the LXX, where *prosōpon lambanein* is used. The Old Testament background is judicial, where Israel's God is declared not to be partial to the rich and forbids his representatives to so act (Deut 10:17ff. *thaumadzei prosōpon*). See Davids, *James*, for further argument, though I do not agree with him that this passage deals with a judicial assembly.

43. In section 3 of this chapter, we will explore the evidence that the new paradigm was challenged and resisted, both in Jesus' training process and in Paul's new communities. We can see James facing the problem here.

in his humiliation (*tapeinōsei*). Similarly, in 4: 6,10, James quoted the same passage from Prov 3:34 which Peter used to "wrap" his admonitions to fellow elders (1 Pet 5:6). This proverb contrasts the arrogant (*huperēphanois*), who are opposed by God, and the humble (*tapeinois*), who are given favor. In v. 10, James articulated a principle virtually identical to that which Peter had attached to the proverb. One must humble oneself in order to receive an exalted place from God. To whom would this imperative be most pertinent? Either those who already "had place" and were used to enjoying the same, or those who because of their present privilege in the community were inclined to learn to enjoy a place just attained. In either case, both Peter and James are emphasizing the redirected paradigm of the great and small, as we have seen it defined by Jesus of Nazareth.

Finally, in the long passage with two parts which commence with "come now" (4:13—5:6), James expands his focus on this matter. To set this diatribe in context, note that earlier in chapter 4, James had warned against "friendship" with the world, as constituting hostility to God (vv. 4ff.). Verse 5 pointed to the residing Spirit of God as the reason why one cannot be in mutual reciprocity with both God and the world. Who gives the favor that counts? Verse 6 answers the implicit question: God gives a greater favor. It is a favor that cannot be mixed with alternate sources, especially if it involves pride and the life of public honor (v. 16). The serial injunctions of vv. 7ff. pointed to the restoration of the appropriate attitude toward God, which allows divine favor to be restored.

James identified three different aspects of "friendship" with the world: acquisitive hedonism (4:1ff.), commercial activity (4:13ff.), and the gathering of wealth (5:1ff.). In the case of the first two, members of the community are clearly in view, for one cannot be an "adulteress" (4:4) without having made a commitment, and knowing the right thing to do (v. 17). What is clear is that some were evading a pattern of behavior that accepted the canons of the Patron, and fulfilled them by the presence of the Spirit. "Doing the good" (v. 17) is not living with an eye to making and spending profit, it is seeking a new profit.

With regard to the last section, members of the congregation do not seem specifically in view, unless they would be new members who could have fulfilled vv. 4 and 6 prior to becoming a part of the new community.[44] What then is the purpose of this passage, except to warn

---

44. The commentaries on James—Dibelius and Greeven (Hermeneia, 1976), Davids (New International Greek New Testament, 1982), Reicke (Anchor Bible, 1964) as well

the Christian community against a class who represent the antithesis of the values of their God? Thus, the values here mentioned cannot be accepted in the church, and those who belong to this class should not be welcomed because of their wealth. It must be noted that the terms of this passage express a distinct echo of Jesus' Sermon (Matt 6:19–34). In these several instructions, James is congruent with the concerns of Jesus of Nazareth in a decisive redirection of the benefaction ideal and honor, as we have seen Peter to be.

In the Mission of Paul of Tarsus

More data is available to us regarding the mission of Paul than those of the figures just presented. I will begin by indicating some of the conclusions of scholars who have considered Paul's way of seeing patronage. Maier and Kloppenborg have seen Paul as "not ideologically opposed to the patron/client relationship." Judge has identified a large circle of supporters in various roles, including patrons. John Chow explored the evidence with regard to Corinth and concluded that Paul accepted from patrons a variety of favors: food and lodging, legal responsibility, gifts for expenses.[45] Marshall saw Paul more in the mode of friendship, accepting favors from individuals of his own rank, yet in a manner that went beyond the normal conventions. For example, the usual three days of hospitality stretched into much longer periods, and the relationships then developed were more intimate, long-term (?), and particular. Indeed, it does not seem clear whether the relations between Paul and his associates, both individual and corporate, followed the pattern of patrons with clients or those of friends, or even if any of these accepted patterns quite fit.

Two vignettes included by Luke in Acts illustrate the manner in which mutually supportive relations operated. In the beginning phase of the mission in Philippi, related in Acts 16:12ff., Paul encountered a well-placed woman named Lydia, who declared herself and her house-

---

as Luke Timothy Johnson (Anchor Bible, 1995)—agree that this is a general class of rich being addressed in a prophetic oracle or diatribe. The parallels from *1 Enoch* and prophetic literature, while not irrelevant, are not as significant as that from the Sermon on the Mount.

45. Kloppenborg, "*Philadelphia*," 276 n. 46 ; Maier, *Social Setting of the Ministry* 35; Chow, *Patronage and Power*, 102. For Edwin Judge, see Marshall, *Enmity*, 144.

hold for the new community of God.⁴⁶ A dealer in purple, and for that reason well connected among the elite of Philippi, she appealed rather forcefully (*parebiasato*) to the apostles to stay in her house. She did not, however, assume that she would be accepted as host, but requested the privilege based on their evaluation of her (*ei kekrinate me pistin tō kuriō*). The favor they granted (access to the truth and to God) was answered by that offered by Lydia, a base of operations and probable access to social networks in the city. She could be considered a client who was answering a favor with another. However, if they were considered somewhat equivalent in status, she could be considered a friend who was answering a great favor with a valuable one. By accepting her hospitality, Paul and Silas acknowledged her friendship, before a watching world.

In Thessalonika, a new disciple named Jason offered a similar favor (Acts 17:5ff.), though the manner in which the arrangement was made is not given. This *charis* resulted in Jason being seized during disturbances that followed the proclamation of the new favor of God by Paul and his team. The accusation against Jason included "welcoming" (*hupodechomai* = act as host) Paul and his followers. Being held responsible as host, he posted a "peace-bond" (*hikanos*), to guarantee an end to the problems.

In the sphere of the Corinthian community, two figures are known to have done significant favors for Paul. Phoebe of Cenchrea is declared to have been a *prostatis* of many, including Paul (Rom 16:3). The term was most likely to mean a patroness, though the actions are not specified. Women of means are well known to have acted as patrons of communities, building buildings and providing protection in circles of influence.⁴⁷ Phoebe had proven herself to be a strong leader and supporter. Gaius' favor is clearer, consisting of hospitality for Paul and for the whole church undoubtedly in several different ways (Rom 16:23).

---

46. Most of the evidence with regard to the name Lydia makes it likely that she was a freedwoman with resources, the head of her own house and business. See *New Docs.*, vol. 2, p. 27, for relevant documentation regarding the rarity of the name in inscriptions, and the likelihood that she received it as a slave, because she was from Thyatira in Lydia. However, Hemer in *New Docs.*, vol. 3, #53–55, #17) documents some use of Lydia among women of higher rank.

47. See *New Docs.* vol. 1, #25. Bartchy has made the case for "leader" in his *Call No Man Father* (forthcoming).

In all these interpersonal relations, Paul apparently accepted favors from those willing to offer them. The terms under which the relation worked must be made clear from the epistles, but first the function of communities should be briefly noted.

Favors done for or solicited by Paul are clear in the case of at least three communities. First, the church at Antioch served as a "home-base" for the mission trips for the bulk of his known ministry. Hospitality and support can safely be assumed. Second, the Philippian congregation sent gifts for Paul's support more than once (Phil 4:15–18).[48] The repeated gifts will have spanned several years. Third, Paul was apparently looking to the community in Rome to be a "home base,"[49] for further mission to the west. He intended to form a bond with them by giving and receiving (Rom 1:11–12). He hoped to be "sent forth" with their support, on his way to Spain. This favor could be asked for Paul or for others, as shown by 1 Cor 16:6, 11. So one can see favors being done for Paul, either asked or requested, by individuals or by communities.

How did Paul understand the significance of these exchanges of favor? Even more than in Luke's works, *charis* and other members of its word family frame the understanding of the work of Jesus in the epistles of Paul.[50]

Every epistle in the Pauline corpus begins with a greeting that includes *charis* wished from the Father and from Jesus. Paul's usage, along with "peace," combines epistolary conventions and gives to them a new focus appropriate to the Christian community. The wide use of

---

48. Reumann, "Contributions," 438–57. Reumann sees the Philippian community acting as a client when it makes its contributions. Sampley sees the relationship as modeled on that of a consensual society (*koinōnia*), building upon the use of *koinōneō* as meaning "entered into partnership" and *apechō* as meaning "paid in full"; *Pauline Partnership*, 53. While interesting, Sampley's model does not account for the full breadth of the language: giving and receiving (4:15), the gift, the supply of God (v. 19), all which belong to the vocabulary of patronage.

49. "Sending on" (*propempthēnai* Rom.15:24) became a technical term for the support of all kinds given by the churches to those in mission. See Dunn, *Romans 9–16*, 872 for a full listing of usages in the New Testament. Third John 6 is particularly interesting—*hous kalōs poiēseis propempsas axiōs tou theou*.

50. As before, the later freighted translation of "grace" will be avoided so that we can highlight the manner in which Paul used the word family. Malina and Rohrbaugh have insisted that "the language of grace is the language of patronage," *Synoptic Gospels*, 390. I fully agree, and will regard the word family as denoting favor given, expressed, received, answered, and passed on.

the *charis* word family in Paul's writings does, however, invest his greeting with greater depth.

In Romans 5 and 6, Paul uses *charis* and *dōrea* with reference to the endowment of God for life in the new community. The florid language of Paul is striking, using comparative terminology like "much more" (*pollō mallon*, 5:15, 17), the verb "reign as king" (*basileuō*) to refer to the effect of the "gift of favor" (*charisma*) in the future (5:17, 21), and "overflow, abundant, super-overflow" (*perisseuō, tēn perisseian, huperperisseuō*, 5:15, 17, 21). The power of v. 17, "those who receive the abundance of favor and of the gift (*tēs dōreas*) of righteousness will reign in life through the one Jesus Christ," sets the groundwork for Paul's exposition in chapter 6, which made clear the response which was appropriate to the gift.

The challenge at the beginning of Romans 6 began the argument that an appropriate response to the overwhelming endowment of God through Christ was not simply a religious matter of accepting repeated forgiveness. Gratitude was expressed in an altered means and manner of living. Paul included several aspects to this response: accepting the obligation of rightous behavior (*edoulōthēte tē dikaiosunē*, 6:18),[51] recognizing their changed privileges (*logizesthe heautous. . . zōntas tō theō en Christō Iēsou*, 6:11), presenting their members to God as instruments of accomplishing righteousness (6:13), presenting themselves to God as those with (new) life. Note in passing that a further and final favor is indicated as the goal (*to telos*, 6:23) of the process, eternal life.[52]

Another standard usage which framed the Pauline work was the phrase "thanks be to God" (*charis tō theō*), used repeatedly with regard to the gifts of God and their effect in the lives of the recipients.[53] Verbal praise was, of course, a standard response to benefaction. Paul used

---

51. The use of *douleuō* here is Paul's convention, indicating not that the people should become slaves, but Paul's way of indicating the strength and humility inherent in the bond. It is important in this regard to remember the diversity of terms referring to the privileges and place of God's new people, including fictive kinship and workplace vocabularies. Lull cites Dio Chrysostom as using *douleuō* and *latreuō* as appropriate for the behavior of the exemplary monarch in "Servant-Benefactor" 297.

52. Similarly florid language is used in the salvation hymn that opens the epistle to the Ephesians (1:3–14) and for the same reason, to exalt the patrons and to arouse gratitude that is then answered in various ways. Danker notes that the periodic style of Ephesians is most similar to the rhetoric of inscriptions; *Benefactor*, 451.

53. Rom 6:17; 7:25; 1 Cor 15:57; 2 Cor 8:16; 9:15.

the repeated phrase "to the praise of His glory" in Eph 1:6, 12, 14. In 2 Corinthians, Paul defined a more concrete form of expressing gratitude, giving to others in a systematic manner.

In 2 Corinthians 8, vv. 1–7 identify and commend a specific form of gratitude, giving a gift to others. This gift answered, not repaid, the great favor that God has brought to the Macedonian Christians. Paul spoke of the *charis* of God that had been given in the Macedonian churches. It is clear that this was not the original gift of favor, but rather was a gift that arose from that gift of God; thus it was also "of God." The description is striking, for the group was described in language often used to describe individual patrons:[54] "a wealth of generosity" (*to ploutos tēs haplotētos*), "according to . . . and beyond their power" (*kata . . . kai para dunamin*), of their own will (*authairetoi*)[55] and "they gave themselves." The context of the giving made it all the more powerful: contrasting "abundance of joy" (*tēs perisseia tēs charas*) and "deep poverty" (*bathous ptōcheia*) in v. 2. Of course, the fact that this was a dominantly Greek group sending money to a dominantly Jewish one is neither to be overemphasized nor lost. Verses 6 and 7 commended this *charis* for the Corinthian community as well. By use of the word "authentic" (*gnēsion*) in v. 8, Paul shows that he considered this aspect of the behavior of the Macedonians to be an expected part of their extension of God's favor. Any Christian community was to act as a benefactor corporately, and was honored as such; but the honor was framed by the endowment of God through Christ (v. 9) and by the fact that finally this gift should bring credit ("glory") to the Lord in particular (v. 19).[56]

Before examining the instruction of Paul affecting the various communities over which he exercised authority, the nature of that authority should be noted, with regard to the term "apostle" and its verbal correlate. In the New Testament, Paul and his occasional associate

---

54. My thanks to a colleague, Dr. Jerry McCant, for making available to me his research on 2 Corinthians 8–9, in a manuscript soon to be published. There the use of much language related to patronage is documented, as well as the rhetorical form in which it is communicated.

55. This adjective is reinforced strongly then by the statement of v. 4, where again in florid terms Paul asserted the eagerness of the Macedonians to help.

56. The remainder of 2 Corinthians 8 and 9 is liberally sprinkled with the vocabulary of benefaction, including the word families which derive from *spoudē, prothumia, epichorēgeō, eucharistian, charis.*

Luke use this family dominantly.[57] Unlike its classical and Hellenistic usage, which more often simply denoted "messenger," Paul reflected the Hebrew term *shaliach*, investing the term with weight and implying commission. It would then function as an extension of that which we have described as the brokering role of Jesus. First Thessalonians 2:4ff. delineates the dynamics of the role. Paul there declared an investment by God (*dedokimasmetha upo tou theou pisteuthēnai*) with attendant accountability to God, who examined the hearts and was witness to authenticity (vv. 4–5). To cater to humanity or to seek glory from them was expressly excluded (vv. 4, 6), while the praise and glory belongs to God, whether for the gift of divine truth and favor or for its effects (vv. 12–13). Thus it can be seen that the function of the apostolate in Paul's thinking shares the dynamics of the new paradigm.[58]

It remains to examine the instruction which Paul gave to the communities and note there a new structure of honor, and the manner in which it differs from the standard language of honor.

Marshall notes the absence of the terms "friend and friendship" (*philos, philia*) in Paul.[59] He quotes Edwin Judge as suggesting that Paul wished to avoid the status implications of friendship terms: "We must watch with great care the way in which Paul talks about his relations with people and their relations with one another and watch as he draws the line between what would have been the natural outworking of the status system and the outworking of the quite different principle of relationships which he is promoting.[60] The language of honor which can be seen in Paul follows the inversion which we have already traced in Jesus and other early leaders. To describe his associates and the mission in which they were involved, Paul used terms drawn from the workplace (*sudzugoi, sunergoi, kopos, mochthos, hoi kopiōntes*), the household (*diakonia, huperētas, oikonomia, episkopoi*), the family (*adelphē, adel-*

---

57. Of 79 usages, 68 belong to Paul and Luke. Rengstorf, "*apostellō*."

58. Of course, Paul has occasion to speak much about the authenticity of his apostolate, but our concern is the honor he expects, and to whom it should be given. See 2 Cor 4:1–5, where again the ministry is defined as given in trust, while the results of the shared favor of God (*hē charis pleonasasa dia tōn pleionōn*, v. 15) are intentionally focused on the extensive giving of thanks to the glory of God (*tēn eucharistian perisseusē eis tēn doxan tou theou*).

59. Marshall, *Enmity*, 133.

60. From Judge, "Paul as a Radical Critic of Society," quoted in Marshall, *Enmity*, 133. For similar sentiments, see Sevenster, *Paul and Seneca*, 178.

phos) and servitude (*doulos, douleuō*).[61] Even those who already had the means to perform benefits for Paul and his mission companions were denoted by these terms. No exalted terms were either borrowed or created, to be invested with a dignity that placed status distinctions within the community. In fact, considerable effort was exerted to avoid just such separations.

In addition to the new vocabulary, Paul's exhortation was directed to bringing about the new dynamics in relationships. If Paul did not wish typical social dynamics, what did he wish to take their place? First Corinthians 12 provides a window into his intentions.

In dealing with a very troubled church, Paul worked with the image of a body as analogy for the community, with many members, interrelated but united in function. In the opening verses, the authority and endowment of God through Christ was stated unequivocally, with a variety of gifts of favor (*charismata*) given, bringing distinctions among the members and a tendency toward value judgment. While Paul recognized certain members as having more weight and visibility than others, he emphatically redirected the honor process in the community. After forbidding either self-aggrandizement or self-denigration with regard to others (vv. 15–18), Paul inverted the honor process. Rather than making sure that the more attractive and important members receive honor, it is the ones who would not be normally honored, who are "shameful" (*aschēmona*) who were to receive overflowing honor (*perissoteran timēn*). Those who have the greater gifts, resources or status Paul mentioned as the "presentable" (*euschēmona*, v. 24); it is implied that they already have honor. This was not a leveling process in the sense of denying distinctions, for the apostles were first, followed by others. However, the honor process was refocused, first to God and then to all other members of the community, with special care for those not usually honored.

In the final paranetic section of the epistle to the Romans, several directions are given which illuminate both the redirection of honor and the nature of the new community as a corporate benefactor. In 12:10, the community was admonished to make sure that all the members were honored, in language sometimes a bit unusual.[62] In v. 16, the members

---

61. See Marshall, *Enmity*, for a full discussion.

62. While there is some disagreement concerning the precise meaning of *tē timē allēlous proēgoumenoi*, either "consider one another first in honor" or "lead the way to

were counseled not to "think of high things," an obscure phrase clarified by its alternative, "being led to the humble ones."[63] The opening clause of the verse, "be of the same mind toward one another," was an imperative that addressed the normal social categorizing which occurred in the minds of both the honored and dishonored. In this context, Paul's admonition in 15:7 of the same epistle is germane. He there directed the Roman Christians to "accept one another, just as Christ accepted us, to the glory of God." The clause that qualifies the direction was decisive, for in terms of comparative status and resources, Jesus would have been far above anyone else. His example, as both method and goal, was critical to understanding the dynamics of the new community.

Two further passages from Romans are also suggestive. In 12:13, mutual help and hospitality for members in need was indicated, illustrating the broad-scale benevolence we have already observed. In 13:8, Paul commended detachment from the usual patron/client system with the words: "owe nothing to anyone except to love another." In so speaking, Paul directed the Roman Christians against a dependence model of social interaction in favor of an interactive benevolent one that does not rest on obligation to humanity, but on gratitude to God. Benevolence was to proceed as an extension of God's gift, and as answer to the same.[64]

Dislocations in and Resistance to the Revised Paradigm

As may be expected, a significant reorientation of social dynamics was not effected in early Christianity without some opposition and resistance. In this section I would like to note the resistance of Jesus' original

---

one another in honor" inverts the normal honor process both by considering all honorable and by seeking the honor of others rather than oneself.

63. *tois tapeinois sunapagomenoi*. The verb can mean either "led astray" or "carried away." The obscurity of this phrase of v. 16 may well derive from the attempt of Paul to speak of social realities quite novel. James Dunn suggests that the meaning of "uninhibited wholeheartedness" is intended by Paul, so extending and rejoicing in the honor that has come to those who were "out of the loop," *Romans 9–16*, 747. The thought here may be clarified as well by the challenge of v. 3, which asks the members to reconsider their importance in light of the giving of God to each.

64. The brief epistle of Paul to Philemon serves as a cameo of how he retained the language of honor and obligation, but transcended it in light of the larger work of God.

disciples, the problems that can be seen in Corinth and a different sort of problem in Thessalonica.

Within the company of disciples who were closest to Jesus, a competition emerged (*philotimia*). In Matt 20:20–28 (Mark 10:42ff.; Luke 22:24ff.), an argument swirled among the disciples concerning who would be the greatest in the Kingdom.[65] James and John actually acted upon their ambition and asked for the highest places, which gave rise to deep resentment from the others, the argument and a rather clear instruction from their leader. Jesus summarized the normal paradigm in terms of honor given and status clearly recognized, even using the term "Benefactor" (*euergetēs*) in the Lukan version. He then simply directed an inversion which began with an humbling of those who already have position (*ho meidzōn*) by taking the position of the young, and of those who lead (*ho hēgoumenos*) by taking the position of the one who serves (*ho diakonōn*). In v. 27 of Luke's version, Jesus finalized this instruction by reference to the honor that accrues to the great ones, who reclined at table, and to the servers who served them. He asked his disciples which are the greater, in the normal paradigm. The answer, those who were served, was contrasted with Jesus himself, who was "among you (pl.) as the server." In a most specific fashion, Jesus confronted the honor game that would normally take place among the disciples. Peter, James and John were the most likely candidates, for they were interpersonally closer to Jesus, with more instruction and privilege granted than the other disciples. We can see that some struggle with a redirection of the paradigm of benefaction is visible in earliest Christianity.

The strongest resistance to the new paradigm that can be traced in the New Testament is the conflict in the church at Corinth. Party strife was connected with certain figures who seemed to have exceptional importance: Peter, Paul, Apollos or Christ.[66] Chapter 1 reveals the desire of some members to give excessive honor to them and to claim some importance by one's relation to the honored ones (chapters 1 and 2). Apollos was described in Acts as powerful in speech and as commended by the brothers to the church in Corinth (Acts 18:27). Chow reminds

65. The parallel in Mark also alludes to the agenda of the sons of Zebedee, though presented to Jesus by their mother, while it is absent from Luke's version. We may be assured that the question had arisen before; see the pericope recorded in Mark 9:34 and Luke 9:46.

66. For a fuller discussion, see John Chow, *Patronage and Power*. I will simply show some indicators.

us that the wealthy were particularly fond of rhetoric and those gifted in it, often giving them significant support in exchange for their talents in action. Paul took occasion in 1 Corinthians to deny the importance of rhetoric for his mission.[67] One cannot say that Apollos became the favorite of the elite in Corinth, but Paul made quite a point of not accepting support from the Corinthians. Since he stated his right to do so, and accepted support from others, why did he not accept it from the Corinthians? Chow suggests that he did not accept it because to do so would have confirmed lines of power that were already a problem.[68] However, refusing patronage usually earned one the antagonism of the party that offered it, shaming them before their peers.[69]

What evidence exists to indicate a group who would wish to continue the standard paradigm? In the first epistle, the correction of legal abuses among members (6:1–11) would indicate that some of the more typical business and social interactions were continuing. The elite were able to function more effectively by their connections, both to advocates and to presiding officers. The abuse of the common table, corrected by Paul in chapter 11, more strongly points to the continuing of strong social distinctions. In that environment, where honor could be most easily demonstrated, shame and dishonor resulted from obvious social differences played out in seating and food portions. As Marshall has noted,[70] the language of Paul is very sharp in countering the evident status distinctions in Corinth.[71] Paul describes his opponents there as "kings" (1 Cor 4:8), while he is "scum" (*perikatharmata*). In this passage Paul set up several other contrasts which would ring bells with those who knew the language of patronage: *mōroiphronoi, astheneis/ischuroi, atimoi/endoxoi*. This evidence indicates that Paul is struggling with a group who are not quite ready to implement a redirection of the honor game.

In this context, the commendation of the household of Stephanas in 1 Cor 16:15ff. is most interesting. Why did Paul consider that exhortation necessary? The possibility that Stephanas was being slighted as

---

67. 1 Cor 1:17; 2:1–5; 4:19–20; Chow, *Patronage and Power*, 104–9.
68. Chow, *Patronage and Power*, 109
69. See Marshall, *Enmity*, 62–66.
70. Marshall, *Enmity*, 135.
71. See Bartchy, "Table Fellowship," for a full discussion of the issues and dynamics involved.

a patron because of the egalitarian nature of the community falls with the evidence above, which shows that the community was anything but egalitarian. I would insist that Stephanas, while faithful and hardworking, did not have enough "image" to be respected as leader. He did not commend himself by the usual standards. Paul's commendation of him, and others like him, was based on their functions and attitude. They ordered themselves to the service of the saints (*eis diakonian tois hagiois etaxan heautous*); they were working and laboring (*sunerhounti kai kopiōnti*) to accomplish good in the need of others. For these reasons, Paul directed submission to and recognition of them.

Paul faced a similar issue when he wrote the latter portion of 2 Corinthians. He had an "image" problem, for he did not cultivate the approval of the Corinthians or a persona that impressed them as "apostolic" (11:10–18). Particularly interesting is the protest that Paul made in 11:5ff. He spoke of the "extraordinary apostles" (*huperlian apostolōn*), asserting more than once that he was not inferior to them. That protest was connected with his "mistake" of humbling himself and not accepting support. If the "superapostles" followed the patronage paradigm of the day, they commended themselves to those with resources and accepted support from them, while speaking well of those who granted support, and perhaps did favors for them outside of the church environment. Paul was struggling to maintain a paradigm of leadership that differed from the methods of many teachers, *rhetors*, and religious figures. Since he did not appear worthy of respect in traditional terms, others filled that position.

Paul went on to defend the integrity of his mission, showing that this reorientation was integral to the new community. For that reason even extraordinary religious privilege, such as the vision spoken of in chapter 12, had no value in establishing the mission's authenticity. Paul had different criteria:[72] the power of God for others (12:11–13), the sufferings willingly accepted for others (11:23–33) and the attitude of serving (11:2, 9; 12:14–15). His opponents were clear by their actions and attitudes: self-promotion and abuse of others (10:12, 15; 11:18–20).

Finally, the question of patronage and its modification may illuminate a thorny issue in the understanding of Paul's Thessalonian letters, by showing a dislocation in the effects of the new paradigm. In both let-

---

72. Note also 2 Cor 11:7—*emauton tapeinōn hina humeis hupsōthēte, hoti dōrean to tou theou euēngelsamēn hēmin.*

ters, a group of individuals were referred to as the "disorderly" (*ataktoi*),[73] who did not work and who acted as "busybodies" (*periergadzomenous*). Who were these individuals? It is likely that they had lived toward the bottom social rank, living in partial or complete dependence on the largesse of the elite. When they were taken away from that relationship, as we see Paul indicating in Rom 13:8, they had not followed the example which he both exemplified and commanded (2 Thess 3:7–9). They formed a new class that was dependent on the new community to meet their needs for the long term.[74] Perhaps some of them were still in the typical patron/client relation. In either case, Paul's injunctions in both letters (1 Thess 4:9–12; 2 Thess 3:12–13) encouraged a combination of responsible personal productivity and benevolent behavior towards others (*ergadzesthai tais idiais chersin humōn, tēs philadelphias kalopoiountes*). The exhortation to "quietness" is striking in this context. This quiet dignity should be seen as a withdrawal from the "busyness" of public support inherent to the patronage system, and that was to be an ambition (*philotimeisthai*) for the Thessalonian Christians. In carefully chosen language, Paul instructed a withdrawal from the usual patron/client system and the development of the parallel one inaugurated by Jesus. If we are right, some of the Thessalonians were either remaining in a prior patron/client relation, or were replacing their former patron with the new community, remaining dependent and disorderly.

Paul indicated that the new pattern was to result in behavior "presentable" (*euschēmonōs*) to those outside the community. I think that the "outsiders" (*tous exō*) would include former patrons as well as the general public. I do not agree with Winter that former clients would earn respect from the former patrons, at least in the beginning.[75] They would be initially perceived as *ingratus*; only later perhaps would they see some grudging respect.[76] In the eyes of the general public, how-

---

73. 1 Thess 5:14; 2 Thess 3:6, 11. For most of this theme, I am indebted to Winter, *Seek the Welfare*, 42–49. My disagreements will be noted in passing, but my appreciation is great.

74. Winter does not seem to think that the elite made clients among the poor (*Seek the Welfare*, 45). Who else would be motivated by a barely adequate *sportula*? He does however suggest that the *ataktoi* might have been imitating Cynic mendicants, which could be an viable alternative to disrupted patronage, and equally contrary to the new paradigm.

75. Winter, *Seek the Welfare*, 51.

76. In these passages, there is a word-play between "work" (*ergadzō*) and "being a busybody" (*periergadzō*). This contrast is present in Demosthenes (*First Philippic* 7),

ever, a change from being a client to self-support would garner some immediate respect. If that work also issued in a type of broad-scale benevolence, even more approval could result.[77] In Thessalonica the implementation of the new paradigm of patronage may have led to this problem of the "unruly," an unforeseen dislocation in its application. Before leaving this chapter, some conclusions about the New Testament critique of the standard paradigm and its redirection are due.

A Revised Paradigm of Patronage for the Patristic Project

As the basis for a continuing examination of early Christianity, I would like to offer the following conclusions, based on the previous chapter.

1. Patronage—in the sense of a pattern of social favors, with the recipients answering in gratitude and that constituted a continuing bond—was not abolished per se in early Christianity. Both Winter and Lull concur in seeing no bar to Christians acting as patrons in Luke 22:25, and most of the figures of early Christianity received favors. Nor is the functioning of the early community an egalitarian one, for there continue to be those who have recognized positions and authority.

2. The accepted paradigm of patronage was, however, critiqued by Jesus and other leaders with regard to the way in which it operated. The aspects rejected were primarily the motives behind the exchanges (love of glory or honor), the excessive honor-giving granted to the patrons, and the consequent degrading of the clientele. To these points, Paul added instruction that directed a breaking of dependence and obligation (Romans 13:8), while refusing to be dependent on figures in Corinth

---

and similar sentiments can be seen in Plato (*Republic* 433ab) and Epictetus (*Discourses* III,22,97). The elite often regarded work as something for the lower classes, thus *ergadzō* could be used in a rather pejorative manner.

77. "Mutual support between ordinary citizens linked by kinship, proximity of residence or friendship and exemplified in the interest-free loan, was a defense against poverty, hardship and the personal patronage of the wealthy." P. Garnsey *Famine and Food*, as quoted by Winter (*Seek the Welfare*, 55). This phenomenon is similar to the broad-scale benevolence visible in the early Christian community, yet smaller in scope and more restricted to social peers. In both volume and extension across social boundaries, that of early Christianity must be recognized as distinct. The purposes were also different in origin and purpose.

that would have perpetuated strong status differences there. James went somewhat further when he directed avoidance of "friendship" with the world, which had serious implications for the conduct of business.

3. The paradigm was redirected by Jesus and continued to be so by Peter, James and Paul in the following ways: (a) The God of Israel should be recognized as the supreme Patron, from whom all benefits come, and to whom all credit is due in a primary sense; (b) Consequently, individuals who usually acted as patrons could be a part of the new community and act as patrons only with the abandonment of the *cursus honorum* as their motivation. They were not automatically to take a first place in the community, with attendant privileges, titles and position. All would be subordinate to the majesty of God; (c) Those who emerge within the community as especially gifted, or chosen for leadership and authority, were not to be excessively honored nor to receive exalted titles and privileges. Their designations were drawn from the lower estates.

4. The redirected paradigm also included a radical inversion of the typical honor-game, extending honor precisely to those within the community (and perhaps outside of it) who were beyond conventional consideration. Both language and behavior were to be deliberately humble for those either used to honor or in a position where it would quickly accrue. These individuals did receive honor, along with the rest, and perhaps in a greater measure than some, but not in either an exaggerated or exclusive manner, nor were they to seek it or expect it as such.

5. Benefaction takes on a new character, as all the members of the new community were to see themselves as benefactors of a new order, in any manner in which they were capable either individually or corporately. One ambition appropriate to their identity was to seek to be capable by diligence and forethought. Thus a new broad-scale benevolence, which extended the gifts of God to others as a credit to God and intended by arousing more gratitude to extend and validate the community of God, was to be created. As Winter states, it constituted the most visible signal to the society of its day of a new community in which a function of all able-bodied members of this new community was to do good. This created a new class of benefactors. They did good because good needed to be done and did so without expectations of reciprocity or repayment.[78]

78. Winter, *Seek the Welfare*, 60.

The benefits included both those of everyday material matters, to qualities of moral and social life and to the spiritual gifts that relate to a more heavenly sphere.

With this revision of the original paradigm in mind, I will now move into the patristic period to investigate to what extent this new paradigm was honored or practiced in the early Christian community. The successive chapters will move around the Mediterranean, from Rome to Carthage.

3

Early Church Order Documents

CHAPTERS SUBSEQUENT TO THIS ONE WILL TRACE THE PARALLEL HIStories of activities, teaching and leadership in various geographical areas of the Roman Empire. Some texts, however, have not been placed securely with regard to their authorship nor area of provenance. Five of these texts are the subjects of this chapter: the Pastoral Epistles (1 and 2 Timothy and Titus in the New Testament), the *Didache* and the *Epistle of Barnabas*. All deal with practical church order.

The *Didache* and *Barnabas* will be treated together, since there is clearly a distinguishable literary relationship between the two, even to the point of having identical sections. The question of one being a source for the other has not been settled. A common source for both is also a likely possibility. It is generally agreed that both represent aspects of the church in the first half of the second century. The Pastoral Epistles represent developments of the later first century, so I will present their evidence first.

The Pastoral Epistles

The benefaction of God, though not discussed in cosmic terms as elsewhere in the New Testament, was clearly stated with regard to religious life, in terms now familiar. "The Favor (*charis*) of God has appeared, [with] salvation for all men (*sōtērias pasin anthrōpois*) . . ." (Titus 2:11). That message was allocated to select servants: "according to the gospel of the glory of the blessed God[1] with which I have been entrusted"

---

1. Only here in the Pastorals in the New Testament is *makarios* used in its classical sense, with regard to a god. But this is to be contrasted with a derived usage in Titus 2:13, where it modifies "hope," a usage that would have developed as "insider" language.

(*ho episteuthēn egō*) ... 1 Tim 1:11). This formulation, so Pauline in mood, should also be put together with the statement of the following verse, which offered thanks (*charin*) to God for trusting the writer with the "service" (*diakonian*). Along with God as the benefactor of first order, both Jesus and the writer as trusted brokers of divine benefits are foundational concepts visible here. Using the word "service," repeated with regard to Onesiphorus in 2 Tim 1:18, concerning his serving the community at Ephesus (*diēkonēsen*), shows a continuing inversion of honorific language, as does the use of "slave" (*doulos*, 2 Tim 2:24) and "workman" (*ergatēn*, 2:15). These designations referred to Timothy and other prominent individuals in the community.

What then was expected of those who have received the mediated benefits? They were expected to offer prayer and thanksgiving for "all humanity" to the God who wishes the same "all" to be saved (1 Tim 2:1, 4). Kings and prominent citizens (*tōn en huperochē ontōn*) were particularly mentioned as objects of prayer "so that we may lead a tranquil and quiet life in all godliness and dignity" (1 Tim 2:2-3). Though it is not mentioned here, this description of living condition was connected in the Thessalonian correspondence to "working with one's hands" and being prepared to help others (I,4:9ff.). A similar passage in Titus 2:12 indicates that the expected effect of the salvation is living "sensibly, righteously and godly" (*sōphronōs, dikaiōs, kai eusebōs*) and the construction ends with the phrase "zealous of good works" (*zēlōtēv kalōn ergōn*) in verse 14. What was meant by those good works, at least in part, was defined in Titus 3:14, where the process of discipleship includes learning to "lead" in good works aimed at urgent needs.[2] This was the normal fruit of their life. Thus we can see that disciplined lives were intended to be productive of the means of assisting those who were in need. These instructions point to a continuing community of broad scale benevolence. To this point, our evidence from the Pastorals seems quite congruent with the redirection of the patronage paradigm explored in chapter 2,[3] and with Paul in particular, though we can see

---

The use of *charis* cited just above is also a developed form of referral to Jesus, not paralleled in Paul's writings.

2. *manthanetōsan de kai oi hēmeteroi kalōn ergōn proistasthai eis tas anagkaias chreias, hina mē ōsin akarpoi.*

3. Without entering into the debate concerning how this writer modifies the place of women, let it be noted in passing that Christian women in general were to be noted for good works (1 Tim 2:9-10) and that one of the criteria for "recognized widows"

some "domestication" of critical terms such as *charis* and *makarios*. The motive of gratitude behind the benevolence was not mentioned. Either it was being lost, or was simply assumed. Two subjects, however, can be adduced to indicate some difficulty in the pattern.

First, the writer addressed the question of the rich in the church and those who were aiming to join them, in 1 Timothy 6. Those who were planning to become rich (*hoi boulomenoi ploutein*) should be strenuously warned against it, for many have encountered great problems with "love of money," the "root of all evil" (vv. 9–10). To achieve that goal, one would typically have to enter into the standard paradigm of patronage, which has been declared unacceptable to followers of Jesus. Verse 10 stated that some have already wandered away from the faith. The warning was apt.

In that same chapter the writer spoke regarding those who already were rich,[4] and assumedly within the community (vv. 17ff.). The focus of their attention was to be redirected away from themselves and their riches (*mē hupsēlophronein*), to the person of God as first order benefactor.[54] The results in action were "to do good, to be rich in good works, to be generous, ready to share" (*agathoergein, ploutein en ergois kalois, eumetadotous einai, koinōnikous*, v. 18). By so doing, they were trading present benefaction, at least in part, for future reward (v. 19), as Jesus had directed in the "Sermon". Note that divestiture of wealth in its entirety is not hinted, and the presence of the wealthy is presumed. Again, benefaction as a grateful answer to God's benevolence, or as imitation of the same, is not clearly stated. Second, in addition to this complex of instruction regarding wealth, a new element appears in reference to the office of bishop. Two words in 1 Tim 3:1 at least point in the direction of ambition. The verb *oregomai* would indicate strong desire, as does *epithumeō*. While not necessarily implying poor motives, seeking the office had been viewed rather negatively. By this point, ambition for the office was accepted, though the long following list of qualifications may demonstrate that great care was to be exercised in the confirmation of

---

is that they have a reputation for good works (*en ergois kalois martutoumenē*) 1 Tim 5:10).

4. "Instruct the rich" (v. 17), and the instruction does not seem that which would have been addressed to nonbelievers, unlike the more generic warning in James. Note that the reference to quite expensive attire in 1 Tim 2:9 may also point to upper class individuals.

the same. This could be a step back toward the former paradigm, acceptable ambition.

The *Didache* and the *Epistle of Barnabas*

Moving to the two related church order documents of the second century, the *Didache* and the *Epistle to Barnabas*, some thinking consistent with the new paradigm can be found. Though not extensively stated, the nature of their God as the first-order Benefactor underlay the thinking of these guides to spiritual life. This God was recognized as "the one who made you" (*Barn*. XIX,2; *Did*. I,2), and the resources from which benevolence proceeds were "his own gifts of favor" (*tōn idiōn charismatōn Did*. I,5). Nevertheless, it is in reference to benefits in the religious sphere that their language flows most freely. "Exceedingly and abundantly do I rejoice over your blessed and glorious spirit for the greatness and richness of God's ordinances towards you; so innate a grace of the gift of the Spirit have you received."[6] The character of this God is also revealed in a passage in which the writer of the *Didache* instructs masters to treat their slave or housemaid without bitterness, in a clear awareness of the God who is "over you both, for He comes not to call men with respect of persons (*kata prosōpon*), but those whom the Spirit has prepared" (IV, 10; *Barn*. XIX, 7).[7] Impartiality by this community and its God subverted the normal patronage process, but facilitated broad scale benevolence.

Those whom God had enriched, in any fashion, were then instructed to avoid the attitudes and relationships of the *cursus honorum*.[8] Both works instruct their readers not to exalt themselves or to permit a bold

---

6. *Megalōn men ontōn kai plousiōn tōn tou theou dikaiōmatōn eis humas, huper ti kai kath' huperbolēn hupereuphrainomai epi tois makariois kai endoxois humōn pneumasin; houtōs emphuton tēs dōreas pneumatikēs eilēphate. Barn*. I,2. Unless otherwise noted, English translation and Greek text will be taken from *The Apostolic Fathers*, LCL. If from Kleist's ET, ACW will be included in its citation. When I have given a new translation, it will be in italics with ABW following.

7. This impartiality was also the task of the Christian: "thou shalt give righteous judgment; thou shalt favor no man's person (*ou lēmpsē prosōpon*) in reproving transgression." *Did*. IV,3; *Barn*. XIX, 4.

8. *ouch hupsōseis seauton oude dōseis tē psuchē sou thrasos. Ou kollēthēsetai hē psuchē sou meta hupsēlōn, alla meta dikaiōn kai tapeinōn anastraphēsē. Did*. III,9. Cf. *Barn*. XIX,3,6. This normative vocabulary is congruent in both patterns and denotation with those which we have identified from the redirected paradigm in both Jesus and Paul.

or arrogant attitude. Both forbid bonding with "the exalted," but command "walking with the humble and the righteous." "Barnabas" specifically exhorts his readers to become "gentle and quiet" (*praus, hēsuchios*) and to be "humble-minded towards all" (*tapeinophrōn kata panta*, XIX,3–4). These injunctions, if carried out, would prevent involvement with ambitious individuals, both inside and outside the community, as well as the pursuit of personal gain and recognition.

Both continuity and novelty were present in instruction with regard to patterns of giving to the needy. The command of Jesus to give without requiring or expecting reciprocation was reiterated. This action reflects the will of God, the Father who "wishes [goods] of his own gifts of favor to be given to all" (*Did.* I,5).[9] A statement from both works reinforced the understanding that the resources given were considered still to be under divine direction: "share all things with your neighbor and . . . not say that they are your own, for if you are sharers in that which is incorruptible, how much more in *corruptible things*" (*Barn.* XIX,8; *Did.* IV,8).[10] An extended quote of Isa 58:6–10 was appended to indicate that the shape of religious observance could be redefined as broad scale benevolence toward the needy. This privilege would be done by all the members, including those with more material resources, but definitely not limited to those individuals (*Barn.* III,1ff.).

The instructions given, however, point to difficulties in the operation of a community of broad-scale benevolence. Some members had either ceased or become doubtful of its effectiveness. To these members, both works forbid hesitation and grumbling in the practice, adding that God had secured it with promise of a future reward, being the "good paymaster of the reward" (*ho tou misthou kalos antapodotēs Barn.* XIX,11; *Did.* IV,7). To this, "Barnabas" adds the inappropriateness of not answering gifts by giving (XIX,9). Finally, there is a hint that such giving may actually have an integral relation to forgiveness received from God in the future, in a saying found in both works: "Of whatever you have gained by your hands, you shall give a ransom for your sins" (*Did.* IV,6; par. *Barn.* XIX,10). If believed, this would be high motivation. The

---

9. My translation . . . *pasi gar thelei didsthai ho patēr ek tōn idiōn charismatōn*. ACW—"for the Father wants His own bounties to be shared with all."

10. Note that "the incorruptible" (*tō aphthartō*) is singular, while I have translated "corruptible things" (*tois aphthartois*) as plural to show that it refers to mundane goods whose importance has been redefined.

concept of redemptive almsgiving becomes an integral element in the Christian community of the third century, and may have been especially embraced by those who were wealthier.[11] At this point, however, there is no clear focus on a particular group, wealthy or otherwise.

It is necessary to address the issue of dependent members who do not work. After an initial welcome, a certain limit to hospitality for travelers was set, two or three days (*Did.* XII,1–2). If one wished to stay, they were to work according to their ability. If they were trained workers (*teknitai*), work was sought immediately. If not, discretion was exercised while some employment was found (XII,3ff.). Idleness was not an option; an idle dependent was a "Christmonger" (*Christemporos*). The detail of these instructions demonstrates that contemporary problems needed to be addressed.

Continuing an agenda we have seen in the Pauline epistles, these two works encourage the body of Christians to be consistent workers as is appropriate, for that work was assumed to be adequate in productivity for assistance to the needy. "Barnabas" allegorically interprets the Hebrew scripture about unclean birds of prey in Lev 11:13 as follows: "You shall not . . . join yourself or make yourself like such men as do not know how to gain their food by their labor and sweat, but plunder other people's property in their iniquity and lay wait for it" (X,4). Whether this last description refers to avaricious wealthy individuals or to thieves is not clear, but the same verb ("join to," *kollaō*) is used in another passage about being bound together with "the exalted" (XIX,6). Clearly, gaining by labor and sweat is commended, while it was despised among the class who were typically patrons. In this community, work provides benefit in excess of one's needs, to be given to others in the name of God.

Some of the factors included in a catalogue of the Way of Death, included in both works, confirm the aspects of early Christianity discussed above. Included in the long list were such designations as "far

---

11. *Lutrōsin* would not appear here to have any different significance than usual. It has been noted that this notion does not fit well with the predominant theory of atonement in New Testament writings. In this period, it is a minor thought which probably is rooted in the Septuagint form of some Old Testament and intertestamental works. See Garrison, *Redemptive Almsgiving*, 52ff., for clear delineation of the emergence of such language in Dan 4:27; Prov 15:27a; Tob 1:3; and 4:11. Other discussions of redemptive almsgiving may be found in Maier, *Social Setting*, 60, and Countryman, *Rich Christian*, 105–9. I find their attempts to root this notion in the New Testament completely unconvincing, but one cannot deny that it is a developing concern in the second and third century Christian Community.

from gentleness and perseverance," "not having mercy for the poor," "turning away the needy," "oppressing the afflicted," being "lawless judges of the poor" and "not working for the oppressed"[12] (*Did.* V,2; *Barn.* XX,2). All of these contradict the broad-scale benevolence advocated for Christians, and it is the last mentioned which, in reverse form, confirms that Christians were expected to work for the benefit of the oppressed (*ponountes epi kataponountes*).

Finally, in our discussion of the *Didache* and the Epistle of Barnabas, some developments were emerging with regard to leaders in the community, though the data here available comes only from the *Didache*.

First, the reader of the *Didache* was counseled to remember constantly "the one who Speaks the Word of God to you." This individual, who is not here given a specific title, was to be honored "as the Lord" (*hōs kurion* IV,1). In itself, this would not be surprising, except for the absence of the generalized honor language which we observed in the New Testament. Late in the work, the writer gave instructions concerning officers in the church, and though requiring values consonant with the above, designates the officers as "the honorable men among you" (*hoi tetimēmenoi humōn*, XV,2). Do we see here a movement towards a limiting of honor? This will bear careful watching.[13]

Second, the writer counsels care in the evaluation of prophets, either resident or itinerant. Within the early community, prophets were understood to be able to speak either in an exalted way under divine inspiration or perhaps in an ecstatic mode. In any case, the writer explicitly gave some practical guidelines that reveal his understanding of the work of God's Spirit. "But whoever shall say in a spirit 'give me money, or something else', you shall not listen to him; but if he tells you to give on behalf of others in want, let no one judge him" (XI,12). It was an inherent contradiction for one led of God's Spirit to seek one's own benefit and inherently consistent for the Spirit to seek the benefit of others. This is congruent with the evidence of the new paradigm as framed in Luke's portrayal of the early community in Acts 2–4.

Third, the writer of the *Didache* speaks of the giving of "first fruits" (*aparchēn* XIII,3). In a primary sense, these were for the support of

---

12. In terms of connection with the standard paradigm of patronage, this list also included "lovers of vanity, those who pursue reward, and advocates of the rich."

13. Cf. "double honor" for elders: 1 Tim 5:17.

prophets and teachers within the community (XIII,1–2). If, however, one did not have a prophet, the first-fruits were to be given to the poor (*ptōchos*). Towards the end of this chapter, a variety of resources were listed as that from which one should "give according to the commandment," which would make one "honored" (*makarios*). This would seem to point back to the support of the prophets and teachers, but the parallel clause in I,5 has reference to broad-scale benevolence, and I would insist on that orientation here.[14] This passage addresses, therefore, both the support of gifted individuals and compassion for the poor, as two related aspects of community benevolence.

Conclusions

1. The God of the Christians is recognized as a first order benefactor, from whom benefits of all types originate. Jesus is recognized as the first order broker of these benefits, while teachers and other officials of the community are now receiving increased honor. The language of honor to be given in general terms to all humanity is not seen.

2. Use of Paul's vocabulary which used deliberately inverted honorifics derived from the workplace and servile status is still visible in the Pastoral Epistles, but not in the two second century documents. Increased prominence was given to those who bore official titles: teacher, prophet, elder, and bishop. Some ambition was acceptable with regard to advancement in these offices, especially in the Pastoral Epistles.

3. The people of the new community are still viewed as a group whose identity necessarily involves "good works," which included the giving of help and gifts to the needy, as well as spiritual benefits such as prayer and the handing on of spiritual truth or life. The work of the Holy Spirit is understood to be foundational and integral to this continuing broad-scale benevolence. Credit and honor should be directed to the Patron and broker of first order. Short-term honor and long-term reward accrue to the people from their God. The *charis* word family was "domes-

---

14. Much of the instruction which we have detailed here is from the teaching of Jesus, and both terms *makarios* and *entolē*, are much more prominent in the Gospels than in the epistles of Paul. This exhortation points then to Jesus' emphasis on the poor, rather than the more Pauline support for resident ministers. Neither is, of course, exclusive.

ticated" and refers almost exclusively to the original endowment, quite rarely to any response or extension of gratitude.

4. The people of this community are increasingly directed to lead quiet, working lives, with specific warnings against involvement in ambitious projects or with the highly placed individuals who move in that arena. Special regard for those with high profile or status is specifically forbidden, for partiality towards such persons is not the agenda of this God or his community. If anything, members of the humble class are to remain in focus and to be preferred. Yet, the presence of the wealthy was acknowledged, at least in the Pastorals; and specific direction was given to them.

5. Specific directions that address doubt about the validity of the new paradigm, visible in the two second-century documents, confirm that the paradigm was being implemented with some difficulty. Both doubt on the part of believers and abuse by unscrupulous individuals were problems which needed to be addressed.

4

The Christian Communities at Rome

IN THIS CHAPTER, I WILL LOOK THROUGH SEVERAL WINDOWS IN ORDER to see how the new paradigm fared in the congregations of Rome. I will begin with the epistle attributed to Clement of Rome, then examine the unusual *Shepherd of Hermas*, the apologies of Justin and Minucius and the voluminous works of Hippolytus, including the church order document called *The Apostolic Tradition*, also attributed to Hippolytus. From these various windows, I will show both practices and tendencies of this church.

Clement Speaks from and for the Communities at Rome

The letter called First Clement was sent by the church at Rome to the church of Corinth, sometime during the last third of the first century CE.[1] Tradition unanimously attributed it to a leader named Clement, who also was included in a list of early bishops of Rome and who gained enough stature to call forth a large body of hagiographic literature, written too late to be considered for this project. The letter was written to address a serious division in the church at Corinth from the standpoint of a sister congregation at peace. The supposition that the "sudden and repeated misfortunes and calamities" (I,1) referred to serious problems within the Roman community is still theoretical, even in view of the mention of disagreement in XLVII,6.[2]

---

1. All citations of *1 Clement*, both English and Greek, will be from *The Apostolic Fathers I* in LCL. The edition of Jaubert (SC 167) was consulted with regard to the Greek text. It is my assumption that in these early centuries, there were multiple congregations of Christians in every large city, since they could not build large public buildings. Therefore, the "church" would be inclusive of these small congregations.

2. Argued by Bowe, *Church in Crisis*.

Leaving aside the debate concerning Clement's contribution to a theory of succession, it is clear that he assumed a hierarchy. Clement used the order of the Old Testament priesthood (XL,5) as well as the various levels of army commanders (XXXVII) to affirm levels of authority, privilege and power. This order (*taxis*) was essential to the expression of the benevolence of God, in a larger sense than just in human society. It was clear in the order of nature. How did Clement understand this benevolence?

In expressive fashion, Clement affirmed the creating, sustaining and ordering work of God as beneficent to all (XX). Both to and through the created order, the goodness of God was received, especially since the various components of that order do what God intended "without dissension" (*mē dichostasousa*), as the Ruler "does good to all" (*euergetōn ta panta*). Order was essential to benevolence.

Divine benevolence was also given in the work of Jesus of Nazareth, through whom a variety of benefits were made available, fulfilling promises made through the Hebrew prophets (XX; VII,4; VIII; Isa 1:16ff.). Divine favor (*charin*) was offered to the entire world.

This divine benevolence Clement described eloquently with regard to the condition of the Corinthian church before the division. Their name was "venerable and famous, worthy of the love of all men," their faith "most excellent (*panareton*) and steadfast" and their customary action "magnificent (*megaloprepēs*) in hospitality" (I,1-2).[3] Further, "a profound and rich peace was given to all, you had an insatiable desire to do good, and the Holy Spirit was poured out in abundance on you all," which was expressed in practical charity toward humanity both within the church and outside of it (II).

Distinct interpersonal values accompanied this benevolent community life, in the view of Clement. One essential value was to approach "all things without respect of persons" (*aprosōpolēmptōs*) (I,3). This aspect of characteristic Christian behavior should not surprise us, since we have seen this to be a dominant interest of their God. In Clement's words, He humbles the lofty (*hupsēlous*) and their pride (*huperēphanōn*), while enriching the humble with holiness, training and honor (LIX,3).

---

3. This kind of language is clearly of the type that would be used to describe and flatter benefactors and is here used in the service of the new paradigm. Note also that hospitality is a prime virtue for clement, who commends examples of that virtue: Abraham (X), Lot (XI), and Rahab (XII), from the heritage of the Hebrew Bible.

Indeed, Clement did not simply mention this theme, which clearly subverts the traditional *cursus honorum*, but emphasized it with reference to the behavior of the whole community, including those who ruled it or had high status.

Humility and submission were primary values for Clement, transforming the function of the levels of order in the community, to correspond to this God's interests. The opening statement of ch.II, prior to the florid description given just above, states that all in Corinth were humble-minded and not arrogant, "submitting rather than forcing submission, more gladly giving than receiving" (II,1).[4] Clement supported this by presenting Jesus as the prime Example. Though Jesus was indisputably deserving of honor and status in the Christian view, Clement reminded his readers that Jesus "thought humbly" (*etapeinophronēsen*), challenging them to do the same, since "we ... have come under the yoke of his favor" (*charitos* XVI,17). Since Christ was the mediator of God's favor, those who continue in that work ("yoke") must continue it with the same values, and preeminent among those values was humility.[5] With reference not only to the schismatics in Corinth but also to those they were displacing, Clement comments: "Christ belongs to those who are humble-minded *(tapeinophronountōn)*, not to those who exalt themselves over his flock" (XVI,1). Later he added: "let us give offence (*proskopsōmen*) to those who exalt themselves and boast in the pride of their word" (XXI,5). The context makes it clear that he was not speaking just to the moment; thus such sentiments should be understood to apply to general behavior, (as do the moral admonitions which follow them).

---

4. *Pantes te etapeinophoneite mēden aladzoneuomenoi, hupotassomenoi mallon hē hupotassontes, hēdion diontes ē lambanontes).* Note that the idea of submission includes the idea of an order, since both derive from *tassō*, to accept an established order, and to place oneself under its authority or importance. In the case of the Christian community, the question is the appropriate function of leadership in God's order. The example of Jesus serves to reveal that leading function and its pattern.

5. Note the many usages of this word-family. The adjective *tapeinos* occurs in XXX,2; LV,6; LIX,3–4 the substantive of process *tapeinōsis* in XVI,7; LIII,2; LV,6. The verb form occurs in XVIII,7; XIX,1; LIX,3 (twice). The compound form *tapeinophroneō* and its cognates occur a total of 18 times: the verb in II,1; XIII,1,3; XVI,1,2,17; XVII,2; XXX,3; XLVIII,6; LXII,2; the substantive *tapeinophrosunē* in XXI,8; XXX,8; XXXI,4; XLIV,3; LVI,1; LVIII,2; *tapeinophrōn* in XIX,1; XXXVIII,2. Bowe (1988,112) compares these 30 usages with 22 in the New Testament and 18 in the rest of the Apostolic Fathers.

Clement goes to some lengths to define a type of nobility which is distinct from that based on birth or acquired status. Rather than call his exemplars "noble," he refers to them as "attested," using past participles of *martureō*.[6] All are from the Hebrew Bible, and include David, Job, Moses, Elijah and Abraham (chaps. XVII, XIX). Quotations that Clement cited deliberately included testimony by the individuals to their own unworthiness. In conjunction with this series of examples, note that Clement clearly forbade self-praise, but affirms praise by others (XXX).[7] Even the latter, however, is not to be arranged or expected. Clement's orientation can be illustrated by his saying: "the greater he seems to be, so much the more should he be humble (*tosoutō . . . mallon tapeinophronein*), and seek the common good (*koinōpheles*) and not his own" (XLVII, 6).[8] Clement's presentation of honoring significantly differed from the revised paradigm, however, in that honor for everyone was never in sight, but rather primarily for the elders and the leaders.

If honor seemed more limited than in the New Testament revision of the paradigm, what of the community of broad scale benevolence? Were the resources and their extension to others also restricted in scope, more in the hands of the increasingly honored leadership?

One might expect the leaders to be emphasized as "second level" brokers of God's benefits, but such is not the case. Clement had a broader view in this respect. "Let the whole body be saved; let each be subject to his neighbor just as he was placed in his gifts of favor (*en tō charismati*)" XXXVIII,1).[9] The gifts of God then determined the relative function

---

6. Clement used the term *gennaios* in three chapters. In V and VI, it referred to Peter, Paul and women martyrs, thus those who have received their reward. In appealing to the schismatics (LIV), he used the term in order to persuade them that to submit or resign would be "noble."

7. In ch. XIII, Clement buttressed his principle by quoting Jer. 9:23f, "let not the wise man boast in his wisdom," and attributed it to the Holy Spirit. Paul had quoted it similarly in 1 Cor 1:31 and 2 Cor 10:17.

8. I found helpful the position of Bowe, quoting K. Thieme, to the effect that humblemindedness was "the readiness for a lower position, lesser regard, the absence of any desire to be great or distinguished, to have eternal honor or public esteem or a name, to mean something." It is then to be distinguished from inferiority or self-disparagement or servility "with which it has nothing whatsoever to do." *Church in Crisis*, 114.

9. Again, "submit" (*hupotassō*) here had the significance of declaring the importance of all who were in an order (*taxis*) which did not belong to those higher placed, but to the One who placed all members. Both arrogance and servility were excluded by the nature of the arrangement.

of action and benevolence. The "strong," who were not limited to the rulers, were to show careful attention (*tēmeleitō*) to the "weak," while the "weak" were to respect (*entrepō*) the former. Rich members were to consider themselves a resource (*epichoregeitō*) for the poor, while the poor were to give thanks to God for the ones who supplied their needs. The wise were urged to demonstrate (*endeiknusthō*) their wisdom in good deeds, rather than (just?) in words (XXXVIII,2). By using these general categories, Clement spoke to and about the entire community, and it was from the full community that both benevolence and thanksgiving were expected. Note the conclusion of the entire chapter: "Since therefore we have everything from him, we ought in everything to give him thanks, to whom be glory for ever and ever" (XXXVIII,4). We have seen that this gratitude took several forms.

Other passages of I Clement make it clear that the expected response was not only verbal.[10] The benefits given by God were appropriately answered by commendable actions (*ta kala kai euaresta*) which were done worthy of him (*axiōs autou* XXI,1). "Doing good" was not only God's business, but very much the business of God's people, as Clement showed by strong encouragement and warnings of accountability. An example of the extent to which "well-doing" was taken was given by Clement in a discussion of those who sacrifice for the common good, mentioning individuals within the Christian community who had sacrificed their freedom for others, selling themselves into slavery so that the price could purchase food for others (LV,2).[11]

---

10. "Shall we be lazy about well-doing and abandon love? May the Lord never permit this to happen to us; rather let us be eager to accomplish every good work with intensity and readiness" (*argēsōmen apo tēs agathopoiias kai egkratalipōmen tēn agapēn; mēthamōs touto easai ho despotēs eph' hēmin ge genēthēnai, alla speusōmen meta ekteneias kai prothumias pan ergon agathon epitelein* XXXIII,1); "Let us observe that all the righteous ones have been adorned with good works; and the Lord himself rejoiced while adorning himself with good works. Since we have this pattern, let us be occupied with his will without hesitation. (*Idōmen, hoti en ergois agathois pantes ekosmēthēsan hoi dikaioi, kai autos de ho kurios ergois agathois heauton kosmēsas echarē. Echontes oun touton ton hupogrmmon aoknōs proselthōmen tō thelēmati autou ... ex holēs tēs ischuos hēmōn ergasōmetha ergon dikaiosunēs*, XXXIII,7–8). My translation. See also XXXIV,1–4.

11. See Bartchy, "Slave, Slavery," especially section 3.3, for notation of the use of two former imperial slaves, Claudius Ephebus and Valerius Bito, to carry this letter to Corinth and this matter of self-sale as integral to the inversion of social patterns.

Before going on to the next "window," a summary evaluation of the evidence in Clement is in order. The subversion of the standard paradigm of patronage is clear, by the forbidding of favoritism to those who would normally be favored. Heavy emphasis on humility and mutual submission also would, if taken seriously, seriously redirect the plans and ambitions of some individuals. God is clearly seen as a first order benefactor, with divine benefits and characteristics mediated through Jesus and his community. So is anything missing in the revision of the paradigm?

Clement did not alter the inversion by speaking of a hierarchy, for that is clearly present in New Testament materials. His analogies from the Hebrew Bible and the Roman army, by which the orders of authority were under-stood, may have been unfortunate. Both the Hebrew cultus and the military sphere have logic appropriate to their function, while the Christian community was directed at an end that transcends either. Clement did not, finally, emphasize important balancing elements to the function of that hierarchy, such as to "honor everyone" (Peter), to "give greater honor to the less presentable" (Paul) or to seek the good of the "little ones" (Jesus). These radical injunctions were at the heart of this new community. It is not clear to me whether Clement lacked these perspectives, or whether they were not included due to the nature or length of the epistle.

"Hermas" Speaks from the Church at Rome

Our next window into the church at Rome is courtesy of the extensive and challenging *Shepherd of Hermas*. Written over a period of time, perhaps a couple of decades, by a single author with significant connection to the leadership of the church at Rome, yet the complaints of Hermas seem to reflect a view of the church closer to the average Christian person in the first half of the second century. Unlike many of the writers of the early who wrote moderate or high quality Greek, Hermas' writing shows no serious training. He was not apparently of the elite, nor in a highly trained part of an elite household.[12]

---

12. All quotations, English and Greek, will be from *The Apostolic Fathers II* in LCL. Joly's edition (SC 53) has been consulted for Greek text. Citations are parenthetically identified as Visions, Mandates and Similitudes. Inconsistencies in thought and variations in structure have led to several attempts to establish multiple authorship over

The first matter to be noted from Hermas is the lack of language that explicitly identified either the God of the Hebrews, or Jesus of Nazareth, as supreme benefactors. One may assume that Hermas believed that all good comes from God, but it is striking that he did not mention it, since it was so strong in all levels of New Testament writing. Hermas did, however, focus upon the actions of church members, and confronted patterns of behavior that connect with the concerns of this project.

Hermas was quite insistent that some Christians were trying to continue the pattern of living inherent to the prevailing patron/client paradigm. While claiming to be members of this new community, they did not show a pattern of values and behavior that made sense to Hermas. His assessment was that they "have never inquired concerning the truth nor made search concerning divinity" and are "mixed up with business deals and riches and heathen friendships and many other business matters of this age."[13] He challenged those who "obtain this world for themselves and glory in their wealth and do not lay hold of the good things to come" (*Vis.* I,1,8). Those who "take a pig's share" (*metalambanete ek katachumatos*) were confronted, since they were hurting even themselves at the table, while others were suffering from not having enough.[14] In method and behavior, these members of the Roman community were not xpressing the new paradigm.

To whom and of whom was Hermas speaking? At this point, Carolyn Osiek's study of Hermas helps us. As she saw, Hermas spoke in first person to the rich, but in third person about the poor.[15] In the

---

a period of time. For evaluation of these theories, see Reiling *Hermas and Christian Prophecy*, who concluded (22ff.) that the evidence was best explained by a single author over a period of time. Wilson, while confirming the irregularities, also postulates one author, due to linguistic consistency and overarching themes (*Reassessment* 7). Maier (*Social Setting* 56) sees the inconsistencies as simply reflective of the unsettled nature of second century Christianity. I would agree, and add that Hermas was perhaps not trained in either thought or expression.

13. *empephurmenoi de pragmateias kai ploutō kai philias ethnikais kai allais pollais pragmateias tou aiōnas toutou Mand.* X,1,4.

14. *Vis.* III,9,2–3. In verse 5 of the same section, he mentions those who "overpossess" (*hoi huperechontes*). Compare 1 Cor. 7:30: "let those who buy be as those who do not possess" (*hoi agoradzontes hōs mē katechontes*). First Cor 11:20ff., 30 condemns similar demeaning actions at the table

15. Carolyn Osiek, *Rich and Poor*. The content of this paragraph reflects her discussions and conclusions on 37, 55, and 127–28.

first half of the second century, it is unlikely that he was speaking to members of the top two orders. Who would be most likely to be described in terms of social climbing? The most likely candidates would be those who had little or no chance before, but who could now rise within the growing openness and prosperity of the Empire under the "good emperors." Many slaves were part of the early Christian community, and when they became free, they could take advantage of new opportunities. Hermas was one of this class, and it is most likely that he spoke primarily to his peers, who had looked forward to being on the "profit side" of this patronage paradigm. It is understandable that they resisted surrendering their new advantage.

The relationship of the ambitious Christian to the larger community was mentioned several times. An abandonment of the faithful was noted: "these are those who had become faithful, but became rich and honored before the nations. They put on great haughtiness (*huperēphanian*) and became highminded (*hupsēlophronēs*) ... and did not cleave to the righteous, rather they lived with the heathen, and this way suited them better" (*Sim.* VIII,9,1). Again Hermas comments: "These then who are engaged in many and various businesses do not cleave to the slaves of God, but being choked by their work, go astray. And the rich cleave with difficulty to the slaves of God, fearing that they will be asked for something by them."[16] A couple of related problems can be seen here. First, Hermas saw a class of believers who he believed were involved with the prevailing paradigm. Their means of gaining wealth involved close relationships with those clearly not in sympathy with the new community, accompanied by pursuit of honor. Second, they were withdrawing from other Christians, consciously rejecting the new paradigm because it required a response to requests by the needy.[17] Both their understanding of appropriate means of gaining wealth as well as its value or use were contrary to Hermas' understanding of the

---

16. *Sim.* IX,20,2. *houtoi oun, oi en pollais kai poikiliais pragmateias emperphurmenoi, ou kollōntai tois doulois tou theou, all' apoplanōntai pnigomenoi hupo tōn praxeōn autōn hoi de plousioi duskolōs kollōntai tois doulois tou theou, phoboumenoi, mē aitisthōsin hup' autōn.* See also *Vis.* III,6,5, which insists that the wealthy deny the Lord in times of tribulation because of business matters (*pragmateias*).

17. I would assume that their means of proving themselves worthy associates of their chosen group would include benefaction. Does their refusal here indicate that a lack of the usual reciprocation disenchanted them? Did they not accept the principle that credit belongs to God?

new paradigm. Was then the gaining and possession of wealth categorically excluded within Hermas' understanding?

One passage would seem to indicate such a position. In order for the wealthy to be useful for the Lord, said the Lady to Hermas, their wealth must be cut (*perikopē Vis.* III,6.6). If this means the surrender of wealth, however, how then could the rich be expected to meet the needs of the poor? How could the rich be symbolized as an elm tree, which because of its stable position and conservation of water, be the support and supplier of the poor, symbolized as a vine in the extended analogy of *Sim.* II,5? I would contend that *perikopē* be understood as "pruned" or "shaped" by the removal of some material, and that the accompanying image of the stone which must be shaped, in order to be a useful wheel, supports that translation of the word. Certainly, modifications in the use and perception of resources were advocated.

Hermas must have been speaking to an ambitious group when he challenged them to stop spending their money on "lands and expensive furnishings and buildings and empty dwellings" (*Sim.* I,1,1), the accoutrement of the pursuit of honor and recognition. Is it not that spending pattern, and the motivations behind it that are to be "cut away"? Instead, Hermas indicated that one who has large resources should spend them in ways that purchase "afflicted souls" and look out for widows and orphans. "For this reason did the Master make you rich, that you may fulfill these ministries for him" (I,1,8–9). Thus they would "build houses" in the City which is to come. The reflection of Jesus' parable of the unjust steward was unmistakable: "make friends by means of unrighteous mammon . . . that they may receive you into eternal dwellings" (Luke 16:9).

Hermas found it necessary to address quite directly "those who take pride in your wealth," admonishing them not to be indifferent to those who are in need. He warned the rich that they could be "locked out" of the church, which he symbolized by a Tower (*Vis.* III,9,6). This warning was immediately followed by strong words addressed to the leaders (*tois proēgoumenois*) of the church and to those who have the chief seats (*tois prōtokathedritais*), who carry "charms and poison" in their hearts. Their impurity then is apparently associated with division (*dichostasiai*) in the Christian community. The entire section deals with the disparity between the rich and poor and the fact that those who should be actively participating in the new paradigm, (which is assumed as the basis of the dissension), have not learned the meaning of their wealth in this new perspective (*Vis.* III,9,1–7).

In this last section, we saw that Hermas connected the leadership of the Roman church to the improper functioning of the new paradigm. Hermas spoke of a Shepherd of Luxury and Deceit, who destroyed the bondslaves of God by misleading them into a pattern of behavior which is self-indulgent and useless (*truphais mataiais, Sim.* VI,9,1–2). Like the leaders who had poison and charms to give the followers, this was an anti-benefaction in Christian terms, both in the leaders and in those who did not properly use their resources because they were following the prevailing paradigm, not the revised one. Rather than seeing that which God had to them as a privilege to be used for others, they simply used those resources for their own pleasure and glory.

A different issue surfaced in Hermas' perception of two groups within the community who were ambitious to move up to a position of prominence. First, he described self-appointed teachers" (*ethelodidaskaloi*) who were filled with presumption (*authadeian*), thinking highly of themselves (*hupsēlophrosunē*) and exalting themselves (*hupsountes heautous, Sim.* IX, 22,1ff.). Secondly, he described a group who sought the first place (*prōteiōn*), though these were called faithful and good (*Sim.* VIII,7,4). Both groups were proceeding in a manner contrary to the new paradigm, though the latter seemed to him to be less dangerous. Some levels of distinction seem to be inevitable, but to seek to be advanced higher belonged to the traditional paradigm.

Hermas also spoke of false leaders within the church, who "devoured the life of widows and orphans," making their service a matter of personal profit (*Sim.* IX,26,2), a clear reversal of the new paradigm. Others whom he labeled "false prophets" allowed weak Christians (the "doubleminded" *dipsuchoi*) to approach them seeking information about the future and insisted on being paid well for their help. Concomitant to that agenda, these individuals sought the "first place" (*prōtokathedrian*), lacked dignity and lived in luxury (*Mand.* XI,2).

Hermas exercised a prophetic voice in his work, confronting several lingering uses of the prevailing model of patronage. In every case, his critiques assume the new paradigm. He did, however, have something positive to say about the new paradigm, in terms of instruction about its application.

First, the person who has the Spirit of God, and thereby some place and respect in the community, will show that fact by aspects of attitude and behavior. Gentleness, quietness and thinking humbly were immediately mentioned.[18] Other prescriptions connect with the themes we have been exploring. Spiritual persons not be anxious to give answers to every question and should make themselves poorer (*endeesteron*) than others, abstaining from the "useless desire of this age."[19] Each of these, if followed, would have an impact on honor-seeking.

Further, Hermas gave strong indication that the community of broad scale benevolence was still the ideal, at least for that part of the Roman community that Hermas represented. Consider the universal scope, work and simplicity of attitude in the following quote: "Do good and of all your toil which God gives you, give in simplicity (*didou haplōs*) to all who need, not doubting to whom you should give and to whom not, for to all God wishes gifts to be made of his own gifts."[20] Here the flow of favor was clear, for even the work one did came from the person of God. Out of the product of that work, those who are in need were to receive divine benefit through the members of the new community. The command not to hesitate contrasts strongly with the behavior of some of the wealthy in the community, who were not even sure they wished to give to other members of the Christian community. No one was to try to discern whether one was worthy of the gifts, for in the line of favor, those who have already received were understood not to be worthy.

---

18 See *Mand.* VI,2,2 for an extended treatment of the qualities of attitude and action to be understood as righteousness. These qualities, which we saw promoted by Jesus and his immediate successors, are pre-eminent here as well. See *Mand.* VIII,3 and 10 for further lists.

19. *epithumias mataias tou aiōnas toutou* (*Mand.* IX,8). The words echo with regard to Hermas' discussion of the retreat to the old ways, in which the pursuit is considered "useless." Compare *Mand.* IX,4—*matataiōtatōn tou aiōnas*.

20. *Mand.* II,4. In this section of Hermas, the word family rooted in *hapl* is used a number of times. The adverb, used above, occurs three times in s.4 & 6 [**AQ: what is the "s" in this citation?**], while a substantive (*haplotēti*) occur in s.1 & 7 of this Mandate, as well as in *Vis.* III,1,6 and III,9,1 (along with *akakia kai semnotēti*). Meaning either simplicity or generosity, the latter meaning is particularly apropos to the matter of giving, which is in view in these passages. Pertinent as well is the use of *haplous* by Jesus in Matt 6:22, to describe the healthy eye, in the middle of a complex of teaching about the appropriate use of possessions.

Attitudes and actions appropriate to this new community were linked by Hermas in a long passage, which can be summarized as follows. "Believers" were to be generous, blessed and without malice or grudges. They were to "rejoice in the slaves of God" (*doulois*), being clothed with the Holy Spirit. Practical applications were specified. They would always have compassion for every person (*pantote splangchnon echontes epi panta anthrōpon*). From the gain of their work, they would function as God's supply for everyone (*echorēgēsan panti anthrōpō*) without prejudging them (*anoneidistōs kai adistaktōs Sim*.IX,24,2–3). Hermas insists that the response of God would be to give them prosperity in further favor (*eplēthunen autous ... kai echaritōsen autous*), having approved their manner of living.[21] Hermas also gave a striking and practical example of how those who were not well off might gain resources for such benevolence: fasting in order to save money which could be used for orphans and widows, who would have benefit beyond the material aid, for the receiving party would "fill his soul" (*Sim*. V,3,6).[22] Let it be noted that this is very broad-scale, for every level of socio-economic strata were to be active in both giving and receiving.

In one final way, Hermas well represents essential aspects of the revised paradigm. Jesus had spoken of an honor from God, which accrues to those who participate in the community that has received this revised paradigm, and even of great reward. Hermas assured those whom he hoped to influence that their benevolence is and will be answered by their status as honored (*endoxos, Mand*. II,6). In another statement,[23] he insists that actions that go beyond the strict commands of God gain greater approval. So the glory that may not be sought from humanity can be gained by the response of the pleased Patron.

To summarize the evidence from the *Shepherd of Hermas*, let me observe the following.

---

21. The substantives used here to describe the true believers are *haplotēti kai nēpiotēti*. The former has already been commented on; the latter clearly connects with the redirection of the paradigm as represented in the instruction of Jesus in Matt. 11:25, where the receivers of the favor of God are called *nēpioi*.

22. This is quite comparable to the practice mentioned by Clement, in which Christians sold themselves into slavery to gain the resources to benefit others (*1 Clem*. LV,2).

23. *Sim*. V,3,3. *ean ti agathon poiēsēs ektos tēs entolēs tou theou seautō peripoiēs doxan perssoterran kai esē endoxoteros tō theō ou emelles einai.*

1. The presupposition of God as first order benefactor and Jesus as prime "broker" was not emphasized. In this case, unlike *1 Clement*, the work is large enough to expect significant assertion of this foundational matter.

2. The new paradigm, which Hermas definitely has in mind, was experiencing difficulties on several levels, among the Christians at Rome. Some members had not abandoned prior patterns and others had returned to previous patterns. In both cases, the purposes were profit and recognition.

3. Some of the current leadership as well as some who aspired for office and influence were conducting themselves in a way that pushed the Roman community in directions that clearly reflected the old paradigm.

4. The community of benevolence is well in view, but those most equipped with resources were hesitant to act within the community and to extend themselves without distinction outside it. They had not learned the meaning of their resources. Whether they had been taught it in theory is not clear.

Defenders of the Community

Justin the Teacher

Another window into the Roman community is provided by the Apologists, Justin Martyr and Minucius Felix. Both Clement and Hermas wrote to and for the members of their own community, so their work has the character of "insider" literature. They reveal the tensions and issues of an emerging movement. Justin's *Apology* and *Dialogue with Trypho*, as well as Minucius' *Octavius*, on the other hand, were intended to be read by nonmembers, as well as members. Along with defending the new group, they tried to present an attractive picture of Christianity, in order to commend its way to educated Romans and Jews, even the good emperors of the second century, to whom several apologies were addressed. By their very nature, these works do not reveal the shortcomings of the community detailed by Hermas in his prophetic and therefore confrontational work, or Clement's pastoral corrections to the community at Corinth. For the purposes of this project, I will assume that Justin and Minucius spoke of the ideals of the Christian community, as they had been taught them and as they had experienced them. Their testimony must be balanced by the evidence of others. Unlike Hermas, Justin clearly acknowledged the God of the Christians as a first-order benefactor, as well as a source of the particular benefits mediated through Jesus.[24] "And Father and God and Creator and Lord and Master are not names, but rather emerge out of his good deeds (*ek tōn eupoiin 2 Apol.* 6). The very creation was a benevolence, "created in his goodness ... for the sake of humanity," *1 Apol.* 10). Justin understood this God to be the Giver of all, to all humanity, even those who do not please him, "who makes his sun to shine on sinners, on the just and the wicked," quoting from the Sermon on the Mount (*1 Apol.* 15; Matt 5:45). Within this context of universal benevolence, God sent Jesus to "broker" spiritual benefits.

Justin understood Jesus' function in three ways. First, he was the teacher of the truth, "for the change and restoration of humanity" (*ep' allagē kai epanagōgē tou anthrōpeiou*, *1 Apol.* 23). Second, he was understood to be the "sacrifice for all sinners who wish to repent and fast the fast which Isaiah prescribed, when they scatter the knots of forced contracts."[25] Third, he was understood to be the present mediator of a new covenant which, as compared to the Jewish Law, was "for all (humanity) generously" (*ho de pantōn haplōs*, *Dial.* XI,2). The breadth of benefit, in both effect and intended group, is quite clear.

What then was the shape of the community based upon these benefits? Justin the layman, (for he was not titled as clergy), referred to no high positions. The titles of prominent leaders were simple: deacons and "presidents." The latter was simply a present participle of *proistanō*, "one who presides." No indication was given that anyone, however gifted with various resources, was given exclusive place. The "president" would have been able to read and speak well enough to exhort and improvise

24. The two *Apologies* of Justin will be cited in English from Falls' translation in the Fathers of the Church series, and in Greek from Gildersleeve's edition. *The Dialogue with Trypho* will be cited in English from Williams' translation, and the Greek edition of Goodspeed.

25. My translation. . . . *prosphora ēn huper pantōn tōn metanoein boulomenōn hamartolōn kai nēsteuontōn heōn katalegei Esaias nēsteian, diaspōntes strangalias biaōn sunallagmatōn*. See also chap. XV, where Justin enlarges on the passage from Isaiah to which he alludes here (Isa 58:3–12) with a wide variety of social benefits.

prayer, but all Christians are members of a "true high-priestly race" (*archieratikon to alēthinon genos semen tou theou Dial.* 116,3), who offer up pure sacrifices among all nations. Justin described his own position as one of privilege and responsibility, one who had been given a favor (*charis*) by God to understand the Scriptures. He invited "everyone to share in that favor without charge or grudge" (*amisthōti kai aphronōs, Dial.* 58,1).

In his description of baptismal rites, Justin showed that not only were the new initiates not tied specifically to the leaders; the opposite seems true. The whole community shared in the preparation and celebration of their entrance, fasting along with the prospective member (*1 Apol.* 61). Justin saw the whole community and its way as "full of the divine Spirit, gushing forth with power and flourishing with favor" (*mestois pneumatos theiou kai dunamei bruousi kai tethēlosi chariti, Dial.* IX,1). The context of that remark shows that Justin clearly spoke from experience and observation.

In chapters 15 and 16 of the *First Apology*, Justin echoed the language of Jesus in the Sermon, both from Matthew and Luke. He addressed both the actions and the attitude, representing the new paradigm cogently. However, he added that their accompanying qualities of life conquer the violence and shame of their neighbors. In material gifts, the moral or spiritual depth of their lives and the over-coming of racial or ethnic walls, the favor of God was to be handed on through all the members of the community.

Both ambition and the seeking of honor were explicitly excluded, both in a prohibition ("do nothing for glory" *mēden pros doxan poiein, 1 Apol.* 15,10), as well as by a redirection of honor-giving. Both the believers themselves, as well as those who witness the good works, should direct glory to the Father in heaven. Ambitious acquisition, as well, was to be transformed into an extension of benevolence: "We who loved above all else the ways of acquiring riches and possessions now hand over to a community fund what we have and share it with every needy person." (... *chrōmatōn de kai ktēmatōn hoi porous pantos mallon stergountes, nin kai ha echomeneis koinon phrontes kaipanti deomenō koinōnountes, 1 Apol.* 14,2). The use of possessions in this way constituted an alternative form of honor or worship, in which the "sacrifices" were put to use in the lives of the needy rather than being offered on an altar or given to a special priestly caste (*1 Apol.* 13,1).²⁶

One aspect of this community benevolence, which will cast a long shadow, was putting the community fund in the hands of the "president," to disburse to the sick, orphans and widows, the needy and the strangers (*1 Apol.* 67). To these folks, he would look and feel like a patron. Though they might be aware that the funds were from the whole community, the nature of the culture as well as the discretion of the president would tend to create a personal following. If there should happen to be an unscrupulous figure in that office, the possibilities would not be missed. Hermas' polemic pointed to precisely that problem.

Minucius Felix

Evidence from Hermas and Justin has shown us that the ideal of the revised paradigm is alive in the Roman community in the middle of the second century. However, the concerns of Hermas showed varying realities in terms of realizing that ideal. Before moving to the end of this century, evidence may be adduced from the third-century apologist Minucius Felix, whose arguments reveal that some aspects of the new paradigm were still important and functioning.²⁷

Minucius' beautiful dialogue *Octavius* defends the Christian way by recreating a debate between two friends concerning the truth of Christianity. Octavius represented the Christian cause, answering the accusations and objections of Caecilius. Both protagonists were from North Africa, but their elegant interaction took place in Ostia, on a day of relaxation. Minucius himself took the role of moderator, and he is represented as a Roman. In the scene, the content and the quality of the dialogue, Minucius represents the movement of Christianity among higher social classes during the third century.

Octavius identified himself as a former prosecutor of Christians who "bent the rules" to force them to recant. At the time of the dialogue,

---

26. Justin used two words in the Apology to refer to those who had more resources, "we who have" (*hoi echontes*) and who help (*epikouroumen*) the needy, and "those who prosper" (*hoi euporountes*) who bring gifts to the common fund (67,1–3). Strikingly, terms that unequivocally identify wealthy individuals are absent.

27. Unless otherwise noted, English citations will be from LCL 250, listed in our bibliography under Tertullian; Latin citations are from the edition of Kytzler. Quispel's edition was also consulted.

however, his opponent called him "prince of bakers" (XIV,1). He had apparently lost his position as an official and as an advocate, reduced in Caecilius' eyes to the drudgery of baking. Is this simply "window dressing" for the dialogue? Perhaps, but the picture correlates well with the accusations leveled at the Christian community by Caecilius: "Is it not deplorable that a gang (excuse my vehemence in using strong language for the cause I advocate) a gang, I say, of discredited and proscribed desperadoes band themselves against the gods? Fellows who gather together illiterates from the dregs of the populace and credulous women with the instability natural to their sex ... they despise titles and robes of honor, going themselves half-naked! (VIII,3–4)."[28] Within the obvious polemic, aspects of the perception of Christian community seem apparent. First, the bulk of the members were described as unskilled or illiterate men along with credulous women. Second, the gatherers of this crowd were apparently not of the same class; thus the adjectives which point to their fallen lot. Third, the *cursus honorum* has been rejected. Octavius denied none of these points, but confirmed them as appropriate.

To the accusation that this movement was composed of unworthy individuals, Octavius answered that the poor and ignorant were uniquely equipped to understand the deeper things of life, not being distracted by gold. Further, he asserted that "all humanity, without distinction of age, sex or rank, were created with the capacity and power of reasoning; wisdom is not acquired by fortune but implanted by nature" (XVI,5). So among the Christians, "we call ourselves 'brethren', to which you object, as members of one family in God, as partners in one faith, as joint heirs in hope" (XXXI,8). Here then were the bases for a continuing honor for all humanity prior to entrance into the community, as well as mutual honor within it.

Minucius also inverted the estimation of wealth and poverty; the latter was more healthful in mental and spiritual terms. He asserted that Christians are free from want and envy of others, for they are dependent upon the daily supply of the Lord. Uniting common wisdom with

28. *homines (sustinebitis enim me impetum susceptae actionis liberius exserentem) homines, inquam, deploratae, inlicitae ac desperatae factionis grassari in deos no ingemescendum est? Qui de ultima faece collectis inperitioribus et mulieribus cerulis sui facilitate labentibus plebem profanae coniurationis instituunt ... honores et purpuras despiciunt, ipsi seminudi!*

the admonitions of the gospels,[29] Minucius argued that wealth was a burden,[30] yet some *could* be useful, if it were to be used for the benefit of others.

In this slender work, Minucius showed that some of the aspects of the new paradigm continue into the third century. Issues regarding leaders and their connection both to the means of God's favor and to the function of broadscale benevolence, are not visible in his work.

Hippolytus and a Changing Community

Toward the end of the second century and well into the third, considerable insight[31] into the community at Rome is provided in the voluminous works of Hippolytus, who was the first of several men who were elected to be an alternative bishop to a leader already functioning in the bishop's office at Rome. I would argue that part of the reason for the proliferation of figures and groups competing for power and honor may be found in Hippolytus' work called the *Apostolic Tradition*.

The Apostolic Tradition

In this detailed work, Hippolytus gave startling instructions for a carefully and strictly graded community. Though the benefaction of God to members of the community was mentioned, as well as divine "respect for the lowly" (*Ap. Tr.* Proem; I,3), new constructs and language put the bishop and deacons in a decidedly different position.

In the ordination prayer for bishops (I,3), God was asked to "pour forth of that power, which is . . . of thy ruling (*principalis/ hēgemonikos*)

---

29. "he who walks lightest walks with the most ease."

30. "Yet for resources, if we consider them useful, we may ask of God, and he who holds the whole may indulge us with a substantial portion. However, we would prefer to despise rather than hold it; we desire innocence more; we seek patience more; we prefer to be good rather than prodigal" (my translation). *Et tamen facultates, si utiles putaremus, a deo posceremus: utique indulgere posset aliquantum cuius est totum. Sed nos contemnere malamus opes quam continere, innocentiam magis cupimus, magis patientiam flagitamus, malamus nos bonos esse quam prodigos* (XXXVI,3). Here Minucius illustrates that ambivalence regarding wealth and its use, which is so critical in Clement of Alexandria.

31. *The Apostolic Tradition of Hippolytus* is cited in English from the translation of Easton. The Latin text is cited from the edition of Botte (SC 11).

Spirit" (I,3). Here the adjective "ruling" is quite at odds with framing of the new paradigm. What was meant by "power" was quickly made clear. The word "servant" (*servus*) denoted a leader who filled a high priestly[32] role with reference to the people of God, to obtain mercy and to bring gifts from the church. The forgiveness of sin was also the prerogative of the bishop, by apostolic authority. Without doubt, these prerogatives established the bishop as a spiritual broker at a much higher level than previously.

The ordination of the presbyters seems unexceptional. They were to receive a spirit of grace and counsel appropriate to presbyters (I,7). More significant changes were reserved for deacons and confessors.

The sacrifice of having been in bonds for Christ qualified the confessors for "the honor of the presbyterate," but not that of the episcopacy (I,10). Such a statement is valuable in two ways. First, it indicates that levels of honor were attached to offices, a re-establishing of the honor system which the new paradigm was aimed at revising. Second, it gives early evidence for the ascribing of high status to those who had been highlighted by local persecutions, a growing trend. Note that this is separate from the measures of endowment by God or of the characteristics of the new euergetism, though the suffering could be regarded as honor given back to the Patron.

Section I,8 indicated that the deacons, while ordained, do not receive "the Spirit that is possessed by the presbytery." Such hierarchical grading with regard to the receiving of God's Spirit contradicts the normative power of the prophecy that Peter quoted on the day of Pentecost (Acts 2:17–18), as well as Paul's construction in 1 Corinthians 12, which spoke of many gifts but the same Spirit. Endowment of the members of this community was to be received in a broad manner, definitely not in a hierarchical scale.

This strict grading becomes even clearer when the position of the deacon was defined as not priestly, but rather as "serving the bishop" (*in ministerio episcopi*) and "carrying out his commands" (*faciat ea quae ab ipso iubentur*). That which he received and did was "confided to him under the bishop's authority" (*sub potestate episcopi est creditum*). It is

---

32. ... *primatum sacerdotii tibi* ... *incessante repropitiari vultum tuum et offere dona sanctae ecclesiae tuae/ archierateuein soi amamptōs* ... *adialeiptōs te ilaskestai tō prosōpō* ... Also in III,6 with reference to ministry to the sick.

clear that the deacons are no longer seen primarily as servants of God or humanity, but of the bishop in particular.

What then of the people of God? Their primary role in this document is to participate in the liturgical and catechetical patterns. They are to hasten to do good works, but this was mentioned only in passing (II,23). Diligence in handing over the first fruits to the bishop was also emphasized, but they are not support, but "offerings." What should be done with them is not mentioned.

Further, the path to being baptized was a long catechumenate, during which the aspiring Christians were to pray separately from the "believers." (It is to be noted that in the same context the women were also separate from the "believers," II,17–18)! After this long training, the catechumens were to be exorcized by the bishop and baptized. When the women were allowed the privilege of worshipping with the believers is not addressed. Again we can see several levels of privilege and honor established.

In this paradigm, the clergy have clearly become the holders of a patron role, or a greatly enlarged brokering role. The function of the people of God has become much less active with regard to God's favor in the world and much more dependent upon the clergy. The latter have become the nearly exclusive brokers of both spiritual and material benefits. With this enlarged power and authority has come much enlarged honor, which is no longer given to all humanity, and is even reduced within the community, with newer believers and women placed in a marginal position relative to the men and the clergy. The vision of the new paradigm, a community of broad scale endowment and benevolence, had become rather vague.[33] When one combines this loss of vision with the strictures that we isolated from Hermas, one is in a better position to understand the conflict between Callistus, bishop of Rome (217–222), and Hippolytus. A position that controlled a great deal of money and influence would understandably be fought over. Both the fight and its underlying reasons are revealing.

---

33. The only anomaly in this structure are the "instructors," who while being laymen, have charge of the catechumens for three years and then release them by the laying on of hands (II,19). Could these teachers have been teaching the catechumens the dynamics of the new paradigm? It is difficult to see how it would have made any sense in the framework that is seen in the *Apostolic Tradition*.

The "Season of Callistus"

In the huge *Refutatio Omnium Haeresium* of Hippolytus, there is much that has no relevance to this present work, with the exception that he attributes self-magnification to several of them, to the effect that their gifts[34] or receiving of visions[35] or ascetic lifestyle[36] qualified them for special regard by all of the "ordinary" Christians. The issue is not whether they in fact had these gifts, but to whom the honor would be given and in what measure. If Hippolytus was not just engaging in polemics, such a search for honor did in fact contradict something critical to the inversion of the original paradigm. For my purposes, it is significant that Hippolytus considered honor-seeking to be reprehensible. It is in reference to the conflict with Callistus, however, that we gain a view into the Roman church in the early third century.

The story is well known. Callistus was the overcomer of a series of reverses, and after becoming a central figure in the Roman church through the favor of bishop Zephyrinus (fl.199–217), Callistus succeeded him as the bishop of Rome. Both his behavior and his doctrine offended Hippolytus, who opposed him and was eventually the focus of a group who elected him as an alternative bishop. In examining the story, one must be careful, remembering that our evidence comes from only one side, that of Hippolytus.

Hippolytus related with considerable detail[37] the events prior to Callistus' rise to influence, which Frend describes as "unenviable."[38] A

---

34. The Montanists claimed to have "something superior to Christ" (*Ref. Haer.* VIII,12), according to Hippolytus. We will see that that is an inappropriate evaluation of this movement. See chapter 6 below for a full discussion of Montanism.

35. The heretic Marcus, discussed by Hippolytus in *Ref. Haer.* VI,37. He was more extensively discussed by Irenaeus; see the supplement to chapter 5 on Irenaeus below.

36. The Encratites, said Hippolytus, are really behaving as Cynics, while holding many beliefs in common with the Church (*Ref. Haer.* VIII,13).

37. English citations from the *Refutatio Omnium Haeresium* will be from the ANF, and the Greek or Latin citations will be from the edition of Marcovich. The story of Callistus is related in Book IX, chapters 7–12, and is strikingly anecdotal in style and detail, quite different from the remainder of the work, largely philosophical in character.

38. Frend, *Early Church*, 78. In a work from his Montanist period, *On Modesty*, Tertullian engaged in an extended polemic against an unnamed figure who, if not Callistus, at least espoused a similar method and outlook. In his first chapter, Tertullian designated his opponent, sarcastically, as Pontifex Maximus and "bishop of bishops." Though it is too early for these titles to echo the actual claims of the Roman bishop, it is certainly the most logical denotation for the first. Since Tertullian will have been

domestic slave (*oiketēs*) of Carpophorus, a Christian and an imperial freedman, Callistus received a large sum of money from his owner for the purposes of "banking." Callistus was either inept or unscrupulous and lost his owner's money as well as the deposits of a number of other Christians, who apparently thought that they were safe because he was of Carpophorus' household. He was apprehended trying to escape and disciplined, released on a false pretext and apprehended again, and sent to Sardinia by the prefect of Rome. Upon being released as part of a favor to the church arranged by Marcia, Commodus' "concubine," he was sent away from Rome by bishop Victor, who did not wish to antagonize those who had suffered from his duplicity, including and perhaps especially Carpophorus.

Carpophorus is really more interesting at this point than Callistus. The investors had great respect for the freedman, and he easily had Callistus punished. Twice Callistus was apprehended because informers rather quickly brought him helpful information. He was apparently on personal terms with the prefect. Yet he does not seem to have had any exalted position in the church, and no special influence is mentioned.

Victor was succeeded by Zephyrinus, about whom Hippolytus waxed eloquent, describing him as a man who only "imagines that he administers the affairs of the church—an uninformed and shamefully corrupt man," who was easily persuaded by gifts and financial gain (IX,2 and 6). Granting some exaggeration by polemic, this testimony is quite striking, when connected with the testimony from Hippolytus' own *Apostolic Tradition*, which showed that the episcopal office had become a focus of privilege and access to the favor of God. It is not difficult to see how divine favor could be exchanged for honor given in the form of gifts. In this process, Callistus was Zephyrinus' advisor and to Hippolytus' eyes, his director. The actions of Callistus, however, give us specific examples how this favor could be given as a benefaction. Callistus had been recalled to Rome by Zephyrinus and put in charge of the cemetery. During the latter's pontificate, Callistus would have been able to deal with many people in difficult and vulnerable situations. When a new bishop was to be chosen, he was elected with no difficulty. We do know something of Callistus' actions as bishop, since Hippolytus carefully described them. Here are the main points of the indictment:

---

writing near the time of the transition from Zephyrinus to Callistus, and since their interests were similar, Tertullian may have been speaking of either one.

1. Callistus at least received (perhaps solicited) those who had been thrown out of sects (*hairesiōn*), as well as those condemned and expelled from other churches, offering to all relatively unqualified absolution for sin.[39]

2. Callistus accepted clergy who had married twice or even three times, and allowed single clergy to marry after their ordination, something apparently under dispute.

3. Callistus created an arrangement with men for the forgiveness of "sins of pleasure."[40] This policy, said Hippolytus, resulted in crowds of adherents.

4. Callistus granted permission for women of high station and of great resources to have unions with slaves and freedmen. The latter would be "considered a husband." Hippolytus also alleged that pregnancies resulting from these unions were terminated by the use of drugs and binding the abdomen, so that the women would have no children by "unworthy" partners.[41]

How are such accusations to be understood? In view of the extraordinary value placed on virginity by both Hippolytus and Tertullian, overstatement of the actions and agenda of Callistus cannot be excluded. Allowing for that, we can still conclude that Callistus was emphasizing forgiveness in a manner extreme to his own environment. Callistus' defense was that the Church should be a sanctuary for sinners, and only God really knows who is truly repentant.[42] Leaving aside the question whether Callistus had a point in opposing the rigorists who

---

39. Given the functional structure of urban Christianity, being a plurality of house-churches, this would result in the numerical and financial strength of Callistus' own house. By contravening actions taken by other presbyters, he was building a clientele at their expense. That the effect reached to suburbicarian areas and even other nearby municipalities cannot be ruled out.

40. *kai prō tos ta(s) pros tas hēdonas (hamartias) tois anthrōpois sugchōrein epenoēse, legōn pasin hup' autō aphiesthai hamartias* (*Ref. Haer.* IX,12,122–23).

41. Hippolytus spoke of the destruction of their dignity (*axian*) and of their "nobility and enormous property" (*tēn eugeneian kai huperogkon ousian*). This indictment is found in *Ref Haer.* IX,12,127–35.

42. He cited the analogy of the Ark, which contained both clean and unclean animals, and the Parable of the Wheat and Tares, where true and untrue grew together. Callistus finally rested on Rom 14:4, "who are you who judges another man's servant" (*Ref. Haer.* IX,12,119–21)? Tertullian also noted that scripture as characteristic of the group he is criticizing (*On Modesty* II).

were denigrating sexuality and denying forgiveness for selected sins, two factors indicate that Callistus saw opportunity to expand his sphere of influence. If it is true that Callistus was not just forgiving sexual sin, but arranging (*sugchōrein epenoēse*) it in advance, he was building an contradictory honor base by acting as spiritual patron for those who had no intention of being other than sinners. Again though some justification could be raised for marital unions across the boundaries of estate, Callistus' spiritual patronage was extending permission to influential and wealthy women to engage in illicit relationships and building a support base in that action. In so doing, both the moral content and the revision of the patronage paradigm were subverted.

On both sides of this conflict, the loss of the ideal is clear. Hippolytus had lost sight of both the revised paradigm in the model of church life revealed in the *Apostolic Tradition*, and with the dynamic of the broad-scale community of benevolence. Callistus shared this defect, and added to it a reversion to a most political model. Both were clearly ambitious, and their conflict was a harbinger of many such conflicts to come in the next three centuries.

New Heroes and Their Titles: Bishops and Martyrs

One final line of observation in the community at Rome derives from literature arising from persecutions and those who suffered in them. Strong emotions and admiration were aroused by such events, and they were expressed in honorific language. Once used, that language could more easily be applied to those alive, even to those who had not suffered.

Note the language which Clement used with regard to the apostles Peter and Paul, as a beginning point. Peter went to "the place of glory which was owed to him" (*eis ton opheilomenon topon tēs doxēs*, 1 *Clem.* V,4). Paul "received the noble fame of his faith" (*to gennaion tēs pisteōs autou kleos*, V,5), and was listed as "the greatest example of endurance" (*hupomonēs genomenos meistos hupogrammos*, V,7).

The martyrdom document relating the examination of Justin and several companions is significantly shy with regard to such honorific language. They are simply called holy martyrs who have glorified God and perfected their testimony.[43] The testimony about twenty years

43. Musurillo, *The Acts*, 42–61.

later concerning Apollonius is significant in two ways. First, he bore a nickname, Sakkeas, which is mentioned three times in the document and appears to denote stature as an ascetic. Second, the hortatory summary of the document used such honorifics as "glorious" (*endoxos*), "generous heart" (*prothumō kardia*) and "most holy victor" (*hagiōtatos athlophoros*).[44]

That such language did in fact come to be applied to the living is shown by letter 30 of Cyprian's corpus. To Cyprian from the elders of the church at Rome, it addressed Cyprian as the "most honored and glorious papa."[45] If such a designation had become accepted, a statement made by Cyprian becomes more understandable. According to Letter 37 of Cyprian's corpus, Decius stated that he would rather face a challenger to his throne than see another bishop seated in Rome. The bishops of the great cities were now being addressed in language that belonged to the elite.

Conclusions

The Christian churches as communities of broad scale benevolence, rooted in the first-order benefaction of God and mediated religious/social benefaction through Jesus of Nazareth, are clearly presented as normative in all writers through the middle of the second century. Clement uses the normative power of the new paradigm as an argument for the restoration of the same in Corinth. Strong expression of the paradigm is found in the apologies of Justin, with echoes in the Octavius of Minucius Felix, which takes us into the third century. Hermas assumed the revised paradigm as basis for his confrontation of those in Rome who were not following it.

In the writings of Hippolytus, however, there is little hint of it. The revised paradigm is simply not visible in either the Apostolic Tradition or in the Refutatio. The period between 165 and 215 is a time of loss that can be confirmed by other trends.

A second matter worth attention is the honor and power given to the leaders of this community. The revised paradigm reversed the honor pattern of Roman society within the community, while advocating a generalized honor for all humanity. Clement's use of the hierarchy

---

44. Ibid., 100–101.
45. Cyprian, *Letters of St. Cyprian*, ed. Clarke, vol. 2.

of the Hebrew priesthood and of the ranks of the Roman army to justify the authority and honor of the leaders in the church was unfortunate, for these were precisely the models which the new paradigm was intended to replace. To be fair, we must note that he emphasized mutual submission and humility, which would give balance to their authority. He noted a rising conflict over the position of bishop, and that aspect of competition is more notable in the Shepherd of Hermas. Further, the use of honorific titles and adjectives for departed heroes and recent martyrs is demonstrably applied to current leaders by the third century. This is paralleled by the gradual loss of both universal honor envisioned toward all humanity, and inverted honor patterns within the community.

The writings of Hippolytus illustrate the loss of the function of a community of broad-scale benevolence. Neither in their own lives nor in relation to the rest of humanity are the people of God directly involved with benevolence. They receive benefit by dependence on the clergy, and grant it through the clergy. The community funds, present in the beginning (Acts 4:34–35) and visible in Justin's note about a common chest under the control of the "president," have eclipsed a broad-scale interpersonal benevolence, which Jesus had clearly taught. Now both the range of spiritual benefit and material help were concentrated in the hierarchy.

In the Roman community, both description and action within the revised paradigm are visible through the middle of the second century. Serious loss occurred in three areas during the later second and early third century: enunciation of the revised paradigm, inversion of the honor paradigm, and extension of benevolence from every member of the community to a broad spectrum of humanity in a direct interpersonal manner.

5

The Work of Irenaeus of Lyons

I HAVE CHOSEN TO INCLUDE HERE MY TREATMENT OF IRENAEUS, ONE of the most prolific writers of the second century, because he had strong ties to the Aegean churches through his training (Eusebius, *H.E.* 5,20,5-7). Though he lived in Lyons, closer to Rome than to the Aegean, his orientation to the practice of Christianity is much closer to the Asian churches.

Irenaeus was first a presbyter, then bishop of the church at Lyons in Gaul. He missed, narrowly it would seem, a firestorm of persecution in 178–179 CE, and led the church after that traumatic experience for an indeterminate period of time. His major work was directed against those who divided the community by their thought and actions, and it is with his assessment of their lives that I will begin.

Assessing the Public Actions of "Heretic" Leaders

Like Hippolytus, Irenaeus spent a great deal of time dealing with the intellectual inadequacies of heretics, especially the Gnostics.[1] His critique of their method of "doing business" is more useful, however, for this project.

In general, Irenaeus saw the heretics as pursuing an honor in the religious field that aimed at establishing a higher position: "numbers of them, indeed we may say all, desire to be teachers ... " (*Adv. Haer.* I,28,1); "for every one of these men ... is not ashamed to preach himself" (III,2,1). The basis for this claim was the discovery and control of truth greater than that of the presbyters and apostles of the Christian faith

---

1. His *Adversus Haereses* will be cited in English from ANF, with some correction of archaic verb forms. Original languages, both Greek and Latin, will be cited from the editions of Rousseau and Doutreleau in SC.

(III,2,2), as well as access to power beyond the "princes and makers" (*principibus et fabricatoribus*) of this present world (I,25,3). The source of their power and knowledge was understood to be an essentially private gift of Jesus (I,25,5). In all aspects of their self-understanding, Irenaeus held them to be decisively different from the broad-scale and public activities of the Christian community and their leaders. In other words, his critique assumed the revised paradigm.

> They have good reason, as seems to me, why they should not feel inclined to teach these things to all in public, but only to such as are able to pay a high price for an acquaintance with such profound mysteries. For these doctrines are not at all similar to those of which our Lord said, "Freely you have received, freely give." They are, on the contrary, abstruse and portentious and profound mysteries, to be got at only with great labor by such as are in love with falsehood. For who would not expend all that he possessed, if only he might learn in return, that from the tears of the *enthymesis* of the Aeon involved in passion, seas and fountains and rivers and every liquid substance derived its origin...?
> (*Adv. Haer.* I,4,3)

As an example of the pride of the heretics, Irenaeus suggested Tatian, "excited and puffed up (*elatus et inflatus*) by the thought of being a teacher" (I,28,1).

Irenaeus gave significant evidence about a certain Marcus, who illustrated some of the general characteristics of these false leaders (I,13). Marcus used "magic" and elaborate ritual to attract a sizable following of both sexes, who were given gifts of (or through?) a feminine figure, Charis, and were invited to prophesy. The purpose of the prophesying was not indicated by Irenaeus. He described a ritual for us, consisting of the giving of cups of consecrated wine to each participant. The wine received the "blood" of Charis when it was consecrated and then would be drunk by each participant. Following that participation in the life of Charis, the women were asked to consecrate small cups of wine, which were ritually poured into a large and eventually overflowing cup, while Marcus prayed: "May that Charis who is before all things and who transcends all knowledge and speech, fill your inner man, and multiply her own knowledge in you, by sowing the grain of mustard seed as in good soil." So far, the clear reflection of Christian terminology and ideas, though in different form, could make one wonder whether

Marcus might have been misunderstood.[2] His actions with and toward his followers, however, seem decisive.

When one assesses Marcus' actions toward his female followers, if properly understood by Irenaeus, he must be placed outside of Christian practice. Marcus especially attracted women who were "well bred and elegantly attired and of great wealth" and offered them his Charis, saying "receive from me." He asked them to "prepare yourself as a bride" in order to be prophetesses. They would reward him both materially and by sexual favors. One might discount this as rumor, except that one of the entourage was the wife of a deacon at the church at Lyons, which would explain the details that Irenaeus can give us.

In addition to the example of Marcus, Irenaeus isolated the self exaltation, the lack of gratitude to God and the assumption that the benefits only come to and through a small elite, as characteristics of the social actions of the heretics (II,19,7; III,2,2; V,28,10–12). Thus the basis for his critique includes the revised paradigm of benefaction, which he considered normative for Christians.

Irenaeus on the Flow of Benefaction

The God whom Jesus called Father was acknowledged to be the universal and supreme Benefactor, in a long and florid list of titles, attributes and actions (II,30,9).[3] The scope of such benefaction was both cosmic and religious.

Jesus was clearly identified as the one who mediated all benefits with regard to reconciliation and concord between God and humanity, "to present man to God while he revealed God to man" (III,18,7). The work of Christ was contrasted with that of the heretics, who "confer no real profit or advantage (*fructum aut utilitatem*) on those over whom they declared that they exert power," while Jesus did real and enduring works of benefit (II,32,3–4).

Benefits continued to be mediated to and through the members of the new community, according to Irenaeus. They responded first with gratitude: "for the receptacle of His goodness and the instrument of

---

2. *Illa que est ante omnia inexcogitabilis et inenarrabilis Gratia adimpleat tuum intus hominem et multiplicet in te agnitionem suam, inseminans granum sinapis in bonam terram* (I,13,2).

3. See also *Adv. Haer.* I,10,3; II,34,3; and IV,20,7.

his glorification is the person who is grateful to Him that made him" (IV,11,2).[4] Further, the true disciples receive favor (*gratia*) from Jesus, including the power to perform exorcisms, healings and foreknowledge, even resurrection (II,32,4; III,1,1). These were understood to be "in his name" and "to promote the welfare (*perficiunt ad beneficia*)" of others. Finally, God will "give very much to those always bringing forth fruit and more to those who have the Lord's money." Was the community expected to do more than supernatural events? What was involved in "having the Lord's money"?[5] How did the practice of benefaction shape the community at Lyons? Irenaeus clearly sees this work as constitutive.

The Shape of the Generous Community

I will begin with a broad statement from Irenaeus, in which he indicates both purpose and attitudes of giving. "It is not possible to name the number of the gifts which the Church throughout the world has received from God in the name of Jesus Christ . . . and which she exerts day by day for the benefit of the nations (*dies in opitulationem gentium perficit*) neither practicing deception nor taking any reward (*pecuniam*)."[6] Among those gifts were material resources that could be used to benefit the needy. In a variety of ways, Irenaeus indicated that the social expression of God's favor was clearly understood. He stated that the offering was given to the poor: "we need to offer something to God, as Solomon says, 'he that has pity on the poor, lends to the Lord.' For God, who stands in need of nothing, takes our good works to Himself for this purpose, that He may grant us a recompense of His good works . . ."[7] Irenaeus also cited Isa 58:6–7, as indicating that in the community of the Christians, the religious fast of the Jews has been transformed into benevolence toward the unfortunate (IV,17,3). Though he made no specific references there to current practices in the church, he does so with reference to the transformation of the tithe, which he considered fulfilled in the

---

4. See also *Adv. Haer.* II,34,3; and IV,20,7.

5. *Adv. Haer.* IV,11,2, citing Matthew 25:21, where Jesus promises more resources for faithful use of those already given.

6. *Adv. Haer.* II,32,3. Irenaeus cited Matt 10:8—"Freely you have received, freely give."

7. *Adv. Haer.* IV,18,6. He cited Matt 25:34ff., where the final approval of God reflects the public benevolence of the disciples, *precisely as a gift to God.*

provisions of Jesus' Sermon on the Mount (Matthew 5–7): "to share our possessions with the poor, and not to love our neighbors only, but also our enemies, and not merely to be liberal bestowers and givers, but even that we should present a gratuitous gift to those who take away our goods" (IV,13,4). A certain alteration in values and pattern of consumption would accompany this pattern of giving. Luxurious and ostentatious consumption should be refused as inappropriate (IV,2,4); and by deliberately distributing possessions to the poor, one negated a pattern of desire and competition (IV,12,5). But was this ideal, still affirmed by Irenaeus, accepted by the "leading men" in his community?

Irenaeus did not speak of the wealthy except with regard to the inappropriate patronage of the heretics, but he does speak both of the ideal of Christian leadership and of some problems among those who held a more prominent place in the Christian community at Lyons. Some were inclined to serve themselves, behave with contempt towards others and be proud of holding the chief seat. Such attitudes disqualified them from the office of presbyter (IV,26,3). They had lost an essential component of leadership.

Irenaeus was struggling with the still developing idea of "apostolic succession." If an essential element of legitimate office is some connection with the apostles through a line of successors, as Irenaeus does seem to assume, how does one prevent that from becoming an "old boys" network? That would be a important component of the traditional paradigm of honor and power, and contrary to the revision inaugurated by Jesus.

In Irenaeus, we can see two additional and non-negotiable sources of legitimacy. When he contends that leaders may be disqualified by the behavior patterns just mentioned, he recognizes a moral legitimacy as essential. That moral component clearly reflects the revised paradigm. Even the highly gifted among the leaders recognized that both gifts and message were from One who was infinitely greater, therefore exaltation was excluded (I,10,2). A second source of legitimacy, which balances the concept of "apostolic succession," was the gift of prophecy for both female and male (III,11, 9). An authority was conferred on "those to whom God sends his grace from above . . . a divinely bestowed power of prophesying" (I,13,4).

Finally, in spite of his obvious intellectual interests, Irenaeus did not consider either ability nor accomplishment to be decisive in the

Christian community, for it is "better to belong to the simple and unlettered class, and by means of love to attain to nearness to God, than by imagining ourselves learned and skillful, to be found among those who are blasphemous against their own God,"[8] supporting his teaching by quoting Paul from 1 Cor 8:1: "knowledge inflates but love builds up."

Martyrs and Honorific Language in Lyons

Some of the language used by Irenaeus and the community at Lyons may have unwittingly been contradictory to the ideals we have just described. Irenaeus used some rather traditional honorific language to describe both the church at Rome and its putative founders, Peter and Paul. That church was "very great" and "very ancient" and its founders were "most glorious." In that very same context, the bishops of Rome were denoted as the successors of those "blessed apostles" (III,3,2–3). Further, he spoke of Polycarp as "gloriously and most nobly (*gloriosissime et noblissime*) suffering martyrdom" (III,3,4). This kind of language was also characteristic of documents issued by the churches of Lyons concerning the persecution of 177.

The brief but wrenching attack against Christians in this district produced diverse responses. Those who were actually suffering refused to be called "martyrs" while they were still living, for that title should be reserved for Christ and those who had already died for the cause.[9] Yet letters were sent in their name, with some sort of weight, to back the opponents of the Montanists in Asia and Phrygia. The famous document on which Eusebius based his account of the persecution was written by the churches of Lyons to those of Western Asian Minor. It was packed with honorific language about the martyrs.[10] Both Irenaeus and the people he served apparently would freely use strong honorific language about the departed, which would not be used for those now present.

---

8. *Adv. Haer.* II,26,1. *Melius est ergo et utilius idiotas et parm scientes exsistare et per caritatem proximum fiere Deo* . . .

9. Eusebius *H.E.* V,2,2ff. Their titles should be "the confessors, the disciplined and humble" (*homologoi, metroi kaitapeinoi*).

10. Eusebius, *H.E.* V,1, sections 6–7, 13, 16–19, 41–42, 45. The martyrs were "steadfast pillars" (*stulous hedraious*), struggled "nobly" (*gennaiōs*) "as if they were Christ" and were called the "worthy ones" (*hoi axioi*). Blandina, a slave who apparently stood out among the suffering, received special attention. She was seen as a noble competitor (*gennaios athlētēs*), describes as bearing the image of Christ, giving great zeal (*pollēn prothumian*) to the other contenders and grace to the fallen.

Conclusions

In conclusion, Irenaeus and the community he headed seem to have the revised paradigm clearly in mind, rooted in the teachings of Jesus and the prophets that gave promise of a new community. Irenaeus' critique of the heretics focused very much on the aspects of their ways that contradicted that ideal. Elitism was inherent both in the roles and status that the heretics adopted for themselves as leaders, and the target of their recruitment, an economic elite.

In two matters, Irenaeus seems to move backwards from the revised paradigm of the Christian community: his emphasis on "apostolic succession," which tends toward a "great men" model of leadership; and his use of honorific language for the martyrs. I would see that danger in the sense that language once applied, even to those now dead, can more easily be used for those yet living, but of higher rank in the church. Yet that danger was balanced by Irenaeus's emphasis on broad-scale benevolence, the dynamic of the gift of prophecy and the breadth of gifts given. It was important as well that he insisted that the disciples chosen by Jesus included those usually considered poor candidates for leadership (II,19,7). In this regard, it is significant that at least one person of more than average status held no high position in this church.[11] The community, as represented in his writings, appears to have been well on track in maintaining the revised paradigm. After Irenaeus, the church in Lyons passes from sight for more than a century, and beyond the time frame of this project. We now move to consider the churches of the Aegean, where Irenaeus had been trained, beginning with the pastors Polycarp and Melito.

---

11. Vettius Epagathus, described as a prominent (*episēmos*) young man, rose up to give advocacy for the Christians in Lyons during the persecution. No office or position is indicated in the narrative for him.

6

The Christian Communities around the Aegean

THE CHRISTIAN COMMUNITIES AROUND THE AEGEAN SEA WILL BE EXamined in this chapter. Unfortunately, though it was a very vital area, especially in the province of Asia, our evidence is limited to small bits of information in Eusebius and to a few relatively short writings.

Eusebius mentions Dionysius of Corinth, bishop about 170 and prolific writer of letters: to the Roman church, to two bishops in Crete, to the Athenians, to leaders in Nicomedia and to Pontus. Eusebius' snippets of a letter to the Romans reveals only that Dionysius thought highly of that church in general and of their bishop Soter in particular (*H.E.* IV,23,9–10). This bishop he spoke of as "honored" (*makarios*) in a manner that seems to attach to his person or office, not clearly to the manner in which he would exercise it. Such usage points in the direction of granting exceptional honor to the leaders of the community more than to its members, which contradicts the reversal of honor patterns in the revised paradigm.

A similar linguistic pattern is seen in the quote from Polycrates of Ephesus, who also wrote towards the end of the second century. He mentions a number of outstanding leaders in the communities of Asia. These included prophetesses, martyr bishops and Melito the eunuch, who "lived entirely in the Spirit." Polycrates denoted these leaders as "great luminaries."[1] Unfortunately, other than these fragments in Eusebius, we have only a few writings from which to assess this area. I will begin with the pastors, Polycarp and Melito. Then the apologists must be considered, who give us the most complete works. In the third

---

1. Eusebius, *H.E.* V,24. *Megala stoicheia*. It should be noted that this is a letter between bishops, and Polycrates is citing the greatness of these leaders to build strength for his advocacy of an original date for the celebration of Easter. In speech among the members, he might not have used such exalted language.

section, we must sift through the evidence for Montanism, which is closely related to the Christianity of Asia, and evaluate its significance. A look at Methodius of Olympus and the documents composed on behalf of the martyrs conclude this chapter, showing language that exalted two new classes of Christians, celibates and martyrs. A supplement to the chapter examines Irenaeus of Lyons, who brought a western Anatolian type of Christianity to Provence.

Polycarp and Melito: Pastors with a New Vision?

Irenaeus had been associated with one of the most prominent leaders of the Asian churches, Polycarp. Leader of the church at Smyrna for several decades, he appears to have had a public profile which made him the target of persecution late in life, but also which made the soldiers and procurator reluctant to proceed against him. Irenaeus gave a clue why that might have been, when he noted that one of Polycarp's supporters was a certain Florinus, a member of the royal household.[2] Polycarp's interaction with the proconsul may also show that he not only had a significant public status, but also that he saw himself as much closer to the proconsul than to the people. When invited by the ruler to speak to the people, he responded that while the proconsul deserved an explanation, the people were not worthy of an apology.[3] He was perceived as so revered by his people that the centurion ordered his remains to be burned so that they could not become the centerpiece of a new cult, taking precedence over that of Christ (*Mart. Pol.* XVII,2).

What kind of status did the members of this community acknowledge for Polycarp? Even in his early career, he was denoted as "most honored of God" by the irrepressible Ignatius of Antioch.[4] In the story of his martyrdom, he is repeatedly called "honored." While one could surmise that the usage reflects post-martyrdom adulation, two passages

---

2. Eusebius, *H.E.* V,20,5. The notation is from a letter between Irenaeus and this Florinus, who was "a man of rank in the royal court" (*lamprōs prassonta en tē basiliē aulē*) and "who was endeavoring to stand with" Polycarp (*peirōmenon eudokemaein par' autō*). Polycarp's *Epistle* will be cited parenthetically as *Phil.*, all citations from *The Apostolic Fathers I* in LCL.

3. *Mart. Pol.* X,2. (*Se men kan logou ēxiōsa . . . ekeinous de ouch hēgoumai axios apologeisthai*). All citations are from *The Apostolic Fathers II* in LCL.

4. *To Polycarp* VII,2 (*Theomakaristotate*). All letters of Ignatius will be cited from LCL.

in the document show that an exaggerated honor had been his during his tenure as bishop. One is an aside from the moment of preparation for death: "he put off all his clothes, and tried also to take off his shoes, though he did not do this before because each of the faithful was always zealous which of them might more quickly touch his flesh. For he had been treated with all respect because of his noble

life, even before his martyrdom" (*Mart. Pol.* XIII,2). The second passage occurs in the context of the concerns of imperial authorities that Polycarp might be worshipped: "many desired to do this [take his remains] and to have fellowship with his holy flesh" (XVII,1). In the martyrdom document, then, we find clear indications of Polycarp's exalted status in the community before the authorities, in the eyes of the public and by the evaluation of his people. None of this is from Polycarp himself, except the interchange with the proconsul. Is there any evidence of the revised paradigm from Polycarp's own mouth?

Polycarp's letter to the Philippians is admittedly not enough to draw a full evaluation of the interests and work of a man who was a leader for several decades. At best, some meager conclusions can be drawn.

In greeting the Philippians, Polycarp speaks of "mercy" and "peace," but not of "grace" (*charis*),[5] which we have seen to be so critical in the revision of the paradigm as presented by Luke and Paul. Note also that the word family is not prominent in the New Testament Johannine literature which is associated with this area.

Polycarp presented Christ as the one who suffered for all Christians, and brought full knowledge to all (*Phil.* VIII,1 ; *Mart.Pol.* XIV,1), but the lack of laudatory language for God and Christ is striking. Any apparent presentation of giving honor back in either word or action is also absent, though it is a small document, so that may not be determinative.

Some elements of the revised paradigm are visible in Polycarp's reference to the social dynamics of this new community. They were to "show preference for one another, in the gentleness of the Lord, despising no one" (*mansuetudine domine alterutri praestolantes, nullam despicientes*, *Phil.* X,1). Clearly reflecting St. Paul's injunctions in Rom 12:10 (*tē timē allēlous proēgoumenoi*), this does not point to the universal honor envisioned especially by Peter, but it does point to breadth

---

5 It is also lacking in the opening and closing of the *Martyrdom*, but occurs in XX,2 with regard to the way in which Christ rescues humanity.

of honor inside the community. They were encouraged to continue in love for God, Christ and the neighbor (III,3). They were encouraged to pray for one another (XII,3) and to be in submission to one another (X,2). Though somewhat general, these admonitions would be part of a generalized honor-giving which recognized the importance of each member, thereby undermining status walls.

What about relations with those outside the community? They were to pray for the rulers (*regibus, potestatibus, principibus*) as well as all who persecuted them (XII,3). All members were to continue to give alms, but the reason cited was that giving alms "freed one from death" (X,2), which is not the same as handing on the gifts of God in gratitude and honor, and which approaches the later theory of redemptive almsgiving.

Polycarp did not speak extensively about the officers of the community, who were called by the same titles we saw in Paul: presbyters and servants (*diakonoi*). Jesus was called the "servant of all" (*diakonon pantōn* V,2). The presbyters were specifically directed to care for the wanderers, the weak, the widows, the orphans and the needy (*penētos*). Other instructions for them included not showing favoritism and being far from the love of money (*makran ontes pasēs philargurias* VI,1). This last was a favorite theme of Polycarp, as he reflected the teaching of Jesus.[6] He even mentions a former presbyter, lost because he was destroyed by *avaritia* (XI,1).

Polycarp reflects several aspects of the revised paradigm, especially with regard to humility, mutual respect, not showing favoritism and sharing with the poor. Yet two critical elements are missing: the foundation of these actions: clear acknowledgement of the Patrons in their breadth of giving; and the heart of gratitude which responds in praise and extends the gifts to others. Whether the average member was expected to be benevolent is not clear. To be fair, we must remember that this is a small piece of literature. Polycarp may have not had that aspect of Christian practice in mind, at the moment.

---

6. "But the beginning of all evils is the love of money. Knowing therefore that 'we brought nothing into the world and we can take nothing out of it', let us arm ourselves with the armor of righteousness and let us teach ourselves to walk in the commandment of the Lord" (IV,1). This commandment would be related then to an appropriate use of resources. See II,2; IV,3; V,2. In II,3 he quotes Jesus' Sermon, "honored (*makarios*) are the poor."

Evidence from the Paschal Homily of Melito of Sardis, should be considered at this point, since the Homily is a pastoral work. Though he was also an apologist, his apology survived only in fragments. The more recently discovered Homily has given us a complete work, though only hints of the revised paradigm can be seen in the theological and rhetorical body of the piece.[7]

Christ was seen as a benefactor of the first order, giving to humanity a world in which to live, and it may be assumed, sustaining it (*Pasc. Hom.* 82–83). Much more attention was given to the benefits Christ granted to the sufferers, freeing those who were in slavery to the devil (*Pasc. Hom.* 66–67). His rhetoric swells:

> This is the One who delivered us
> from slavery into freedom
> from darkness into light, from death into life
> from tyranny into an eternal kingdom
> and who made us a new priesthood
> and an eternal people personal to Him. (*Pasc. Hom.* 68; last line from Hall)

It is to be noted that the declaration of priesthood for the people of God applies to all members and implies that they are functioning in a beneficial manner towards the rest of humanity.

After mentioning the benefits of Jesus' miracles (72), Melito castigated the Jewish people at the point of their ingratitude, not just their failure to see or believe.

> Put me a price on the men born blind
> whom he led into light by his voice
> Put me a price on those who lay dead
> whom he raised from the tomb
> Inestimable are the benefits
> that come to you from him
> but you, shamefully,
> have paid him back with ingratitude
> paying him back evil for good
> affliction for favor
> death for life.[8] (*Pasc. Hom.* 90)

---

7. Circa 160 CE. Parenthetically cited as *Pasc. Hom.* with stanza number. ET may come from Hawthorne's translation.

8. *timēsai moi tous ek genetēs tuphlous hous autos parōn etherapeusen ... atimētoi hai par' autou soi dōreai. Su de atimōs antapedōkas eis auton tas charitas. Acharistias antapodous aut?...*

Our evidence at most indicates that Melito saw Christ as a first-order cosmic and religious benefactor, who deserved an appropriate gratitude, with a hint that benefaction continued through the people benefited.

Defenders of the Community: Aristides, Athenagoras, and "Diognetus"

The Christian community of the Aegean produced important defenders against those accusations and actions that faced them. In this portion of the chapter, I will treat the presentations of Aristides, Athenagoras and the anonymous Epistle to Diognetus, whose author we will refer to as "Diognetus."[9] Since they were writing to commend, not to instruct or correct, what they tell us will be the ideal and the best of its fulfillment in their eyes, as we have also assumed to be true of Justin and Minucius Felix.

In his appeal to the emperors to weigh judiciously the dynamics of the Christian community, Athenagoras reveals that the traditional patronage ideal was alive and well, for he noted that the provincials come to the emperors, give obeisance and ask for favors (*Embassy* 16). He was asking for one as well, and so his florid manner of approaching the ruler was a preparation for that favor, a request for fair treatment (I,2). In his conclusion, he promised that the behavior of those who were in this group would not disturb the empire, being "quiet and peaceble" (*ēremon kai hēsuchion*) under normal circumstances. Further, they would pray for the peace of the empire.

The beneficence of God and Christ was not extensively treated by these writers. Athenagoras attributed a creative and sustaining providence (*pronoia*) to God, extending to the work of his angels, including life, order and beauty (*Embassy* 24). He also declared that the rulership of God promoted the health and integrity of humanity, as opposed to the mutilation inherent in some religious practices.[10] God requires

---

9. I am well aware that the provenance of the "Epistle" is unsure, and that it is really an apology, but it seems to fit well with the Aegean writers, so I include it here. Both Aristides and Athenagoras are considered to be from the community of Athens, otherwise undistinguished, and of the Antonine era.

10. *Embassy* 24. Athenagoras cites a proverb: "For when the demon devises evil for a man, he damages his mind beforehand," while "God is ever perfectly good and eternally author of good" (*ho de theos teleiōs agathos ōn aidiōs agathoios estin*).

equal justice for all, though it was not stated that this would also mean honor for all.

"Diognetus" was more specific than Athenagoras, in confirming God as a first-order benefactor: "he gave us all things at once, both to share in his benefits (*tōn euergesiōn*) and to see and understand" (VIII,11). In addition, the forgiveness and melioristic action of Christ was attributed to God (IX,2ff.); and the homily which was appended to the apology (XI–XII) expected the multiplication of *charis* among the members.[11]

"Diognetus" explicitly attributed to Christians a lifestyle that answered the gifts of God in a distinctive manner of living: law-abiding while exceeding the necessary; giving back good will for evil; accepting abuse and dishonor. Meanwhile important principles of the revised paradigm were to continue, for Christians were to seek to "love all humanity," "render [them] honor" and "make many rich" (V,7–15). "Diognetus" called this pattern an "imitation of God" in a passage worth quoting in full.

> But as you love you will be an imitator of his kindness (*chrēstotētos*). And do not wonder whether it is possible for a human being to become an imitator of God; it is possible when he wills. For it is not being happy to hold power over the neighbors nor to have more than the weak, nor to be rich nor to coerce inferiors, nor can anyone in these things be an imitator of God—on the contrary, these things are outside of his majesty (*alla tauta ektos tēs ekeinou megaleiostētos*). Rather, whoever takes up the burden of his neighbor, and wishes to benefit (*euergetein*) another who is worse off in that in which he is the stronger, and by supplying the things which he has received (and holds from God) to those who need them, becomes a god to those who receive them—this one is an imitator of God.[12]

So "Diognetus" makes very specific statements about the revised paradigm, but in his own words.

Aristides did not express the benefactions of God or Christ as the other two apologists had, but he noted the practice of hospitality

---

11. See also the concluding statement in IX,6, which expresses strongly the variety of divine benefits.

12. This is my translation, adapted from that of Lake in LCL. The use of standard terminology (*euergesia, choregeō, chrēstotētos*) was combined effectively with clear elements of the redirected paradigm.

and community care for those who must bury a family member, which is primarily significant if one has racial and social diversity.[13] He also mentioned the attempt to do good, with a positive attitude, to those who are enemies (*Apol.*15).[14] If anyone is needy, those who have resources shared them, even fasting intermittently in order to divert their food to those who needed it (15).

In these presentations, the practice of benevolence does not seem to have been focused in the leaders. Athenagoras made specific reference to benevolence by precisely those folks who once might have expected it from the elite:

> But among us you might find simple folk, artisans and old women (*idiōtas kai cheiroteknas kai graidia*), who if they are unable to furnish in words the assistance they derive from our doctrine, yet show in their deeds the advantage (*opheleianō*) to others that accrues from their resolution. They do not rehearse words but show forth good deeds; struck, they do not strike back; plundered, they do not prosecute; to them who ask they give and they love their neighbors as themselves. (11)

Both Aristides and Athenagoras gave witness that a modest refusal to accept credit for such good deeds is a part of the specific way of "doing business" which belongs to the logic of this community. Aristides said that not only do Christians not broadcast their benefits, but go out of their way to conceal them (*Apol.* 16). Athenagoras gave a summary of this concern, for he indicated that a pattern of life acceptable to God could be described as "modest, benevolent and easily criticized" (*metrion kai philanthrōpou kai eukataphronōton*), willing to accept risk and sacrifice in this sphere, for the future life will be "gentle, benevolent and appropriate to all" (*tou praou philanthrōpou kai epieikous biou, Embassy* 12).

The Aegean apologists contain all the elements of the revised paradigm, though the clearest and most complete statement is in the anonymous Epistle. The only honorific language that is obvious is that which was used to flatter the emperors addressed.

---

13. The context seems to point to benevolence primarily within the community, but the language could point to hospitality as a connection point with outsiders. "If they see a stranger, they take him under their roof and rejoice over him as over a very brother..." *Apol.* 15.

14. See also Athenagoras, *Embassy* 11.

The Montanist Phenomenon: Preserving the Paradigm?

Around the middle of the second century, the public actions of one man and two women produced one of the most dynamic movements in early Christianity.[15] Montanism was named after the man, Montanus, rather than his two associates, Priscilla and Maximilla, though in our sources it is often simply denoted by the area in which it began and was most prominent, as Phrygians or Cataphrygians.[16] The three proclaimed themselves to be prophets, agents in a renewing of the prophetic gift promised in Acts chapter two to both female and male members of the Christian community. Thus another name they acquired was the New Prophecy.

I begin with the testimony of their opponents. Since they sometimes spoke in the first person as the divine voice, they were accused of considering themselves divine. When they confirmed those who listened with blessings and congratulations, they were accused of inflating their followers with their own importance, making them conceited (*chaunoumenous*). They were accused of speaking and acting oddly, in ecstasy or excitement. In practical matters, they were accused of accepting and soliciting gifts from their followers, organizing their leaders with salaries and "bribes." In addition, they were accused of taking a strongly negative attitude toward marriage and of multiplying fasts and eating vegetables.[17]

Accused of considering themselves divine, they could answer that they were in the tradition of ecstatic and prophetic activity among the Hebrews, as well as Christians. Though Epiphanius' unnamed source[18] asserts at length that the other prophets were always of sound mind and action (*Pan.* 48.3.1,4), I am not so sure that their contemporaries would

---

15 The sources cited in this section are Heine, *Montanist Oracles* and Tabbernee, *Montanist Inscriptions,* both cited by page. I found both confirmation and extension of my conclusions about Montanism in Trevett, *Montanism.*

16. Priscilla, as well as the second generation Quintilla and Tertullian, had subgroups named after her.

17. Eusebius, *H.E.* V,16–18; Epiphanius, *Panarion* 48 passim. Along with Hippolytus' *Refutation*, these later writers preserve the earliest contemporary accounts and arguments.

18. *Pan.* 48.1–13. Identified as a unit independently by two scholars in the nineteenth century, it is one of the most extensive witnesses to and arguments against Montanism that appears to be contemporary. Reproduced in Heine, *Montanist Oracles and Testimonia,* 26–51.

have agreed, especially in the case of Ezekiel. More telling, however, was the tradition of inspiration and prophecy in the church of west and central Asia Minor. Prominent in this tradition were John the seer of the Apocalypse and the daughters of Philip, celebrated at Hierapolis for their prophetic work (Eusebius, *H.E* III,31). Quadratus, an associate of the daughters, was notable as well (*H.E.* III,37), while Melito of Sardis, "who lived entirely in the Holy Spirit," is contemporary with the Montanists. Thus active and public work attributed to the direct inspiration of the Spirit can be documented from this area, for both sexes, for some time preceding.

Support for their activity came as well from other areas of the movement. The letter of the churches of Lyons and Vienne gives testimony that such charismata were not unheard of and that many Christians readily concluded that this was appropriate work (*H.E.* V,3,4). Tertullian insisted that the bishop of Rome initially accepted these Prophets (*Adversus Praxean* 1). Irenaeus, that staunch defender of the truth, asserted that those who repressed the "false prophets" were suppressing the work of the Spirit. He connected that work of the Spirit to John and Paul (*Adv. Haer.* III,11,12). Though it seems clear that their statements, often in the first person, were more similar to the "thus saith the Lord" statements of Hebrew Israelite and Judahite prophets, there was no coherent reason for them to be judged false, both from the standpoint either of Hebrew tradition or of Christian practice up to their own time.

What of the other accusations? Looked at carefully, none of these matters were foreign to Christian leadership. A variety of Christian leaders blessed their converts and assured them that they were part of something great, devised new patterns of devotion such as fasts or feasts and took a less than joyful stance toward sexuality and marriage.

In addition, both Hippolytus and Epiphanius, neither noted for generosity to opponents, affirmed that the Montanists affirmed the basic doctrines of the Christian faith and accepted without reservation both parts of the Scripture as defined by the leadership (*Ref. Haer.* 10.25–26; *Pan.* 48.1.3–4).[19] Why then the fierce resistance and actions against the Montanists?

---

19 Accusations of wide ranging doctrinal aberrations arrived much later in the works of theologians, especially those of Alexandria. The earlier writers and sources do not allege such aberrations.

Testimony from Serapion, bishop of Antioch in the late second century, and Eusebius's contemporary source Apolinarius of Hierapolis may help us. Serapion stated in a circular letter that "this false order of the so-called new prophecy has been abhorred by the whole brotherhood throughout the world" (*H.E.* V,16,3) and Apolinarius said that the "inspired spirit" taught the Montanists to condemn the "whole catholic church under heaven" (*H.E.* V,16,9). These statements were not accurate, for there was significant support for the Montanist position in North Africa, Gaul and Rome. The Montanist communities persisted into the early medieval period.[20] Who then are the "whole brotherhood" and the "whole catholic church," to which these two second century authors allude? Serapion's letter was signed by several bishops and a martyr, but none of the leaders of the great Asian churches were mentioned. Leaders from Corinth or Rome were not signers, only figures from Antioch to Thrace. At best, this support group was regional. Why were these bishops so troubled?

Was the episcopate in eastern Asia Minor and Antioch becoming the focus of authority and benevolence, as we have seen it develop in Rome? If so, the strong renewal of ministry and leadership validated by a charism of prophecy would have seemed quite inappropriate to the bishops, even dangerous. The shape of the Christian ministry envisioned by the New Prophets saw the power and work of the spirit of God as coming to and validating Christian people in general. Note this oracle of Montanus: "Why do you call the more excellent man (*ton huper anthrōpon*) saved? For the just will shine a hundred times brighter than the sun, and the little ones (*hoi mikroi*) among you who are saved will shine a hundred times brighter than the moon" (Heine 3). Certainly this statement indicates that a broad spectrum of members of this community will be outstanding in life, and this because God is active in them, which the oracles declare by the direct statement of active residence (*ho theos ho pantokratōr kataginomenos en anthrōpō*) and by the indirect image of a plectron striking a lyre.[21] According to the testimony

---

20. Tabbernee (28–35) has traced the evidence for the destruction of a striking marble shrine to the three original prophets of Montanism by the heresy-hunting bishop, John of Ephesus. This sixth century event is dated between the 27th and 29th year of Justinian by Michel the Syrian, and to the year 550 by (pseudo) Dionysius of Tell Mahre. These medieval chroniclers agree on the main lines of the event, though not on all the details.

21. Heine 3. All these citations are from Epiphanius' source. That source's criticism of the musical image, as being inappropriate (*Pan.* 48.4.3), must be evaluated in light

of Origen, Celsus spoke of "nameless" prophets, who spoke anywhere, claiming to be the agents of God, and enthusiastically inviting hearers to salvation (*Celsum* 7.9). If that were not troubling enough, some of these prophets were women. To accept joyfully women in public positions and actions proved to be the most disturbing aspect of this vision of community. Hippolytus is representative of the horror with which the activities of Montanist women were viewed: "they magnify these weak females above the apostles and every divine greater has occurred in them than in Christ."[22] Origen's argument that the female Biblical models of these women only spoke in private, though historical nonsense and theologically wrong-headed, gives evidence that in the third century, this practice needed to be addressed.[23] Our evidence then leaps to the later fourth century writer Epiphanius, who spoke of women prophets in public worship events, women bishops and presbyters (*Pan.* 49.2–3). Both he and later writers lamented such activity.[24]

We have no record of the benevolent activities of the early Montanist community beyond what appears to be a restoration of expectation that a broad spectrum of members would be invigorated and used of God, but the activities which accompanied that expectation was resisted specifically because it contradicted the growing clerical dominance of the bishops. We should see this movement as a counter to the narrowing of privilege and function.

---

of the image occurring several times in the *Odes of Solomon* (6.1; 14.8; c.f.26.3) and in Clement of Alexandria, *Exhortation* 1,6.

22. *Adv. Haer.* 8.19. Perhaps Hippolytus had forgotten that weakness was really irrelevant, as was status and other obvious advantages, according to St. Paul in 1 Corinthians 1–2. Note that the promise of "something greater" was from Jesus' lips, according to John 14:12.

23. *Catenae on Paul's Epistles to the Corinthians* 14. 36. There can be no doubt that the *shophet* Deborah exercised public ruling and speaking activities for an extended period of time (Judges 4–5). Further, even if it were demonstrable that none of the pre-Christian women were permitted to exercise public functions, new position and privilege had been granted them in the Christian arena.

24. Both Augustine and John of Damascus deplored the admittance of women to the priesthood by Montanist churches (Heine 71). Note the early second century inscription discussed by Tabbernee (66), which reads "*Diogas episcopas for Ammion presbytera in memory*," which may have been Montanist, since it contradicts this opposition to women in leadership positions. It is of interest that the contemporary anonymous source of Epiphanius does not focus on the gender issue.

Martyrs and Honorific Language

Another window into the community and their understanding of honor can be found in the martyrdom documents that arise from the Aegean circle. Not surprisingly, the dominant one is that of the famous Polycarp. Strong honorifics abound in this work.

In addition to the word "honored" (*makarios*), which we have observed becoming a stock word for those highly regarded, these documents utilize the word family based on *gennaios*, a word denoting in the first instance nobility by birth, and then the behavioral qualities expected of the wellborn. The martyrs as a group, said the composers of the Martyrdom of Polycarp, are "noble" (II,1), and those writers asked "who would not be amazed at their nobility." The strengthened form *gennaiotētos* is also used several times, notably with regard to the "most noble Germanicus, who fought with beasts splendidly" (*episēmōs* III,1).

Polycarp was described by adjectives which included splendid, noble, wonderful, great, blessed and prominent (*episēmos, gennaios, thaumasiōtatos, megethos, makarios, exochos*). This language is not surprising, for the emotional intensity of the martyrdoms would call forth some acknowledgement of sacrifice on the part of those who remained. However, we have already noted that extraordinary regard had been given to Polycarp, so the honor given to him was also extraordinary. Indeed, the document tells of the creation of "Polycarp Day" on which they would celebrate the anniversary of his martyrdom (XVIII,2).

Another document from this area presents three martyrs from Pergamum in the time of Decius.[25] All three appear to be of some stature. Carpus gave quite an eloquent attack upon the false gods whom they refuse to serve, and is called a bishop in the conclusion of the Latin recension. Papylus was asked if he were a councillor (*bouloutēs, principalis*) by the examining proconsul, but admitted only to being a citizen. Agathonice was identified as a mother in natural life and as a "servant of God" (*famula dei*). All were hailed in heroic language, similar but more restrained than the account of Polycarp.

In conjunction with the letter of the churches of Lyons and Vienne, composed concerning the martyrs of Gaul in 1789, the descriptions and language of martyrdom documents led to the application of honorific

---

25. Musurillo, *The Acts*, 172.

language to living Christians who had been released after prosecution or imprisonment. This language once would have been used with reluctance and only of the most prominent members of the community after their death. This use of language contributed to an erosion of patterns of honor in which the lesser members were deliberately honored.

Methodius and the Virgin Ideal

Methodius of Olympus in Lycia provides the last window into the Aegean churches, at the very end of the period we are investigating. Well known as one who opposed the speculative theologies of Origen, his largest extant work is a symposium or banquet conversation. The speakers are ten virgins who extol their chosen way of life at considerable length. The evidence his speakers provide is sparse.[26]

Along with the exhortations to chastity, a certain excellence of life was indicated for the virgin ideal, shown by the fact that the person addressed by the virgins was Arete personified. The virgin should "love things which are honorable, and be distinguished among the foremost for wisdom, and addicted to nothing slothful or luxurious ... " (*Banq.* I,2). Building upon Jesus' parable of the Ten Virgins, one virgin says that the oil that they must have is beneficial wisdom and righteousness unto the world, "making its good actions to shine before humanity, so that our Father which is in heaven may be glorified" (*Banq.* VI,3). None of this is peculiar to virginity, but Methodius makes his point clear through another speaker, who misinterprets the words of St. Paul in 1 Cor 15:41–42 and those of Jesus in Matt 5:3–16, to the effect that virginity is a superior order of Christianity.

> And this Paul, too, sets forth saying "There is one glory of the sun and another glory of the moon, and another glory of the stars." And the Lord does not profess to give the same honors to all, but to some He promises that they shall be numbered in the kingdoms of heaven, to others the inheritance of the earth and to others, to see the Father. And here also He announces that the order and holy choir of the virgins shall first enter in company with Him into the rest of the new dispensation ... for

---

26. Methodius will be cited in English from ANF vol.6 and in Greek from the edition of Bonwetsch GCS 27. *The Banquet* will be cited by discourse and chapter (e.g., *Banq.* I,1). I found no pertinent material in his discussion *Concerning Free Will* or in his *Discourse on the Resurrection*.

they were martyrs, not as bearing the sins of the body for a little moment of time, but as enduring them throughout their life. (*Banq.* VII,3)

On behalf of Methodius, the ten virgins articulate the celibate lifestyle as one which should be lauded above the ordinary Christian life. Not only does this not have any justification in the original documents of Christianity, it contradicted the revised paradigm by isolating another group to be especially honored.

Conclusions

Granting that the windows through which the Christian communities in this area can be seen are rather narrow, some hesitant conclusions can be drawn.

1. A growing use of honorific language with regard to the leaders within the church can be seen in the words of Polycrates, Dionysius of Corinth, and especially in the martyrdom account of the death of Polycarp. Though this last almost surely was exaggerated by his very public position and death, an extreme reverence for him preceded the martyrdom.

2. This growing reverence for church leaders seems to find no encouragement in Polycarp's own words, either in his letter or in the martyrdom account. He speaks strongly against church leaders who promote themselves or their own interests, and seemed particularly concerned that they handle material resources appropriately.

3. Two classes of Christians are now the receivers of patterns of honor that set them apart from the bulk of the members. The phenomenon of martyrdom gave rise to strong use of adjectives that were once applied to the elite, especially clear with regard to Polycarp, eroding the pattern of seeing credit as belonging to God and the intermediary, Christ. This language, if used of those who suffered but did not die, later called "confessors," a second higher class of Christians were linguistically separated from the common member. Methodius adds another higher class, the ascetics or virgins, who are expected to achieve a higher level of excellence than the ordinary Christian and are more highly honored both in the present and in the future reward from God.

4. No evidence can be adduced from these slender writings that indicates that any higher rank or honor was given to those who had much more status or resources prior to joining the Christian community.

5. The presentation of God and Christ as supreme benefactors whose gifts must be answered by gratitude and imitation is muted, with the exception of Melito's Homily, though the good works were still expected. The specifically Christian motivation deriving from an revised patron/client paradigm is clearly stated only in the apologist writings, especially "Diognetus." It is also in the apologists that broad-scale benevolence, both in terms of the givers and receivers, is given clear expression.

6. The Montanist phenomenon points strongly to a reaction to increasing clerical dominance, to an insistence that authentic Christian practice included a broad spectrum of participants, including women and to the work of the Holy Spirit as invigorating such breadth of involvement.

7

The Christian Communities of Syria and Osrhoene

MOVING EASTWARD AGAIN, THE NEXT AREA OF INVESTIGATION INcludes the Roman frontier area of Osrhoene and Syria proper. Unlike the Aegean Circle, this area was home to varying Christian groups that not only developed traditions which were in tension, but sometimes actively opposed one another. In the three parts of the first section, I will examine the perspectives of leadership in Antioch, considering Ignatius, Theophilus, and Paul of Samosata. In the second section, I will focus on the heartland of Syriac Christianity, east of Antioch, where Christians of a bilingual culture entertained unique figures like Tatian and Bardaisan, received heartily Marcion's radical version of Christian faith and celebrated Christian life in the unique Odes of Solomon. Finally, in the third section, I will examine an attempt to unify the Syrian church order, in a document which shows both evidence of the center at Antioch and of the diversity of Edessa, the *Didascalia Apostolorum*.

Examining Leaders in Antioch

Ignatius the Martyr

Antioch was the hub of imperial life in the East, and was home to one of the oldest Christian communities. In the early second century, we have evidence of their apparent leader, Ignatius, a fascinating and enigmatic figure.[1] He was a bishop of the church in Antioch, but we know virtually

---

1. All citations of Ignatius' letters are from *The Apostolic Fathers 1* in LCL. Parenthetical documentation will give a shortened version of the community of destination (Ephesians, Trallians, Magnesians, Smyrneans, Philadelphians, Romans) or to Polycarp.

nothing of his relationship to the people in that church. He wrote at least seven letters during the reign of Trajan, which reflect his interest in and relationship to the churches in the province of Asia, as he traveled to Rome with expectations of martyrdom. Within the letters, along with strong echoes of the Gospels and Paul,[2] there is evidence of a strong personality with clear ideas about the shape of Christian community.

Ignatius' letters were shaped by his impending death for his convictions and faith. He seems most grateful for the support advanced by the Asian congregations. As he responded to their representatives and messages of hope, he employed a vocabulary in which "worthy' (*axios*) is frequent, which is prominent in the vocabulary of honor. He referred repeatedly to himself as "not worthy" in general, but often referred to the Asian Christians as "worthy" in several varying expressions.[3] He was quite effusive in his praise for the leaders of the churches and for the churches themselves, a pattern best seen in the openings of his epistles to the Ephesians and to the Romans. Indeed, to the Romans he used no less than 6 compounds of *axios*, but this was simply an extreme example of his regular usage.[4] Superlatives abound: he called Polycarp the "most honored of God" (*theomakaristotate*) and in his letter to the same, challenged him to call together a "most godly council" (*sumboulion agagein theoprepestaton, Poly.* VII,2). How should we evaluate this language?

Since the laudatory language is applied both to the communities and its leaders, this is not simply a revival of elitism. The denial of worthiness for Ignatius himself should probably not be taken too literally, since the tone of the letters clearly assumes a position of leadership and authority. He denied that he "speaks as someone", but as Schoedel points out, this was a literary convention (45). Indeed, since there is evidence in the letters that considerable trouble had been taken to arrange these meetings and the support which was their purpose, I would argue that this is a very traditional use of both self effacing language and flattery,

---

2. Schoedel, *Ignatius of Antioch*, 9.

3. In the seven letters, he used *axios* 17 times and compounds of *axios* 11 times. This kind of usage is not unusual in classical literature, but it is unusual in patristic literature, both in the frequency of usage and in the particular combinations employed. See the listings in Liddell and Scott, and in Lampe's *Patristic Greek Lexicon*.

4. The church at Rome was *axiotheos, axioprepēs, axiomakaristos, axiepainos, axiepiteuktos, axiagnos*. The bishop at Magnesia was called "worthy of God" (*axiotheou* II,1), and "rightly revered" (*axioprepestatou*, XIII,1).

intended to facilitate the bond desired by the author.[5] It has little to do with the core ideas of the revised paradigm, but a great deal to do with the impending martyrdom. He expected and was given honor due to his position and his future glory. He spoke frequently of "attaining to God" (*epitugchanō theou*),[6] a reference to the anticipated martyrdom and saw the honor gathered along the way as increasing the glory given to God by that final moment.

A final expression in which he used the language of mutual honor is the way in which Ignatius begged the church of Rome not to perform an "unseasonable kindness" (*eunoian akairos*, IV,1) and to "grant me this concession" (*suggnōmēn moi echete*, V,3). His point was that they should not impede his martyrdom in any way. In an ongoing pattern, visible throughout the seven letters, Ignatius used traditional honor-based rhetoric to promote what he understood to be a Christian goal, martyrdom.

Among Ignatius' other concerns were doctrinal matters concerning the person of Jesus and the stability of the communities to which he wrote. His well-known emphasis on the hierarchy, especially the bishops, was certainly aimed at these issues. I would strongly disagree with Schoedel, who insists that our author was very close to New Testament models of leadership, strengthened but "not legitimated in terms that are essentially new" (22). Ignatius legitimated the authority of bishops in terms which move decisively outside the honor patterns of the revised paradigm; they are indeed not "new," but predate Christian usage.

The bishop holds the seat of authority in the place of God (*prokathēmenou tou episkopou eis topon theou*) and the presbyters hold the seat of authority in the place of the council of apostles, while the deacons were entrusted with the service of Jesus Christ.[7] The members

---

5. Schoedel (11) discusses Ignatius' oddly circuitous route, which would seem to follow no known travel plan of the day, expecially the movement up the Meander. See also Stevan Davies "The Predicament," for cogent discussion of the terms under which Ignatius was traveling and the punishment he apparently expected.

6. For examples, see *Rom.* I,2; II,1; V,3; IX,2; *Smyr.* IX,2; *Magn.* I; and *Trall.* XII,2; XIII,3. R. A. Brown, "The Meaning of *epitugchano*," shows that *epitugchanō* is clearly rooted in the idea of completion by being united with God. As such, it is larger than the issue of the honor connected specifically with martyrdom, but includes that honor.

7. *Magn.* VI,1. See also a similar passage in *Trall.* II,2 & 3. Ignatius used the same verb (*prokathēmenai*) to describe the ruling power of the Roman church over its *chora* and its ruling precedence in love, in an absolute sense (*Romans* proem).

of the community were to be bound together in one submission (*en mia hupotagē katērtismenoi*) to the bishop and presbyters (*Eph.* II,2). Honor to be given to a bishop is especially clear in the epistle to the Magnesians, where the young age of a bishop invited disrespect. In response, Ignatius used a variety of verbs which belong to the environment of honor given to elite citizens: "it is fitting" (*prepei*), which indicated conformity to a social code; "yield" (*sugchōrountas*), which directed them to give way to their betters; and "granting him all respect" (*pasan entropēn autō aponemein*), which clearly reflects prevailing honor values (III,1-2). Ignatius instructed his younger episcopal peer Polycarp as follows: "let nothing be done without your approval" (*gnōmēs*, IV,1),[8] a sentiment echoed in his statement to the Trallians that "whoever does anything apart from the bishop and presbytery and deacons is not pure in conscience" (VII,2). Here indeed is the familiar world of elite leaders and dependent followers.

To be sure, Ignatius acknowledged that all was intended to honor God finally,[9] but these provisions are a loosely attached qualifier to a complex which functions outside the revised paradigm,[10] following rather the logic and language of the prevailing one. Overall, Ignatius' focus is clearly to bring the community together in the bishop, as he made clear in a striking passage from the epistle to the Philadelphians: "I cried out when I was with you, I spoke with a great voice, the voice of God: 'Pay attention to the bishop and to the presbytery and the deacons'" (*ekraugasa metaxu ōn, elaloun megalē phōnē, theou phōnē, Tō episkopō prosechete kai tō presbuteriō kai diakonois*, VII,1). In all these passages, attention and honor are focused not on God or Jesus, but primarily on a group of leaders, in whom everything centered. Even when Jesus is mentioned, it is primarily for the purpose of doctrinal issues, not as the Giver of gifts or favors.

---

8. This authoritarian rigor may have been aimed at itinerant prophetic activity as well as doctrinal error; it would have a repressive effect even if it were not specifically aimed in that direction. See Trevett, "Prophecy and Anti-episcopal Activity."

9. *Magn.* XV; *Trall.* XII,2; *Poly.* V,2.

10. For example, the use of "blessed" (*makarios*) in *Philad.* X,2, to the effect that an ambassador from Philadelphia to Antioch is blessed to have been found worthy, reflects traditional usage, not the new paradigm. Similarly, for Ignatius the "children" (*nēpiois*) are those who cannot receive heavenly things (*Trall.* V,1), while for Jesus they are *precisely* those whom God trusts with the same (Matt 11:25).

In considerable tension with the themes that we have already identified in Ignatius, he gave some directions to both leaders and people that do reflect the revised paradigm. Humility is for all members, and as such works in powerful ways.

Ignatius instructed Polycarp to "seek everyone by name" and not to treat slaves in a haughty manner (IV,2–3). To the Smyrneans, he insisted: "let not office inflate anyone, for faith and love are everything and nothing has been preferred to them" (*topos mēdena phusioutō; to gar holon estin pistis kai agapē, hōn ouden prokekritai* VI,1). He commended the bishop of Tralles for humility (*praotēs*), which was his power (*dunamis* III,2). Almost immediately, Ignatius commented that he was in need of the same humility, "by which the prince of this world is destroyed" (IV,2). To the Philadelphians, he insisted that the office of bishop was given of God, not for vanity (*kenodoxian*) but rather for the common good (*eis to koinon*, I,1). Ignatius taught the revised paradigm, apparently, for the purposes and mode of leadership, implicitly denying the function of the *cursus honorum* in this community.

Similar prescriptions applied to the people of God in general. They do not have an inflated idea of their own importance (*phusiousthe*), because they "have Jesus Christ in themselves"; and when praised, they become more respectful (*Magn.* XII). Commands to respect one another (*entrepesthe allēlous*) and not to evaluate anyone in the ordinary manner (*kata sarka blepetō*) were rooted in a prior receiveing of the character or conviction of God (*homoētheian theou labontes*, VI,2). Not surprisingly, humility is a prime value for the people as well as for their leaders (*Trall.* VIII,1). Ignatius presents a consistent pattern of instruction.

He did not, however, present a consistent pattern of instruction with regard to privilege.[11] Since the people are not free to do anything without the leader's presence or permission, the privilege of being a direct participant was greatly restricted. Of necessity, this undermined what we have called the community of broad-scale benevolence, and all the more strangely since Ignatius is quite clear that they have been greatly favored and gifted.

---

11. Ignatius used similar prescriptions with words such as *praus* and *phusioō* for both classes, but *entrepō* was reserved for the laity. An injunction to Polycarp seemed to see members of servile status beginning to feel too good about their privileges. "Let them not be puffed up (*phusiousthōsan*) but rather let them endure slavery (*douleuetōsan*) to the glory of God" (*Poly.* IV, 3).

Ignatius' letters are sprinkled with the *charis* word family, which we have seen to be constitutive of the idea of favor and gratitude. Schoedel is of the opinion that *charis* refers to a "whole pattern of life and thought bestowed on the church by God or Christ,"[12] or as a sphere of favor which surrounds the Christian life and from which good deeds flow. I do not see the latter aspect in the work of Ignatius. He used the word in much the way that later writers would, as a gift which conveys religious and spiritual benefits to the individual and the corporate group (*Smyr.* IX,2; *Rom.* proem; *Magn.* proem; VIII,2; *Poly.* I,2; VII,3). Both response and results tended to be religious and moral, with an emphasis on stability and purity. Members of this community should be blameless and unwavering (*Smyr.* proem; *Romans* proem). Apart from general admonitions to love one another, only one indication is given in the entire corpus that this favor should be extended to others in the form of public benevolence, and that in a critique of heretics: "see how contrary they are to the mind of God. For love they have no care, none for the widow, none for the orphan, none for the distressed, none for the afflicted, none for the prisoner or him released from prison, none for the hungry or thirsty" (*Smyr.* VI,2). Since this comment could refer only to a lack of responsibility among the *leaders* of the heretics, it is not at all clear that Ignatius considered benevolence to be at the heart of the Christian community, a community that received and gave gifts on a broad scale.

To summarize, Ignatius shows no awareness of God as general or first order benefactor, nor even of Jesus as prime mediator of benefits even in the religious sphere. To be sure, there are rhetorical flourishes which invoke the favor, mercy and gifts of God, but these seem to function in a rather narrow manner. Concern to preserve moral vitality seems to effectively obscure the larger issue of carrying life, truth and good to a larger world. Deep tension is present between the injunctions to honor and submit to the leaders and the interpersonal relations that were to involve humility. Universal honor for all humanity and the inversion of honor values, as enunciated by Jesus and Paul, are not in view. Gratitude for the gifts of God, to be expressed as worship or doing good to others, is not mentioned. Control by the leadership would inhibit such responses. In short, most of the critical elements of the revised paradigm are conspicuously absent, and those that remain

---

12. Schoedel, *Ignatius of Antioch*, 239–40.

are threatened by the dominance of narrowly religious and hierarchical concerns.

To be fair to Ignatius, these letters probably represent only a small slice of his thinking in an unusual setting. He may have taught much more which was closer to the revised paradigm. It is still significant that both the language and method displayed in our sources are conspicuously different than the main lines of the revision. These epistles will, however, be very influential.

Theophilus: The Bishop/Apologist

A second leader in Antioch whose views can be clearly seen is Theophilus, bishop here toward the end of the period of the five good emperors.[13] He wrote an apology to Autolycus, a figure otherwise unknown, which then was spread in Christian circles. Unlike Ignatius, Theophilus was not a forceful personality. He followed the typical themes of the Apologists: showing the Hebrew roots of Christianity, attacking idolatry and the gods of the pagans, and explaining the ways of the Christians. In so doing, he reveals that his understanding of Christianity included much that we have identified as the revised patronage paradigm.

God was acknowledged by Theophilus in terms that declare primary beneficence. He is "the maker and fashioner (*dēmiourgon*) of the universe, nourisher of all breath" (II,34). God was called Providence (*Pronoia*) with regard to a very active goodness (*agathosunē*, Ad Auto. I,3). Among the adjectives applied to him were "inimitable goodness" and "inexpressible beneficence." These specifics derive from Theophilus' intent to clarify the nature of the Christian God, as distinct from the traditional Greco-Roman gods.[14]

This kind of language is not applied to Jesus, who is not discussed with respect to his historical work, but only in respect to God, and there as the Logos. For that reason, Jesus' historical role as the broker of God's

---

13. Background material and citations are from *Ad Autolycum*, ed. and trans. by R. M. Grant, OECT.

14. "For he is in glory uncontainable, in greatness incomprehensible, in loftiness inconceivable, in strength incomparable, in wisdom unteachable, in goodness inimitable, in beneficence inexpressible" (*dox yar estin achōrētos, megethei akatalēptos, hupsei aperinoētos, ischui asugkritos, sophia asumbibastos, agathōsunē amimētos, kalopoiia anekdiēgētos* . . ., I,3).

goodness was missing, nor could Theophilus present him as an exemplar or continuing benevolence on earth in human community.

Despite that lack, there *is* a chain of benevolence in the thought of Theophilus. Two responses to the person and gifts of God are mentioned. First, worship is to be given only to God, a point mentioned in the context of the question of emperor worship (I,11). Second, an appropriate response to God is a life devoted to purity, holiness and righteousness (I,6–7). In practical terms, that meant honoring one's parents (III,9), broad-scale benevolence to widows and orphans, reaching out to the destitute[15] and doing good to enemies (III,12). Any public boasting or display, as well as the expectation of public honor, were forbidden as inappropriate to the members of this community.[16] Finally, Theophius cited Rom 13:8 in this context: "owe nothing to anyone except to love one another," which negated the system of public obligation but affirmed public benevolence. These words were rooted in Lev 19:18, quoted in Romans 13:9 and central to the ethics of Jesus and to Theophilus here (III,12ff.). Such living patterns made one "useful to God" (*euchrēstos... tō theō*, I,1).

Theophilus was able to speak of the community that followed these patterns as a refreshing sanctuary, using two metaphors about the sea. The law of God and the teaching of the prophets, cherished by Theophilus and early Christians, are streams and rivers "flowing and gushing with sweetness and compassion," which refresh the world sea. The community itself was, he said, an island oasis, offering truth and peace in the conflicts of the world (II,14).

Theophilus lacks some of the elements of the revised paradigm, notably the motive of gratitude that receives and gives through the continuing work of Jesus. However, given that this is an apology, it is quite possible that the missing elements would be present in other works. No glaring contradictions to the revised paradigm are present.

---

15. Here Theophilus quotes two passages from Isaiah (1:16–17; 58:6ff.), as well as Zechariah 7:9f. We have seen these to be characteristic Hebrew Bible sources, alongside the Sermon on the Mount, for the clear understanding of the revised paradigm, in a variety of Christian writers.

16. Theophilus also spoke against showy public speaking. "Fluent speech and euphonius diction produce delight and praise, resulting in empty glory..." *Stōmulon men oun stoma kai phrasis euepēs terpsin parechei kai epainon pros kenēn doxan...*, I,1. One might wonder about the assonance of the quote in note 13 above.

The Curious Case of Paul of Samosata

One further window into the life and practice of the church at Antioch is provided by the events surrounding the work and fall of Paul of Samosata, bishop of the church in Antioch in the decade following Valerian's capture. Opposed by a faction at Antioch led by the presbyter Malchion, Paul was accused of heresy and several types of professional misconduct. Unfortunately, we have only the testimony of his enemies to the situation.[17] He was examined twice by councils of bishops, who excluded him from his church. When he refused to surrender the building, an appeal was sent to Emperor Aurelian, who ordered it to be given to Paul's opponents. His alleged theological errors about the person of Jesus are not germane to this project, but the details of his career certainly are.

One accusation against Paul concerned a most vigorous style of worship, in which the bishop apparently horrified his peers. He used rhetorical methods calculated to appeal to the emotions, such as slapping his thigh and stamping his foot. Congregational reactions was both expected and required. He was also accused of eliminating songs about Jesus, as being recent compositions, but of having songs composed in his own honor. Leaders in sung worship were female, and among his strongest followers.

I have serious doubts about the elimination of songs in praise of Jesus, though I think songs in his own praise quite possible. I can see that female leaders of worship might seem problematic, as women are clearly moving into the background as the second century ends. As far as the rhythmic exuberance is concerned, I am not sure in what sense emotional displays would be considered inappropriate. Is this a clash of eastern and western sensibilities?[18]

A second accusation leveled against Paul centered upon his actions as a judge. He had placed a tribunal and a throne in the central

---

17. Eusebius give us considerable information about Paul, his opponents and their councils and their descriptions of his manner of life, in *H.E.* VII,27ff. Of necessity, we must work from tendentious remains.

18. Virginia Burrus has traced very effectively the similarities between the portrait of Paul in this letter and rhetorical patterns found in Lucian, Quintilian and Cicero. Paul may have seemed an ecclesiastical "new man", who used and sometimes exceeded the accepted methods of rhetorical prowess. See her "Rhetorical Stereotypes." I would not doubt that he did exceed the normal boundaries of dignity.

area of the church, emphasizing his position and power and bringing secular judgments into the church. He had, so they said, become wealthy through his judicial activities and strong rhetorical language accused him of extortion and twisted judgments. Further, his wealth had been used to develop a retinue, both male and female, and to live luxuriously and ostentatiously.

Developing a retinue was not unusual for leaders, even for church leaders, in this era. Inclusion of women, even young and beautiful ones, was not inappropriate, though we have seen various attitudes toward the participation of women in church life. Whether his judgments were twisted would have been debatable in his own day, nor could we with confidence accept the judgments of his opponents in that regard. Being a judge would not be incompatible with the vocation of a Christian servant leader. However, even allowing for exaggeration, it would seem clear that he lived in a manner that contradicted the heart of the new paradigm. Neither motivation by money nor a luxurious lifestyle were consonant with that revision. Had he not been taught it, as I think likely, or had he chosen to ignore that part of Christian tradition?

To complicate matters, the third major accusation raises the question raises the question whether Paul held a secular office of procurator in addition to his episcopal office. He was accused of "thinking of high things" (*hupsēla phronei*) and "lifting himself up" (*huperērtai*), setting himself up in secular honors (*kosmika axiōmata hupoduomenos*) . Paul's public presence included a large group of attendants, including secretaries and bodyguards, as he strode (*sobōn, badiōn*) through the agora of Antioch. Letters were read and composed in public, while self-aggrandizing statements were made. He preferred to be called "ducenarius" rather than bishop. How should we evaluate this presentation?

Again, we must allow for some exaggeration in the description due to the heat of the struggle in Antioch, but allowing for that, such behavior was manifestly out of character for a Christian leader. If it is true that Paul essentially combined the offices of bishop and procurator, he was in a situation that his detractors were not well equipped to evaluate. Were some of his actions simply "normal public presence" for a high level procurator? Would he have said that he was not acting as a bishop when the great pronouncements were made?[19]

19. It seems to me quite likely that he was a procurator during the confused conditions in Syria in the time of the Palmyrene usurpation. The timing is right and his

To be both bishop and procurator and fulfill both roles in their respective cultural contexts would have required extraordinary vision and depth of character, if indeed it was possible at all. Paul was apparently not that person and seems to have assumed that the two offices were roughly equivalent. If so, that also reveals how the bishop's office was being conceived at about 260. I would argue that Paul was simply exercising the traditional paradigm of patronage, with regard to both offices. There is nothing in the description of his activities that suggests that he represented the revised paradigm of Jesus in any serious manner. Paul's opponents assumed the revised paradigm in their criticism of his lack of humility and promotion of honor, yet their manner of opposition deserves its own assessment.

First, the synod that began the examination was convened rather quickly, requesting the attention of bishops such as Firmilian of Cappadocia and Dionysius of Alexandria. Why were these two leaders asked to come, in particular?[20] When the two synods were finished, letters were sent to Dionysius of Rome and Maximus of Alexandria, then to other communities. Can we not see here an understanding of rule within the church that rests on "great men," defined as rulers of prominent, wealthy communities? Most were "great men" even before they became bishops, but were they the best qualified to help, in the sense in which Jesus and his immediate followers defined "greatness"?

When those who condemned Paul were done, they appointed as successor the son of the prior bishop, "adorned (*kekosmēmenon*) with quite all the good things which are suitable (*tois prepousin*) for a bishop" (*H.E.* VII,30,17). One wonders what was considered "suitable" and necessary for a bishop in Antioch in the late third century. Some aspects of the traditional understanding of greatness were apparently shared by

---

hometown of Samosata was under Palmyrene rule. Also, the judgment of Aurelian becomes understandable, for all who cooperated with Zenobia would have been under duress, at the very least. See Bardy, *Paul d'Samosate*, 261ff.; and Norris, "Paul of Samosata," in favor of his serving in this civil role. Millar argues the opposing view in "Paul of Samosata, Zenobia and Aurelian."

20. Dionysius refused to be involved and died before the decisions were reached. Firmilian presided over the first meeting and died on his way to the second. Our window into Firmilian's view of the church can be found, slightly, in letter 75 of Cyprian's corpus, where he either echoes or agrees with Cyprian that the power of the church is in its unity and is vested in those who have the power to baptize and give the Spirit by laying on of hands. Graeme Clarke notes, in his edition of Cyprian's letters, that Firmilian was from Cappadocian aristocracy (Vol. 4, p. 250).

Paul and his opponents. In the actions of neither do we see much regard for the members of the local community, nor a seeking of their good.

Our picture of the leaders in Antioch is, of course, limited. We have no pastoral letters from Ignatius nor from Theophilus. The source for Paul is a conciliar letter clearly colored by opposition and competition. However, within the limits of the sources, it would seem that Theophilus did share the revised paradigm, that Ignatius is in considerable tension with it and neither Paul nor his opponents operate in its defined patterns.

Dynamics of Christianity North and East of Antioch

Attempting to come to a clear focus upon Christianity near the upper Euphrates is notoriously difficult. Historical information is often embedded in documents that seem spurious or hagiographic. Documents and scriptures were translated into Syriac or from Syriac into Greek, and much of the population may have been bilingual, with a corresponding blend of cultures. Edessa, the primary center of this arm of Christianity, was politically under the influence of the Sassanian empire until the time of Caracalla, when it was declared a Roman colony. It was, of course, increasingly affected by Rome both directly and indirectly throughout the second century.[21]

Church Order Documents

My presentation of evidence begins with the indications found in two documents which cannot be precisely dated but which reflect early traditions in Syriac Christianity. One is called the *Teaching of the Apostles* and the other purports to derive from a shadowy "apostle" which the Syriac church associated with their founding, the *Doctrine of Addai*.[22]

---

21. For the background and boundary of this discussion, I am reflecting Burkitt, *Early Eastern Christianity*; various essays by Drijvers in *East of Antioch*; Segal, *Edessa*; Klijn, "Christianity in Esessa"; and of course, the careful work of Millar, *Roman Near East*.

22. I am not convinced that there was no figure by that name in early Eastern Christianity, not that Thaddeus could not have become Addai, as Drijvers argues in "Facts and Problems" (*East of Antioch*, 160–61). Both words and names have a remarkable fluidity in bilingual areas, Drijvers' argument that this Addai was created in the image of a later Manichaean Addai could easily have occurred in the opposite direction.

Though we cannot place them securely into the second century, I would argue that they cannot be placed after the third, because they do not reflect the issues of the emerging imperial church. Asceticism, so important to monasticism, can be seen here, but in a different mix of goals.

The *Teaching* explained the ministry of the church by analogy to the offices of the Hebrews. Deacons and elders were seen as similar to the Levites in general, the bishop as similar to Aaron and the local Ruler was comparable to the combination of gifts and talents in Samuel (sections #5 and 24). Those who had been so invested with trust and authority were not to be haughty, boastful or arrogant about their position (#23). Neither were they to show partiality to anyone (#26). Nothing was commanded in terms of special honor given or required for those who held these positions.

In addition, the *Teaching* showed considerable concern about their attitude toward money and profit. Those invested with ministry were not to be involved in money lending or commerce (#14). In fact, they were to divest themselves of material possessions and not be in pursuit of further gain (#20). This concern was echoed in the *Doctrine*, where Addai refused money from King Abgar and cited "the word of Christ" as reason for the refusal (p.657). "Instead of receiving gold and silver, he himself enriched the church of Christ with the souls of believers" (664). This, the document insists, was accomplished by the handing on the gift of God through speaking the truth (659).

Descriptions of the moral qualities of the followers of Addai included renunciation of sexuality characteristic of some other third century writers and of course, the development of monasticism,[23] but considerable attention was also given to living in "watchfulness touching the ministry, in burden bearing toward the poor, in visitations to the sick ... their noble nature ... was neither subservient through covetousness, nor in bondage under fear of blame" (664). This description apparently

---

Segal (*Edessa*, 65) argues the real possibility that a community was established in this area in the early second century by an Addai. Whether or not Addai was historical, the teachings predicated of him would reflect what the Syriac church thought early leaders would espouse. Both of these documents will be cited from *ANF*, vol.18. The *Teaching* is cited by section numbers; The *Doctrine* by page.

23. The earliest Syrian monastics emphasized the example of Christ as the *Ihidaya*, a designation used to represent one who is utterly devoted to faith, prayer, purity, and simplicity, and therefore separated from sexuality. See Griffith, "Asceticism."

belongs to the men and women of the "formal" ministry. The actions of the general membership of the community are not discussed.

Concerning honor, it was asserted in this context that much public praise resulted from the demeanor and actions of the Christian leaders. That honor was not to be sought, however, inside or outside the community of believers.

> Give heed, therefore, to this ministry which you hold, and with fear and trembling continue in it and minister every day. Minister not in it with neglectful habits, but with the discreetness of faith ... Let not the secret eye of your minds be closed by pride, lest your stumbling blocks be many in the way... Look not for the honor that passes away: for the shepherd that looks to receive honor from his flock: sadly, sadly stands his flock with respect to him. (663)

This last clause indicated the damage that would be done to the community if the leaders were seeking honor rather than guarding against pride.

To summarize, these documents do not present the foundation of the revised paradigm, the first-order benefaction of God or Christ. Nor is there any indication of approval or reward from these first-order benefactors. Roughly speaking, the behavior and attitudes expected of the leaders are congruent with the revision, but the full change in honor values is not present. Whether the other members of the community were expected to be humble and benevolent is not treated. Small pieces of the revised paradigm are clearly stated, but only in reference to the clergy.[24] Were the functions of the people no longer considered important? Even in the Hebrew covenant, which is the putative model in much of this document, the people are addressed seriously, if in a subordinate role.

Tatian the Syrian

Tatian, a figure renowned for his asceticism, profoundly affected Syrian Christianity in the second and third centuries. We can see a clear, if slight, reflection of the revised paradigm in his radically focused Christianity. He began and ended his life in Syria, being strongly influenced by the

---

24. In keeping with this, the *Teaching* declared that believing kings should be allowed to stand at the altar with the priest, like David (#25).

apologist Justin Martyr in the intervening years. His harmony of Gospel accounts, the *Diatessaron*, was extensively used in the Syrian church and a sect of Syrian Christians called Encratites followed his lead in asceticism. His own apologetic *Oration to the Greeks*, the only complete work from his hand, gives an indication of his attitudes.[25]

First, he declared that he would rather be dead than to be ungrateful (*acharistos*) to God by denying his committments (4.1). Second, though he referred to Justin as "most admirable" (*thaumasiōtatos*, 18,3), he appeared to protest the use of public honorifics in this rhetorical question: "Why, if you heal your neighbor, are you called a benefactor" (*euergetēs*, 18,2). Last, he stated fully the rejection of public honor and affirmed the giving of generalized honor to all humanity without regard to the distinctions which usually separated groups.

> With us there is no desire for false glory, nor do we employ subtleties of doctrine ... Withdrawn from public and earthly talk, obedient to God's commands and following the law of the incorruptible Father, we reject all that is based on human opinion. Not only the rich philosophize, but the poor also enjoy teaching without charge, for there is no comparison in exchange value between the truth of God and this world's recompense. Thus we admit all who wish to hear, even if they are old women or youngsters, and in general every age enjoys respect with us ..." (32.1)[26]

These statements clearly address only one of the critical components of the revised paradigm, equality of dignity and participation for all. Tatian only hints at the benevolence of God. Nor does he clearly give evidence that this community is structured for the flow of benevolence through many members to the many who need to receive good. Yet like Theophilus, as well as the *Teaching* and the *Doctrine*, there is no glaring contradictions to the model which was commended in earliest Christianity.

25. Cited from Whittaker's translation in OECT. Translation is cited by chapter and part; Greek by chapter and line.

26. *Par' hēmin de tēs men kenodoxias ho himeros ouk estin, dogmatōn de poikiliasou katechōmetha. Logou yar tou dēmosiou kai epigeiou kechōrismenoi kai paraggelmasi kai nomō patros aphtharsias epomenoi, pan to en doxē keimenon anthrōpinē paraitoumetha, philosophousi te ou monon oi ploutountes, alla kai hoi penētes proika tēs didaskalias apolauousin. Ta gar para theou tēs en kosmō dōreas huper paiei tēn amoibēn. Tous de akroasthai bouloumenous pantas houtōs prosiemetha kan meirakia, pasate hapaxaplōs hēlikia par' hēmin tugchanei timēs.*

Marcion of Sinope, in Syria

Marcion was a profoundly influential figure in second-century Christianity due both to the enormous spread of his followers and the vigor with which his ideas were attacked by a variety of theological opponents. Originating in Sinope of Pontus, he created a great stir in Rome and was rejected by that community. As he traveled east, he apparently planted groups of followers and finally settled in Syria, where communities of his followers were a force until the fourth century, opposed by major figures even in the fifth. None of his works have survived, but from the attacks of his opponents, we may be able to see why he was so successful in creating communities and being viewed as a serious opponent.

With ample financial resources from his father's shipping business, Marcion came to Rome about 137. He brought a large gift of money with him to the Roman church.[27] To the members, he must have looked like a patron. However, when he began to argue his theological interests to the elders of the church, he was rejected, and his money was returned in full. These financial resources, to our knowledge, were never surrendered or renounced, and may be the key to understanding the compelling attraction of his later life.

Ephraem Syrus compared him with Bar Daisan in the words: "Bar Daisan adorns himself with fine clothes and precious stones; Marcion is clothed with the garb of a penitent. In the grottos of Bar Daisan are heard hymns and songs, amusements for the youth; Marcion fasts like a serpent."[28] Ephraem also argued that Marcion saw Christ as an extremely humble warrior who negotiated the purchase of souls for eternity.[29] Now, if humility and simplicity were the form of Marcion's life, as he was spreading his version of Christianity across the northern Mediterranean, and if he were not able to hand over his resources to the church, but continued with that type of wealth, what was he doing with it? The nature of this investigation suggest an answer to that question and also to the question of the wide and quick growth of the

---

27. The testimony is from Tertullian's *Praes.* XXX, which I cite from ANF vol. 3. In spite of the nearly unanimous declaration that this sum was 200,000 sesterces in secondary literature, Tertullian speaks only of 200 (*ducentis sestertiis*). Since this amount would hardly be noticed, I assume that students have taken *ducentis* in its transferred sense, as "a large indefinite amount," but 200,000?

28. *Madrash* 1.12 and 17. Quoted in Bauer, *Orthodoxy and Heresy*, 29.

29. Drijvers, "Christ as Warrior and Merchant," in *East of Antioch*, 73–85.

movement. One must coordinate the nature of his theology with the historical factors.

According to Epiphanius, when Marcion appeared before the Roman leaders, he argued that the new way of Jesus took priority over the former Hebrew heritage, basing his arguments on Luke 5:36 and 6:43 (*Pan.* 42.2). Tertullian says that he rejected the person of a God who not only allows evil, but in some cases even fosters it, in favor of a God who was unqualifiedly good (*alium Deum solius bonitatis*, Praes. XXXIV). Tertullian quoted Marcion as saying that the Hebrew God "ruthlessly pursues" evil men, and was "jealous" in nature. He must be contrasted with the God of Jesus, who overflowing generosity extended towards even those who do not expect or deserve benevolence.[30] Apparently Marcion concluded that the new way must be decisively separated from the Hebrew one, spending many hours editing Christian texts and writing his *Antitheses* to show the impossibility of the God revealed in Jesus' work being the same as the one in the Hebrew Bible.

Tertullian tells us that Marcion followed the Stoics in regarding God as peaceful and immovable, not really involved with this world (*Praes.* VII). The nature of the God which Marcion espoused is better revealed, however, in the following quote from Tertullian: "I am aware of the plea which they will adduce, that that is rather a primary and perfect goodness which is shed voluntarily and freely upon strangers without any obligation of friendship on the principle that we are bidden to love even our enemies . . . The requirement of the undue is an augmentation of the due benevolence" (*Adv. Marc.* I,23,3 & 5).[31] Here Tertullian clearly identifies the controlling principle of Marcion's movement, and it is at the heart of the revised paradigm! This God has "blessing for the poor" (*Adv. Marc.* IV,15), and the manner of life of the members of this community would reflect that agenda. It cannot be a coincidence that the two Scriptural references used by Marcion to argue for a radical goodness in this Kingdom of God come from Luke's version of the Sermon

---

30. *Adversus Marcion* II,13. English citations are from ANF vol.III. Latin citations are from SC #365/368, though the new translation of Evans in OECT was consulted throughout. On *aemulatio* as a key criticism of the Hebrew god, see Mühlenberg, "Marcion's Jealous God."

31. *Scio dicturos atquin hanc esse principalem et perfectam nonitatiem, cum sine ullo debito familiaritatis in extraneos vountaria et libera uffunditur, secundam quam inimico quoque nostros et hoc nomine iam extraneos diligere iubeamur . . . Exaggeratio est debitae bonitatis exactio indebitae.*

on the Mount, where precisely this openhanded flow of resources is commanded (6:33–38).

Returning to the question of the flourishing of this movement, note that Justin complained that they placed great emphasis on being Christian, and that they had spread to all humanity (*1 Apol.* 25.5–6). That assessment comes only ten to fifteen years after Marcion was forced out of the Roman churches. A few decades later, Tertullian stated that the movement had "filled the whole world" (*Adv. Marc.* V,19). Marcionite martyrs are mentioned in several seasons of persecution, and nearly every significant writer considered it their duty to refute their beliefs. Yet they endured; Ephraem the Syrian and Aphraates the Persian both felt compelling to attack them in the fourth century. A Marcionite building labeled as such has been discovered near Damascus and dated to the early fourth century. Theodoret boasted in the fifth century that he had seen to the conversion of more than a thousand to orthodoxy.[32] What could account for this strength and enduring influence?

It was not asceticism alone, nor novel doctrinal ideas which attracted such numbers of adherents. If so, the Encratites and "Gnostics" would also have been much stronger and enduring. I would argue that Marcion embodied a most powerful principle of early Christianity—namely, its radical goodness. When one combines Marcion's concept of God as peaceful and ultimately generous, his affinity for the most radical teachings of Christ and Paul, his personal ascetic lifestyle and the enormous growth, it seems very probable that he invested his resources in the manner that Jesus had taught. In so doing, he would have set the pattern for other members of the elite, as well as those who once aspired to reach that rank. Did this movement, in spite of its problematic intellectual framing and rejection of Jewish heritage, retain and build consistently upon the essence of the revised paradigm and find the profound energy which it releases when practiced?

The Odes of Solomon: *Community Songbook*

Before we consider the attempts to regularize the Christianity of Syria and its sphere of influence, attention to the *Odes of Solomon* is in order. This body of songs originating in the Syriac Christian community, then

---

32. Bauer, *Orthodoxy* 24. Theodoret's boast is from *Epistle* 113, according to Blackman, who cites it in *Marcion and His Influence*, 4.

later translated into Greek and Coptic, reveals some of the central affirmations which would be made by members of the Syriac community in corporate worship. What were they learning as they were singing?

The dominant theme of the *Odes* as a whole is devotional, answering the greatness and beneficence of God with poetry and praise, adoration and love. In patterns and images often strikingly like Biblical psalms, yet more intimate, God is celebrated for life, salvation and gifts. *Ode* 16 speaks of first-order benefaction:

> It is He who made the earth broad
> and placed the waters in the sea.
> He expanded the heaven
> and fixed the stars
> and fixed the creation and set it up,
> then He rested from His works.
>
> And created things run according to their courses
> and work their works
> for they can neither cease nor fail.[33]

This was not a dominant theme, probably because the teaching of Psalms and prophets was assumed. Rather, spiritual and social benefits were emphasized, for example:

> And by Him the generations spoke to one another
> and those who were silent acquired speech.
> And from Him came love and equality
> and they spoke to another that which was theirs.
> And they were stimulated by the Word
> and knew Him who made them,
> because they were in harmony. (12:8–10)
>
> And hatred shall be removed from the earth
> and with it jealousy shall be drowned
> for ignorance was destroyed upon it, because
> the knowledge of the Lord arrived upon it. (7:20–21)

Though the work and presence of God is spoken often as immediate, there is also a figure who mediates between God and humanity, one who "is the opening of everything," who looses all who are bound (17:11–12), and who "continually does good to every one" (28:13). In personal experience:

---

33. Citations are from *The Odes of Solomon*, ed. and trans. by Charlesworth.

> He became like me, that I might receive him
> in form he was considered like me.
> And I trembled not when I saw him
> because he was gracious to me.
> On account of this He was gracious to me
> in his abundant grace
> and allowed me to ask of Him
> and to benefit from His sacrifice. (7:4–5, 10)

The people ("generations") of this person bring God's life to the world, they are the "interpreters of his beauty, the narrators of his glory, the confessors of his purpose, the preachers of his mind, and the teachers of his works" (12:4). They produce fruit from God's life (1, 3, 8, 14), which are defined as truth, grace holiness and praise. Strong social implications can be found, with clear echoes of Isaiah 58.

> The offering of the Lord is righteousness,
> and purity of heart and lips.
> Offer your inward being faultlessly,
> and let not your heart oppress a heart,
> and let not yourself oppress anyone.
>
> You should not purchase a stranger
> because he is like you,
> nor seek to deceive your neighbor
> nor deprive him of the covering for his nakedness.
>
> But put on the Lord generously
> and come into His paradise,
> and make for yourself a crown from His tree.
> The put it on your head and be joyful,
> and recline upon His rest.
>
> For His glory will go before you;
> and you will receive of his kindness and his grace
> and you will be anointed in truth
> with the praise of his holiness.
> Praise and honor to His name. Hallelujah. (20:4–10)

All the elements of the revised paradigm are here, with the exception of universal honor: recognition of first-order benefactors, gratitude for gifts geive expressed in both word and work, all within a broad-scale perspective. God's favor and gifts were expected to flow to and through the many members of this worshipping community.

The Structures of the *Didascalia Apostolorum*

In the fragmentary remains of early Syrian Christianity, there are many stories of heroes of the faith. The famous story of embassies back and forth between King Abgar and Jesus, preserved for us by Eusebius (*H.E.* I,13), is fascinating but historically indefensible. That doubt also applies to many stories of Addai, his successor Aggai and the martyrdoms of Barsamya and Sharbel. These stories have a heroic character reminiscent of later hagiographa and cannot be demonstrated to have a historical core.[34] They are significant, however, as showing that some figures of the Edessene church wished to demonstrate the early origins and heroic nature of their community.

One connection which they attempted to make was to trace the ordination of a late second century bishop, Palut, through the well-known Serapion of Antioch to Zephyrinus of Rome.[35] Unfortunately for their assertion, Serapion significantly antedated the Roman bishop, but the desire of this group to be legitimated through Antioch underlies the inclusion of elements from their tradition in the church order document called the *Didascalia Apostolorum*,[36] compiled in the middle of the third century.

Strikingly, this manual lacks extensive acknowledgement of the gifts of either God the Father or of Jesus. Chapter VII briefly mentions the "gentleness of thy goodness" which promised forgiveness to those

---

34. *The Doctrine of Addai*, *the Acts of Sharbel*, and *the Martyrdom of Barsamya* are in ANF vol. VII. Other than the teaching outlined above, none of the actions of these figures is germane to the issues of this project. It is interesting that Aggai, Sharbel and Barsamya are not listed in the martyr calendar of the Syrian church, while 3 later pre-Constantinian martyrs are: Shamona, Guria, and Habbib the Deacon (Burkitt, op.cit. 22).

35. See Burkitt p.28 and 79, for the circuitous tracings of the tradition about Palut, and the fact that this "orthodox" party were long called Palutians, which may be testimony to the strength of the party of Marcion and perhaps also to that of Tatian, who were recognized as Christian.

36. The *Didascalia* will be cited from Connolly, *Didascalia Apostolorum*, and from Vööbus *The Didascalia Apostolorum in Syriac I*. Citations from chaps. I–IX will be from Vööbus, by chapter, section, and line, while chap. X and following will be from Connolly, cited by chapter and page number.

who repent. That mention is the basis for a much longer exhortation to the bishops to be gentle and patient in the performance of their duties (86,1; 89,14–15). The surrender by Jesus of privilege and power, in order to live and serve in poverty, is mentioned in chapter XIX as support for the challenge: "we who have our Lord for master and teacher, why do we not imitate his teaching and his conversation?"

By contrast, the amount of attention given to bishops as a group is quite large, far more than any other. The proem of the work begins: "we make known that everyone shall stand and confess and believe in that which has been allotted by God ..." Immediately a six part breakdown of church officers is presented, then the people themselves, who are to be "hearers of the words of the Gospel in discipline" (lines 813). The writers used a variety of images to reinforce the exalted position of the bishops: shepherds (VII,73,7); "rams", as opposed to the people, who are "ewes"; high priests and Levites, chiefs, leaders (VII,91, 26–27; IX,99,15–16). More striking yet is the assertion that 1 Sam 8:10ff., which foretells the abusive behavior of the kings who were to come in Israel, is an appropriate description of the role of the Christian bishop. Blithely comments the *Disascalia*: "now this likeness also holds for the bishop" (IX,106). A more thorough return to the paradigm of the "great man" would be difficult to conceive! Yet more: "on this account, bishop, take pains to be pure in your works. And know your place, that you are set in the likeness of God Almighty and do hold the place of God Almighty" (V,52,21ff.). Not surprisingly, the people were to regard him as the "mouth of God", and to honor him "as God" (IX,102ff.; VII,67,15ff.).

Certain of the functions of God also devolved upon him, for he had "authority to judge those who sin" (V,52,27) and to forgive those sins, "for you have put on the person of Christ" (VII,78,6–7). Indeed, the judge was to be in chambers for a variety of settlements on the second day of the week; and a number of guiding principles were given to keep his judgments fair (XI,p.113). In addition, he bore responsibility for the congregation's sin, in a manner which is clearly considered adjunct to the work of Christ (VIII,92,22ff.). In all these functions, his work was sacred, though he was warned that he would answer to God for the integrity of his actions (XI,114–15).

Someone who was taught to insist on such rank and privilege would probably need guiding restraints. Bishops were admonished regularly to cultivate humility and simplicity (III,27,19ff.; IV,40,15–30;

IV,44,20-21).³⁷ They were not to practice favoritism either in their leadership or judging functions (IV,46,28-29; IV,47,1-2; VI,67,3ff.; X, p.106). Clearly, this was not just a matter of self-consciousness, for one canon connects it with a problem which is mentioned frequently:

> But if your mind be not pure—whether it be through respect of persons or the gifts of filthy lucre which you receive, and you endure that an evil person should remain among you... you will have put yourselves in deadly peril of forfeiting eternal life ... because you have pleased men and have turned back from the truth of God, through respect of persons and the habit of receiving empty gifts: and you will have scattered the Catholic Church ..." (X, p.108)

Favoritism was linked with money (V,51,22ff.; VI,65,17ff.), and whoever compiled these guidelines was seriously concerned about motivation in the area of money. In general, the bishop should not be a lover of money, before or after taking office (IV,48,1 & 8; IV,40,15). Further, a warning was considered necessary against accepting money from "the heathen" (IV,47,26-27), for that was "defiled money". Much later in the book, a large section was devoted to detailing the type of persons from whom alms could not be accepted.³⁸ Anticipating the objections, the editors commented: "But if you say, 'these are those alone who give alms; and if we do not receive of them, from what ... ?' God says to you: 'to this end did you receive the gifts of the Levites, that first-fruits and offerings of your people, that you might be sustained and have over and above ...'" (XVIII, p.159). Last, warnings were addressed to the bishops concerning the use of donations for the purposes of luxurious living, though it is clear that their living derived from such a source (VIII,90). One can see how the very exalted position assigned to the bishops would tend toward an elite lifestyle, including friendship with prosperous individuals who would donate to the church for reasons often having much more to do with the traditional paradigm of patronage, than with

---

37. Some of these admonitions are credited as being from the *Doctrine of Addai*. See also IV,454,12ff.

38. "rich persons who keep men shut up in prison, or who mistreat their slaves, or who behave with cruelty or who oppress the poor; those who are lewd or who abuse their bodies, evildoers, forgers, dishonest advocates, false accusers, hypocritical lawyers, painters of pictures, makers of idols, metal workers who are thieves, dishonest taxgatherers, spectators of shows..." XVIII, p. 156ff.

any internal logic of the Christian community. So the many warnings were quite necessary.

Instruction regarding lower ranks of clergy are significant first for their relative brevity. Rooted in a prior source called the *Testamentum Domini*, they type of person to be elected presbyter was "humble, gentle, poor, not a lover of money, having labored much in the services of the weak ... father to the orphans ... has served the poor ... who in all things is noble in piety" (II,28,12ff.).

Those who would be elected deacon could not be "entangled by the business of the world... having no riches" (IV,29,15–16). They were charged even more specifically to be occupied with the needs of the sick, the stranger, the widow, the orphan and the indigent. Further, a deacon's responsibility included informing the church of such needs (IV,30,5–6), and opening his home to the stranger, for his home was the "inn of the church" (V,30,11ff.). Deaconesses were charged with much the same values and roles, but with regard to women in particular. Both deacons and deaconesses were to be eyes and ears for the bishop: "you shall... inform the bishop and be his soul and mind" (XVI, p. 148).

Widows were given significant attention in the *Didascalia*. Receivers of material support from the bishop through the diaconate, their role in the church was primarily one of offering prayer. They were expected to pray for all who needed help, for those who gave assistance, for the bishop through whom the help was administered and for the giver of alms, though they were not to mention the name of the latter (XV, pp. 142–43). Occasionally, they may have accompanied the deacons or deaconesses to the homes of the sick, in order to lay hands on them and pray. In the *Didascalia*, the writers seem to be troubled at the amount of respect thus earned through faith and work. They were being asked serious questions about truth, and were perhaps being seen as good persons to teach or baptize. Widows needed to be shown their place. Chapter XV instructs them not to teach, under danger of judgment for sin, for the non-believers might scoff. (That it is sinful to tell the truth and have someone ridicule it is, of course, self evident.) So their place was clearly defined: "let a widow know that she is the altar of God and let her sit ever at home and not stray or run about among the houses of the faithful to receive. For the altar of God ... is fixed in one place" (XV, p.133). Interestingly, the male orphans were also defined as altars of God (IX,100,14), but were not instructed to stay in one place.

To be fair, there is some indication that some of the widows were out of line. Perhaps "running after gain" may be dismissed as an exaggeration of the understandable desire of people to give effective widows gifts of money beyond that which she received from the clergy. One passage would, however, point to a serious problem: "Now we see that there are widows who esteem the matter as one of traffic, and receive greedily; and instead of doing good works and giving to the bishop for the entertainment of strangers and the refreshment of those in distress, they lend out on bitter usury and they care only for "mammon" (XV, p.136). It may be assumed that such activity would not be done on a widow's stipend, and thus involved gifts from the more prosperous. All cases, however, involve an infringement on the prerogatives of the bishop and those who worked with him.[39] This becomes more likely when one examines the expectations for honor-giving among the members of the community and the shape of the people's work.

First, the people should give strong honor to all the clergy. At the *agapes*, each distinct group received their portion, "the honor which is right to him" (IX,101).[40] The widows portion serves as a standard, then each other rank received a double portion of that standard, while the bishop received a quadruple portion. Such are the gifts, honors and "the reverence of the world" (IX,101,5–25).

When one attended the corporate assembly, one's place was clearly defined: bishop on the throne in the center, surrounded by presbyters, men and women separated, widows and mothers separated, youth and children standing (XII). Yet, with that very structured ranking, some of the old paradigm could be found in rules for the service. If a person of rank (*honorabilior secundum saeculum*) entered the assembly, the bishop was forbidden to halt the service, but a deacon should attend to him. Alternatively, if a destitute person (*egenus aut egena*) entered the service and could not find a place, the bishop should offer them his seat.

At first glance, the expectations for the behavior of the people seem to flow directly from the revised paradigm. They were to work hard with their hands and to be prepared to give for the benefit of others; idleness

---

39. See the cogent assessment of Charlotte Methuen "Widows, Bishops" 197–213.

40. IX,100,10ff. contains a crisp breakdown. "The bishop sits for you in the place of God Almighty ... the deacon in the place of Christ ... the deaconess in the place of the Holy Spirit, the presbyters in the place of the apostles, the widows and orphans in the place of the altar."

was strictly prohibited (II,14,10; VI,34–35; IX,107–8). Attendance to the spectacles was frowned upon, for this people were to be serious workers (XIII,128–29). Women were expected to take seriously the model of the godly wife in Proverbs 31, including "stretching out her hand to the poor" (III,22,2–3). Management of legitimate gain would allow the people to "store up" resources for giving to others (IX,110). Those who would not be likely to have free resources were expected to fast and donate what they would have spent upon themselves (XIX,161). Orphans were put under the guardianship of bishops for training in a craft or domestic role (XVII,152). Thus far, the revised paradigm seems secure with reference to the behavior expected of the people, but two critical factors undermine its function.

First, alms were described as redemption for sins, rather than the expression of gratitude and new identity: "if you have something in your hands, give it as a redemption of your sins ..." (VI,34,29). Second, it seems that the bulk of the resources were funneled through the bishop's office:

> Search and make trial, therefore, that you may be receiving from the faithful, who communicate with the churches and conduct themselves well, to nourish those in distress and not receive from those who are expelled ... and teach your people and tell them that it is written: "Honor the Lord with righteous labor and with the chief of all your increase." Wherefore nourish and clothe those in want from the righteous labor of the faithful ... (XVIII, 159)

These words were addressed to the bishop; it was not permitted for individuals to act on their own initiative or to give with their own hands, especially to the widows (XIV,131). Indeed, the instruction to the folks was "apart from him do not do anything ... that you bring no shame upon him as a despiser of the poor" (IX,103).

Thus the public identity and honor of the bishop were guarded by blocking any intended initiative on the part of the people. They were directed to approach the bishop for permission, but even that only through the deacons, for "not even to the Lord God Almighty can one approach except through Christ" (IX,101,19fff). One suspects that the distance between the bishop/patron and the poor was such that abuse of the program of benevolence could readily be accomplished if one were so inclined, and so it is no surprise that part of chapter XVII is addressed to that very problem. Three disjunctions are enunciated: those who take when not in need, those who manage not to work in order to receive and those who have concluded that this is not a workable agenda and have stopped giving.

We may summarize the perspective of the *Didascalia* by noting first that the rooting of the community in the benevolence of God and Christ is barely hinted. Second, the bishops have pre-empted the place of the supreme benefactors with reference both to the members of the community and also to those outside who may be in need. The place of the bishops was exalted by titles, financial privilege and physical separation, which was shown both in the seating arrangements in the assembly and by the demand that the deacons serve as intermediaries between the people and their bishop.

Numerous injunctions were aimed at the bishops regarding humility, not being partial and not linking themselves with either non-Christian figures or badly behaved Christian ones. These are necessary because their position contradicts the Syriac heritage concerning leaders. There was tremendous tension between the heritage and the current position of the bishop, essentially a return to pre-Christian "great man" ideas of leadership and rule.

Severe restrictions were placed on the freedom and function of the people, who could primarily exercise benevolence only through the office of the bishop. A particularly strong restriction was aimed at the widows.

Conclusions

The *Disascalia* neatly summarizes the development of Christianity as an institution in Syria and Osrhoene. It combines significant traditions from Edessa, which emphasize the humility and servant hood of the clergy, with the powerful exaltation of the clergy which we first saw in Ignatius. Both are developed along the way and seem to me to be in tremendous tension. The place of the people is gradually restricted and channeled through the clergy, most clearly through the bishop. It would not be accidental then, that the people are not really mentioned in the two major works of Edessene Christianity and their place in the *Didascalia* is small. The clergy in general, and the bishop in particular, have become both spiritual and material patrons for this community, and the honor values follow that reality. An inversion of the pattern of honor-giving has been lost and the universal honor envisioned in the New Testament was not even on the horizon. The revised paradigm has been lost.

Another stream of tradition, however, ran parallel to the development of the institution. In the Odes, strong witness to the benevolence of God and Christ was answered by gratitude both verbal and active toward others. These were the songs which the people sang. Both Theophilus and Tatian give strong hints that in a presentation of the essence of this new community, the revised paradigm was quite distinctive and should be highlighted to both opponents and inquirers. As in the case of the Aegean apologists, their interest is quite clear.

Perhaps the struggles associated with two prime "troublemakers" may help clarify matters. The clear ineffectiveness of Syrian Christianity to counter the spread of Marcion's version of the faith should be attributed to the fact that in some very important areas, moral and social issues quite close to the everyday life of "folks," Marcion was clearly closer to the original vision we see in the New Testament than was the institution which was developing in Syria. The attempt of Edessene leaders to claim roots in Rome and Antioch were countered by Marcion's claim to be rooted in Jesus, at his most radical.

In the case of Paul of Samosata, the state of the institution is quite clear. Paul himself clearly accepted, and took to the limit, the sense that the bishop should be a "great man." Enough of the humility and sharing of honor; let the bishop be seen as the one who ruled in glory, "in the place of God." Let him be honored as such. His opponents reached back to the revised paradigm to criticize him, but their actions betray their understandings to be agreeable with his. By invoking the other ecclesiastical "great men" and finally the redoubtable Aurelian, they revealed a return to a traditional Roman model of greatness. The resolution was quite Roman in a most traditional and political way.

In Syrian Christianity, we see a chaotic and perplexing history. The struggle between the revised paradigm of Jesus and a return to the traditional seems to have been lost in the third century, if the sources we have are adequate. We cannot be sure, however, of many small communities of Marcionites and of rural communities not really reflected in our written sources.

8

The Christian Communities in Alexandria and Southern Palestine

IN THIS CHAPTER, I WILL INVESTIGATE THE TREATMENT OF THE REvised paradigm in teachers of the Christian communities in and near Alexandria. Southern Palestine was closely related to the teachers of Alexandria, by borrowed leaders and visiting teachers. While one can be sure that Christianity had arrived in Egypt in the first century, both origins and development are obscure. Eusebius relates a tradition that the church was established by Mark, then enumerates a list of bishops in Alexandria which is rather too precise in the beginning and then too obscure in the second century. He does give substantial information about both Origen and Dionysius of Alexandria, though it is not particularly helpful with regard to this investigation. Finally, the rich collections of papyri discovered in Nag Hammadi and Oxyrhynchus, though from the second and third centuries, tell us less about Christianity than about the complex philosophical environment that challenged it.

Of necessity, this investigation will reflect mostly the thinkers and leaders of urban Alexandria, for the Christianity of the rural areas cannot be seen except through them and in sources later than the third century. The Christian community comes into clear focus with the leadership of Demetrius in Alexandria, about the year 189. At that time, the shadowy figure of Pantaenus was revered in the community for his learning, both Biblical and philosophical, as Eusebius relates (*H.E.* V,10,1 & 4). That combination of learning was consistent for the leaders of Alexandria. Before treating the primary figures of Clement and Origen, I will explore the themes of the *Sentences of Sextus*. This collection of aphorisms originated in Alexandria and added Christian themes to what was probably an already composed body of philosophical sayings. In this method, it well represented Alexandrian Christian teachers.[1]

Wisdom, Gospel and Philosophy: The *Sentences of Sextus*

Because this collection does not aim at either speculative knowledge about God or devotional paeans to divine creativity in the natural sphere, some characteristic themes of God's first order benevolence are not extensively stated. Christ is not mentioned at all. However, two sayings state an assumption for the collection, that God is the source of good in the world.[2] The same assumption is clear in several sayings that direct the reader to understand and seek good, which is ultimately the work and business of God. For example, "consider as good only what is worthy of God" (*Sentences of Sextus* # 131); or "consider only what is noble to be good and only what befits God to be noble" (# 197). This theme continued in a number of sayings[3] that emphasized that the benevolent character of this God is reflected in the attitudes and actions of a good person.

In other sayings, the identity of the good man as the son of God is to be determinative of behavior: "Be worthy of the One who deems you worthy to be called a son, and act always as a son of God" (# 58). God's child will practice magnanimity (*megalopsuchian*, #120), and the imitation (*homoiōma*, #148) of God.[4] That imitation would be the greatest honor that one could give to God, though some verbal credit was apparently also considered appropriate.[5] Two sayings make it clear that behavior toward others help to define the nature of this imitation of

---

1. Citations will be from the translation of Edwards and Wild. For a helpful assessment of the various philosophical and biblical material in this work, see Wilken, "Wisdom and Philosophy."

2. "First of all there is God the benefactor, and second, man the beneficiary" (#33)."An evil man denies the providence of God" (*kakos anēr pronoian theou einai ou thelei* #312).

3. Sayings 122 and 132 alike encourage the good man to see and pray for that which is worthy of God.

4. Note also #221 and 222, which note that calling God "Father" and oneself "son" leads to consciousness of the need of appropriate action.

5. "The knowledge and imitation of God is the best way to honor Him" (#44)."Give God the credit for whatever you do well" (#390).

God. Like God, one would be concerned for the welfare of others (*ho pronoōn anthrōpōn* #372) and pray for them. Conversely, "the greatest impiety toward God is the mistreatment of a human being" (*megistē asebeia eis theon anthrpou kakōsis* #96). The children of God should reflect God in their character.

In a number of sayings, Sextus spoke against the practice of public honor-seeking. Relative to the issue of motives, he condemned the public gift which aims to garner attention (#342), since it is for one's own benefit instead of the benefit of others. Self-love (*philautias*) produces injustice (#138), while the love of glory (*philodoxia*) produces ugly rumours (*kakodoxias* #188). In practice, then, one should not seek to speak first (#164) and should avoid public praise as shameful.[6] Finally, Sextus condemned the common practice of flattery as simply making evil people worse (#149). With regard to both principle and practice, Sextus opposed public honor-seeking and honor-giving as destructive of good.

In his collection, Sextus outlined a functional attitude to possessions that is appropriate to a person who is seeking the noble way of life rooted in God. First, he denied the orientation that goods define the good life. "Do not honor anyone on the basis of his many possessions" (#192).[7] The "good life" is not characterized by luxury,[8] which results in ruin (*olethros*, #73), nor is luxury the purpose of human life. Similarly, hoarding or collecting possessions is contrary to the value of human life (*philanthrōpon*, #300). One should limit one's acquisition by the clear definition of basic needs.[9]

Possessions are to be understood relative to the agenda of God. The philosopher should not consider anything to be his own property (#227), for those who share God in common as Father should as a mat-

---

6. *aischron ēgou logou echōn dia stoma epaineisthai* (#286).

7. Possessions as a defining goal directs the person to avarice (*pleonexias*, #137); they are unworthy because they are temporary (#128); they create a desire which cannot really be fulfilled (274b).

8. "You were not born to luxuriate in what God provides" (*ou gegonas entruphēsan tē tou theou paraskeuē*, #117). See also the warning against physical indulgence in #76: "Love of goods demonstrates love of body."

9. In addition to a broadly utilitarian perspective (#115), Sextus advocated a limiting of needs, so that we are like God who needs nothing (#50, #18, #382). This rationale, which we will also see in Clement, is a philosophical commonplace which I would argue is not rooted in Christian thinking.

ter of course have possessions as a common resource. Not to do so is essentially to lack respect for God (*ouk eusebēs*). To despise worldly goods prepares one for a closer relationship with God (#81) and makes it possible to follow the right teaching (#264). The right use of possessions is to share them (#82b) with the needy (*tois deomenois*, #330), with your neighbor (#17), with the poor person (*tou pteōchou*, #267), and indeed with everyone (#266). Some clear connections to Christian teaching can be seen in the injunction to deny oneself the ordinary food of the day, fasting in order to provide food for those who lack (#267), and to allow the neighbor to take even the last of one's possessions, for this confirms the freedom one enjoys (#17). Finally, one should do these things with alacrity (*prothumōs*, #330),[10] a qualifier which is characteristic of honorific inscriptions. Here it does not apply to the large-scale benefits, but to a more extensive, low key benevolence. Sextus had in mind more people doing smaller benefits.

When our philosopher wrote more broadly of benevolence, he continued to link the motive and action to God. The wise man is a living image of God (*eikona theou zōsan* #190), and is a benefactor after God's example (#176). God is the leader of human well-doing (*anthrōpōn kalōn praxeōn hēgemōn estin*, #104) and confirms their deeds (#304). Further, benefaction is the only suitable offering to God and is therefore connected with the vitality of prayer and a continuing favor of God (#217; 47; 378).

The revision of "greatness" in the estimation of God includes benevolence to all humanity,[11] but especially to the needy (#51, 52). All humanity included enemies (#213) and those who were ungrateful (#328). In what seems an echo of Jesus, Sextus challenged his readers to give as generously (*proika*) as they have received from God (#242).

Other important qualifications to the life of benevolence included thinking about the nature and functions of good things (#56; 100) and spending more time (and priority in time) on deeds than on words (#383; 359).

---

10. Note also #379: "When someone shares food wholeheartedly (*ek holēs psuchēs*) with a needy person, his gift is small but his readiness (*prothumia*) is something great in God's sight."

11. "strive to be a public benefactor to humanity" (*koinos anthrōpois euergetēs*, #260). "Treat all human beings as though you were a public benefactor of humanity" (#210).

Sextus reflected clear streams of current philosophical thinking and his work is not involved with the theological issues of redemption. He did, however, compose a collection of admonitions for "the philosophical life," which has been strengthened with Christian social and moral teaching. What I have been able to show here is how carefully these elements follow what we have called the revised paradigm of benevolence and honor. Sextus challenged his readers to take seriously a Patron of first order magnitude and to respond by becoming benevolent themselves, without reference to honor sought or expected. Honor and good are extended to all, though especially to the poor, as a matter of imitation of God and giving honor to God.

Clement of Alexandria: Teacher and Defender of the Community

By the end of the second century, Alexandria was clearly becoming a unique center of developing didactic work. After the mysterious Pantaenus had finished his career, he was succeeded informally by one of his students, Clement. An avid participant in Hellenistic culture and philosophy prior to his conversion, Clement combined the roles of apologist, polemicist and moralist. I will show that he reflects the revision of the patron/client paradigm in nearly every way, with some hints of a renewed elitism in some parts of the *Stromateis*, the last of his works. However, in his works as a whole, the themes of the revised paradigm are fully expressed and thoroughly interwoven.[12]

God and Christ as First-Order Benefactors

Clement clearly presented the Hebrew-Christian God as a first order benefactor. The life of humanity and whatever spiritual renewal is offered by God are set into the framework of creation and providential order (*Paid.* I,2,6). This Creator, who made the world in strength

---

12. The *Protrepticus* (Exhortation to the Greeks) and the *Quis dives salvetur* (Can the Rich Man be Saved?) will be cited from LCL 92. English citations from The *Paidagogos* (Christ the Educator) will be cited from Wood's translation, and Greek citations will be from the edition of Marrou (SC 70, 108, 158). English citations from the *Stromateis* I–III will be from Ferguson's translation, while books IV, V and VI are from ANF, Vol. II. Greek citations of the *Stromateis* are from the edition of O. Stahlin, GCS 15/17.

(*Protrep.* VIII,181), filled it with "divine benevolence" and "holy powers" (XI,236ff.). Clement quoted Jesus' crisp and defining statement about the Father who "causes his sun to rise upon all men" as a quality which also characterizes the Son, who "attends humanity with equity" (*ep' isēs peripolei tēn anthrōpotēta*, *Protrep.* XI,243). Further, the very nature of the universe, as consistent and orderly, reflects the character of the Creator, who is pleased when humanity also follows that pattern in righteous living.[13] Finally, Clement presented God as a wise Patron, who not only gave life in the beginning, but taught how to live well (*eu zēn*) so that he might supply (*chorēgēsē*) everlasting life.[14]

Clement had much to say about the goodness of God. In the *Stromateis*, he cited a number of passages from the Hebrew Torah to show that God expected kindness towards even animals (II,94,1; Deut 25:4). He saw the Mosaic legislation as a significant revealer of God's varied goodness. Mentioning the command to leave a portion of both the grape and olive harvest, he commented:

> Do you see how the legislation proclaims simultaneously the justice and goodness of the God who provides food unstintingly for all. (*Strom.* II,86,2)

> In fact, the principle of tithing crops and flocks was an education in honoring the divine; not being totally absorbed by profit, but sharing humanely with the neighbor as well (*Strom.* II,86,3)[15]

In addition to a complicated and abstruse discussion of goodness relative to God (*Paid.* I,8,63), in which he showed his affinity for philosophical argument, Clement quoted the book of Psalms to argue for the goodness of God (*Strom.* II,71, 3). His citations teach that God is "full of mercy" (Ps 11:4) and "good to all" (145:9). He saw God as having an "overwhelming love for humanity" (*tēs huperballousēs philanthrōpias Protrep.*VIII,183), and he saw God's love working in both the first cov-

---

13. Clement expressed himself eloquently at this point (*Protrep.* VI,157), rooting his views first in Deut. 25:13ff., where Moses commands God's people to use a consistent set of weights and measures. He followed that with quotes from Plato's *Laws* #715e and 716a, showing the similarities.

14. *Protrep.* I,9. See X, 205 for a similar use of this verb *chorēgeo*, common to inscriptions of benefactors.

15. Clement sees the year of Jubilees as another restriction on the accumulation of possessions, by limiting the time of ownership. He concluded this discussion by quoting three passages from Proverbs (11:26; 14:21; 20:28).

enant with the Hebrews and the second one with followers of Jesus (*Strom.* I,29,2), in discipline as well as beneficial actions. It is clear that Clement shared none of the theoretical disjunction between Hebrew and Christian understandings of God, sometimes seen in early Christian writers. He saw continuity in divine history, life and action.

> There is only one cultivator of the soil within human beings. It is the One who from the first, from the foundation of the universe, has been sowing the seeds with potential growth, who has produced rain on every appropriate occasion in the form of His sovereign Word. *Differences arise from the times and places which receive the Word.* (*Strom.* I,37,2; my emphasis)[16]

Clement clearly saw the activities and character of God as expressing benevolence on the broadest scale, in both the natural and the religious spheres, and throughout time. Before we move on to note how this benevolence continues in the work of Jesus of Nazareth, one connection to other themes of the revised paradigm should be noted.

Though it is intertwined with philosophical notions of self-sufficiency and impassibility, Clement placed strong emphasis on the disinterested nature of God's benevolence. His "benevolence (*eunoia*) consists in wishing good things on others for their own sake . . . a benevolence directed to well-doing" (*pros to eu poiein*, *Strom.* II,28,1ff.). This is important later in the emphasis on the imitation of God. Thus Clement was quite emphatic that God cannot be swayed by threats or promised honor from either friend or enemy, while he engages in "supplying all things to everything that has received being and has wants" (*Strom.* VII,3). Divine approval is granted only to a pattern of life that honors God's gift by doing justice without regard to either gift or threat, that is to say, a pattern of life which imitates God's values in these matters.

With regard to beneficence in the world, that which originates from the hand of God is so interwoven with that which comes through Christ that it is somewhat difficult to distinguish them. In general, however, one may say that in the human sphere, the activities of Christ are more specific, though that is not so in regard to creation.

Building upon the first chapter of the gospel of John, that Christ was the Word (*Logos*), Clement connected him with the beginning of

---

16. Similar sentiments, expressing a variety of actions in which God works with human lives, are found in the following places: *Paid.* I,1,1 and I,7,55; *Strom.* I,173,5; *Quis dives* 7.

all things, as well as actually being the agent of creation (*Paid.* I,11,97; *Protrep.* I,17; John 1:1ff.). Jesus, the New Song of the world, embodies the name of God and thus is in ultimate harmony with the created order, which originated with him (*Protrep.* I,7 & 11).[17]

When Clement presented the multifaceted benevolence of Christ on behalf of humanity, he used several images to elucidate such variety. This quote shows the breadth of conception with regard to benefits, using the image of a singer with a new song.

> What then is the purpose of this instrument, the Word of God and the New Song? To open the eyes of the blind, to unstop the ears of the deaf and to lead the halt and erring into the way of righteousness; to reveal God to foolish men, to make an end to corruption, to vanquish death, to reconcile disobedient sons to the father. The instrument of God is loving to men. The Lord pities, chastens, exhorts, admonishes, saves and guards us. Over and above this, He promises the kingdom of heaven as reward for our discipleship, while the only joy he has of us is that we are saved . . . the truth, like the bee, does no harm to anything in the world . . . (*Protrep.* I,15)

In another place he compared such varied attention to a catalogue of medical practices,[18] and to the intensity of a champion in the arena.[19] When thinking of the story of the good Samaritan, he saw Jesus as the supreme Neighbor and as an example of how to be one (*Quis dives* 29). The image of a teacher and trainer (*paidagogos*) underlay most of the other images, for the speaking Word of God was the dominant conception. He specifically echoed Jesus' words in Matt. 23:8, in asserting that there is only one Teacher, "whether of lecturer or student, and he is the

17. *Protrep.* I,7 & 11. Here he speaks both with philosophical terms like "elements" (*stoicheiōn*), discord/ concert (*diaphōnian, sumphōnias*) and "harmony" (*harmonia*), and with physical terms like sea, land, air and fire. Nor is he shy about associating cosmic expressions like "support of the universe" (*ereisma tōn holōn*) with the fulfillment of the "fatherly counsel of God." The New Song is not then simply a healing or harmonizing phenomenon, but a *return* to cosmic harmony, once written into the fabric of nature, but now disrupted by evil.

18. *Protrep.* I,21. He included the radical ideas of surgery, cautery and amputation, but speaks first of poultices and massage. In *Paid.* I,2,6 he referred to the healing of the soul's passions.

19. *Protrep.* X,237. Note that the Lord is not just a sole combatant (*agonistēs*), but also a fighter together with his people (*sunagonistēs*). In X,211 Clement continued the metaphor, calling his listeners to enter the arena of struggle for the truth, stripped for action.

source of understanding" (*Strom.* I, 12,3), deserving of full credit (*Quis Dives* 6).

In addition, Clement specifically presented the central work of Christ as giving his life a sacrifice which answered for the sins of humanity (*Paid.* III,12,98), and who provides access to the many benefits of God's life through this "shedding of blood" (II,8,73).

> Such is our Educator, good beyond a doubt. "I have not come" he declared, "to be ministered to, but to minister." For that reason He is represented in the gospel as afflicted, for he is afflicted on our account and undertakes "to give his life as a redemption for many." He is generous indeed who gives us the greatest things he has, his own life, and liberal and kind because he willed to be humanity's brother, though he could have been his Lord; so good that he even died for our sake. (I,9,85)

Thus we can see Jesus and the one he called Father as explicitly and extensively described as first-order benefactors in the natural and spiritual spheres. With that in mind, an examination of the responses of those who saw themselves as favored by their benevolence is in order.

Christians as Grateful in Praise and Discipline

Clement insisted that the foundational response of humanity to such benevolence should be gratitude (I,8,74). He saw the acts by which God "saves humanity," however, as the "most noble of all God's acts" (*to megiston kaibasiliskōtaton ergon tou theou*), and thus worthy of the "deepest gratitude" (*tēn megistēn charin* I,12,100). Those who recognize the active goodness of God should be "returning thankful praises to God for His benefits and honoring him through the Word . . ." (*Protrep.* XI,249).[20] Yet both of the passages just cited immediately declare that the expression of this gratitude is really found in a pattern of life that consists of seeking God and adapting one's behavior to God's values.

---

20. In *Quis dives* 27, Clement commented on the great commandment to love God with all one's being as being based in supreme honor: "the only thanks we pay him, a small return for the greatest blessings." Although he saw that to do good to others is something given to Christ (ch.29), he did not quite make the connection that this is an expression of thanks. Countryman (*Rich Christian* 55f) misses the fullness of Clement's exposition when he claims that Clement limited alms to members of the Christian community.

The path that Clement laid out begins with a "longing" for God, focused first on creative Majesty (VI,153), as well as for noble things and "the Word of truth himself."[21] The vision of God that results from this longing is facilitated by righteousness and self-control (*egkrateias*), and leads to a rational path opened up by Christ (1,27). Clement indicated what was primary in his own mind by setting up a sequence of events that begins with deliverance through persuasion. After that, one is healed through discipline then instructed in a higher life

Paid. I,1,3). In *Quis dives* 1, he affirmed that it was "by the Word through the favor of the Savior" (*logō dia tēs charitos tou sōtēros*). At no point is this an autonomous process, however, but at all points is the work of God through Christ.

What were the components of the healing discipline with which one proceeded under the guidance of the Paidagogos? Reverence for God leads to thoughtful self-control, self discipline and piety (*Strom.* I,159,3). A virtual reversal of values occurs, Clement said, because the follower of God "stores up blessedness with God" (*tō theō to makarion thēsaurisas Protrep.* X,227;c.f. *Paid.* III,6, 34). He needs little for this life, and Clement defined "little" in almost exhaustive terms.

For whatever reason, Clement knew a great deal about the lifestyle of the wealthy and how their visibility creates desire in all who observe or participate in it. To place it into perspective, he drew both from the philosophers and from Biblical traditions. He pointed out that even a non-religious investigation of extensive wealth may only show that the person who possesses a great deal is a crook.[22] Still he does not see wealth in itself as an evil to be

eliminated, but as a dangerous condition. Being wealthy must be managed carefully.[23] It is a danger first in reference to the methods

21. *Protrep.* XII,260–61. Clement used *pothos* here for a longing for somethings lost or absent, and *philotimoi . . . pros ta kala . . . genōmetha* to indicate a serious ambition for a style of life which pleases God. He quoted Ezek 18:39, which speaks extensively of justice and compassion, as a "complete description of the Christian life" (*Paid.* I,10,95).

22. *Paid.* II,71,2, quoting Plato *Laws* 5.742.e. It should be noted that Clement echoes the allegorical interpretation of Lev. 11:13–14, found in the *Epistle of Barnabas* 10.4. The unclean animals were seen as types of humans who live by plundering others (*Paid.* III,11,75). Like "Barnabas," Clement forbade association with such persons.

23. Clement carefully denied that total divestiture of good was inherently godly, because: (1) it could be done even for selfish reasons and (2) left one unable to help others or even dependent on others (*Quis dives* 11).Yet if one could not effectively reinterpret the meaning of possessions, they could and should be liquidated, as Jesus commanded the rich young ruler, but not other wealthy persons (24).

deemed necessary for its acquisition, then for the desire which it creates. Clement did not wish to prevent the "proper acquisition of wealth, but its unjust and insatiable acquisition" (*kalōs oun ploutein ou kekōluken, alla gar to adikōs kai haplēstōs ploutein* Strom. III,56,1). Seeing that wealth has an effect both on those who have it and on those who do not, he considered its proper use a critical issue. Clement recommended a balanced moderation between spending and giving (*Paid*. III, 6,35e), supporting his contentions with quotes from Prov 11:24 and Ps 112:9. He concluded with these words: "Therefore it is not he who possesses and retains his wealth who is wealthy, but he who gives; it is giving, not receiving that reveals the happy man. Generosity is a product of the soul, so true wealth is in the soul." Clement had very clear ideas of the use of wealth. We turn now to see how he guided his readers to manage resources.

To spend and consume extensively is to "misuse the gifts of the Father." We should be the lords of our eating habits, for it is "beneath human dignity to humanity to feed themselves like cattle being fattened for slaughter … ever bowed over their tables" (*Paid*. II,1,9). Later he advocated simple food in abundant variety, but without the sauces which "lead us to eat when we are not hungry," with explicit reference to Christ as an example (I,1,14–15).

He recommended simple white garments for both male and female, (though the women would do well to wear veils), for covering, warmth and comfort, though not for pleasure (II, 10,106; III,11,53ff.). The use of gold and silver was not absolutely prohibited, but was seen as dangerous since they exceed the needs of life (II,3,35). Hairstyles should be simple, avoiding elaborate braiding and "extensions," though a decorative brooch was acceptable (III,11,62).

Household utensils come in for their moment of attention, as Clement took aim at fancy beds and beddings, as well as basins and lamps made of precious materials, arguing again that utility is the primary issue (II,3,37; II,9,77). Taking the life of Jesus as an example, he noted the simple drink from the well (John 4), the great but very simple meal eaten on the grass and the washing of the feet of the disciples from a basin "made, be it noted, of no precious silver brought from heaven" (II,3,38).

The use of slaves as part of a self indulgent lifestyle was also attacked, and Clement knew a great deal about slaves and slavery. He compared the life of one who is constantly attended by slaves to the model of the abusive king in 1 Samuel 8 (III,4, 26). In this context, Clement recommended that Christians practice "self-service" (*autodiakonian*), by which he meant physical exercise and manual labor deliberately chosen.

"Self-service" included washing one's own feet and putting on one's own sandals, thus not being constantly served by others. Not asking others to serve you, however, leads to voluntary service for others. One could return a massage for a massage as an act of "communal righteousness" (*dikaiosunēs esti koinōnikēs*). Similar actions include sleeping alongside a sick friend, serving others and providing for those in need in person (III,8, 52).

Clement's understanding of divine discipline saw possessions as valuable tools or accompaniments, but with stringent limits on quantity or luxury. Similar restraint applied to activities. Christians need to practice a "moderate frugality in our journey toward the good life of eternity" (I,12,98).

The final goal of all this work is to "accomplish the original divine command: 'Let us make mankind in our image and likeness'" (I,12,98). After quoting Psalm 112:9, which characterizes the reverent person as one who "scatters" resources and gives to the poor, he commented: "For the words 'after the image and likeness', as we have said before, are not directed to physical matters ... but to intellect and reason, whereby the Lord can stamp his seal appropriately on the likeness related his beneficence and authority (*tēn pros to euergetein kai tēn pros to archein homoiotēta*, Strom. II,102,5). Within this framework, divine benevolence which is freely given to humanity in order to move them through a process which restores a likeness to God in terms of discipline, benevolence and power, I will now examine other aspects of Clement which relate to this investigation.

Christians as Those Who Transform Ambition

The revised paradigm prescribed decisive changes with regard to the search for and granting of honor, and Clement spoke clearly to this issue. First, note that there is a connection with possessions and their social implications. "Follow God, rid of false pretenses, rid of the pomp that perishes, possessing only what is really yours, the good that cannot be taken from you: faith in God, belief in Him who suffered, good works toward men, your most valuable possessions (*Paid.* II,3,35). In the opening of *Quis dives salvetur?*, Clement wrote against flattery of wealthy people, for both those who hold great position and those who admire them need to be released from its attraction. However, would position and flattery continue to be pursued inside the Christian community?

Clement saw a danger in the teaching position.[24] One should be careful that they have not "leaped into teaching hastily or out of jealousy of others; that he is not spreading the word out of personal ambition." One should not look to humanity for approval, but only to God:

> But anyone who is enrolled as a fully grown Christian ought not to even have the desire for recompense. Anyone who boasts of his good actions has his reward already through his reputation. Anyone who performs any of his duties for the sake of his recompense... is surely in the grip of this world's practice. He ought to imitate the Lord as far as possible. The person who does this is serving God's will to the full; he receives a free gift and offers a free gift. (I,9,2)

The behavior of those who follow God finds its motivation in the benefit to others. Clement gave an interesting twist to the saying of Jesus: "I was hungry and you gave me food" (Matt 25:35). He stated that Christ was saying that he was nourished through the benefit given to any person as if that person was Christ himself. In a striking phrase, Clement referred to that person as the "person of his purpose" (*Strom.* II,71,3). What was unstated but clear is that the purposes of God are fulfilled through the action of the Christian disciple, for Christians "learn to share as a result of justice; they pass on to others some of what they have received from God out of a natural attitude of kindliness" (*Strom.* II,71,3).

Clement did not see all members of this Christian community as totally equivalent. He recognized that certain members have more capabilities than others (I,3.1). Men apparently differed from women in his evaluation, though his references to women's place were rare and not onerous. Certainly he ascribed more glory to the higher levels of clergy (*Strom.* VI,13). Yet he insisted that the shape of this new community

---

24. *Strom.* I,6,1. The teacher should have only the good of the hearers and the approval of God in mind. See also I,9,2, where he speaks of writing for "vainglory." The "wide road which leads to destruction," about which Jesus warned, is for Clement simply "love of women, love of glory, ambition and similar passions" (IV,6).

transformed relations between members, of whatever sex or station. "Noone should glory in his superiority in human intelligence" (I,50,1). So Clement stated about what may have been one of his own temptations, quoting both the Hebrew Bible (Jer.9:23f.) and the words of Paul (1 Cor 3:19ff.). Those who seem to be wise to the general public are not to be specially valued or honored (*Strom.* I,88,1-2).[25] Neither God nor his representative prejudges people "according to appearances" (*Paid.* I,7,61), so it is inappropriate as well for the followers. Further, men and women were joined together in a common agenda: "Let us recognize that both men and women practise the same sort of virtue. They who possess life in common, grace in common and salvation in common have also virtue in common and so education too" (I,4,10).

Clement highlighted the term "child" (*nēpiosi*) as a designation of all Christians.[26] "Let us then call him by the one title: Educator of little ones" (*Paid.* I,1,1), he said in regard to Christ. "Children" is a term which referred to all Christians (I,5,12), though he also used animal metaphors such as "colts" or "lambs," with reference to simplicity (I,5,15). Once he gave a rather dubious etymology of *nēpiosi*: "We ought to be in a position to understand that the name "little ones" is not used in the sense of lacking intelligence. Childishness means that, but "little one" really means "one newly become gentle" (*ne + epios* I,5,19). Whatever one thinks of this etymology, it is clear that Clement renewed a critical term in Jesus' revision of the code of greatness and used it precisely in the same sense that Jesus had commended it to his disciples.

Clement also emphasized the common table as a clear sign of the present values of Jesus and of the heavenly future of the community which bears those values. In successive sections of the *Paidagogos*, he addressed several salient points concerning the *agapē*. First, not just any dinner will qualify, especially one which simply is a celebration of fine food. Here Clement worked with the complex of Jesus' teaching (Luke

---

25. See *Strom.* I,48,5 against showy rhetoric.

26. D.K. Buell allows her theory to eclipse the evidence in the conclusion to ch.7 ("A Rhetoric of Christian Unity") of *Making Christians*. She refers to "developmental language in the Paidagogos" as reinforcing power differences among Christians. She saw Clement as portraying catechumens and newer Christians as infants, whereas Christian teachers starred as adults (117). Clement does acknowledge differences in gifts, maturity and rank, but his use of *nēpios* and related terms or images is designed not to reinforce or highlight such differences but to minimize them. See *Quis dives* 31 as well.

14) concerning place and guests at dinners, where one should not seek a place of honor. One should invite "many" but not those who would usually be first choice (II,1,4).

After contrasting "bread" with seasoned delicacies, he then spoke of the supper as "permeated with love, yet not identified with it, but as an expression of mutual and generous good will" (II,1,5). In the process of sharing food with the atypical guests so invited, one samples the kingdom of God, for "from food taken at a common table we become accustomed to the food of eternity" (II,1,7). Clement used the language of honor to comment on the practice of social humiliation at the table, both described and corrected by Paul in I Corinthians 11. A person who eats heartily and neglects the hungry disgraced himself in two ways: adding to the burden of the poor and exposing his lack of temperance before those who are rich. (II,1,12).

In all of this, Clement showed remarkable congruence with the revision of honor values as outlined especially by Jesus. These patterns of behavior accompany the development of broad-scale public benevolence by members of this community.

Patterns of Benevolence

In *Strom*. VII,3, Clement tied together his varied understandings of the gratitude which leads to benevolence, writing of "the beneficence which has us for its object," and of the three great answers which Christians give to that beneficence: worship, teaching and beneficence in deed. He saw clearly that a Christian life responds to the prior goodness of God in gratitude (*Protrep*. X,223) and discipline, then moves on to imitate God's actions by handing on God's gifts to others (*Strom*. II,97).

It is in this imitation of God that benevolence finds its source and guidance: "The man who performs and teaches these things shall be the greatest in the kingdom" says Scripture, imitating God by the generous offer of similar gifts. For God's gifts are available for the benefit of all ..."[27] Clement declared that God's ownership takes priority in substance, and God's giving of all things so overshadows our reception and possession that we should see material goods as belonging more to the

---

27. *Strom*. II,97,2. See also II,100,4 where clement again connects "likeness" (*exomoiōsin*) to following God, quoting Luke 6:36: "Be merciful as your Father is merciful."

human community than to us. So while we earn or inherit them, they are ours only in trust for the common good. The question to be asked is: "I have something, why should I not share it with those in need?" Here Clement brought in the language of honor but with a new application. It was "unbecoming" (*atopon*) for some to live in luxury while many live in poverty. It was "much more honorable" (*eukleesteron*) to serve many than to live in wealth. One will derive more benefit from practicing kindness. One can see that Clement here made the connection between the extensive instruction he has given about frugality, self-denial and the refusal of luxury and a consistent attention to the material needs of others.[28] The disciplines prepare one to meet those needs both in goods and mental orientation.

Of course, from the standpoint of Christianity, material needs are not the only place where benevolence can and should be extended to all. Clement saw light, truth and knowledge as gifts of God to humanity. These gifts, like the material ones, are given to the people of God in trust, to be handed on to others. Clement enunciated a vision of truth flowing from heaven to Zion, the mountain of God, which seems to represent the community faithful to God. From there, it can and must be shared with the whole world, delivering men from error.[29] Instruction is a gift from those who have received (*Strom.* I,38,5).[30] The true sacrifice included both "doctrine and money" given to those in need (VII,8). Clement considered essential the combination of verbal truth and appropriate action, "for the false is not dissipated by merely placing the true beside it; it is driven out and banished by the practice (*tē chrēsei*) of truth (*Protrep.* VIII, 175). Those who speak and those who serve in physical ways should honor one another together, seeing their respective roles as inherently cooperative (*Strom.* II,46,3). Yet he taught a greater way in which evil could be confronted, loving one's enemies.

---

28. *Paid.* II,11,120. Perhaps echoing Jesus' injunction to use money to win friends for eternity (Lk.16:9), Clement noted that it is much more useful to have friends than decorations as ornamentation. In II,11,128 he gave an extended mteaphor of qualities of character as the adornment of life, including "giving of your possessions" and "unhesitating readiness for good deeds."

29. *Protrep.* I,7, reflecting Isaiah 2:3.

30. In *Strom.* I,4,2-3 Clement gave a list of five gifts to be given, of which three focus on truth, investigation and knowledge. He also cited Paul's letter to the Galatians 6:8f, interpreting the principle of sowing and reaping primarily with regard to teaching and preaching.

In two places, Clement cited the words of Jesus about loving one's enemies and desiring good for those who would place a curse upon his disciples (Luke 6). In so acting, one is the child of the Father who is in heaven, says Jesus, and Clement said "Amen" (*Strom.* IV,14; *Paid.* III,12, 29). This is the exercise of great goodness.

Clement wrote briefly of the reward which is given to those who follow such a pattern of life. One saying seems related to the principle of Jesus that one will be treated as one treats others. In a collection of sayings with similar structure, we find: "as you benefit others, so you will receive benefits" (*Strom.* II,91,2). He also quoted the teaching of Jesus from Matt 25:31ff., which speaks of final reward and punishment at God's judgment. The approved will be called *makarios*, and receive the kingdom prepared for them. This is, to my knowledge, the only place where he is quite specific with regard to reward.

As can be seen from the above exposition, Clement continued every theme of the revised paradigm, though he developed some more fully and only mentions some briefly in passing. Overall, the balance and integration of thought and practice is quite impressive. He rooted it in Scripture both Hebrew and Christian[31] and supported it with citations from Greek moralists and other early Christian fathers.[32] It was, however, his own synthesis of thought and heritage.[33]

---

31. Citations which are particularly germane to this investigation include several from Proverbs (3:3, 27; 10:4; 11:24; 13:8, 11; 15:5; 19:17), Lev 19:18, Hag 1:6, Pss 50:19; and 112:9; and of course Isaiah 58 regarding the New Fast as public benevolence. In New Testament writings, Clement seems to favor the gospels of Matthew and Luke, especially the "sermons" on the Mount and Plain (Matthew 5–7; Luke 6). He did, however, also cite Paul's letters in *Paid.* III,12,94 with reference to benevolence and the revision of honor giving (Eph 4:25—5:2; Gal 5:25; 6:9; Rom 12:8ff.).

32. Clement found Clement of Rome helpful, citing 13.2 in *Strom.* II,91,2 and a number of passages in *Strom.* IV,17–18. His love of Plato is also obvious.

33. The only jarring notes would be several passages where Clement counsels his readers not to give the truth to everyone. He gave several reasons: some have a frivolous desire for disputation (*Strom.* I,21,1); the necessity of discerning those who could accept them (I,13,2); the need for not giving pure truth to the impure (I,55,1). One should note that all these passages are from the first book of the *Stromteis* and use vocabulary not used elsewhere, such as "hidden" and "mystery." Was he simply cautioning wisdom in proclamation? Was this incipient elitism, influenced by Gnostics? Given the long debate about the purposes of the *Stromateis*, I am not willing to see the passages as anything more than momentary departures from the main stream of his thought.

Origen: The "Master" Teacher

The last among the leaders of Alexandrian Christianity to be examined is Origen. In his case, we have a variety of works from which to work and much more understanding of the details of his life than we do of either Sextus or Clement. Unlike his predecessor Clement, Origen was not only a teacher, but also a member of the clergy.[34] From a respectable family, Origen was educated in both secular and sacred studies, and taught both in his early career. He was famous in his own time and was called upon by leading citizens such as the governor of Syria and members of the imperial court, who asked him to teach them his Christian philosophy. Our concern, however, is whether he continued the aspect of Christian thought which we have called the revised paradigm.

God and Christ as First Order Benefactors

Origen acknowledged God as the source of good, order and sustenance in the world. In his statement of such, he included creation, benevolence and providence: "at no time was God not Creator, nor benefactor nor providence" (*De prin.* I,4,3). The image here was of a father, who cares for all in a comprehensive manner, a thought also found in chapter 5 of *On Prayer*.[35] In one of his early writings, he asserted that God "multiplies his benefits and grants favors" and "sustains all, anticipating their prayers" (*Exh. Mart.* I,2; II,7).

In critiquing Marcion's rejection of the Hebrew God who both kills and heals, Origen describes his position as seeing "goodness as that sort of disposition by which one is led to do good to all, even when the recipient of the benefit is unworthy and does not deserve our kindness" (*De prin.* II,5,1). Origen acknowledged that extensive goodness was an

---

34. Literature by and about Origin is an industry all it own. For broad perspective concerning his life, I am indebted to Henri Crouzel's *Origen* and Kannengiesser/Peterson, eds. *Origen of Alexandria*. I did not work through the entire Origen corpus, but I did work with commentaries on both Old and New Testament books, homilies from several collections, devotional writings, the *Contra Celsum* and the *De principiis*. My conclusions are therefore based on a representative sample.

35. Origen's *De principiis* is cited from Butterworth's translation, *On First Principles*. His *On Prayer* and *Exhortation to Martyrdom* are cited from the translation of J. O'Meara in ACW vol. 19.

essential part of God's working, but emphasized that it did not exclude justice also being exercised.[36]

Origen spoke of the impartiality of God; but in an interesting twist, it was primarily an impartiality of justice only, giving to each what he deserves, which would be quite different from the disregard for social "face."[37] In fact, he regarded the present status of person as a sign of God's "impartial" judgment of merit (*De prin.* II,9,8), which abandoned precisely the aspect of a vision of God characteristic of Jesus' revision of the patronage ideal.

Of course, Origen spoke of the goodness of God in working with those who have fallen away from "that original unity and harmony in which they [rational beings] were originally created." God "transforms and restores all things, whatever their condition, to some useful purpose and the common advantage of all" (*De prin.* II,1,1–2). In this mat-ter, of course, Jesus Christ and the Spirit are cooperating factors in "superabundant grace" (*On Prayer* preface.)

What is striking in all this, besides the neglect of God's broad-based honor and impartiality, is the rarity with which Origen referred to God in any way pertinent to this discussion; I have cited all the germane passages from more than fifteen hundred pages of text.

Origen presented Jesus primarily as the broker of God's benefits in the spheres of knowledge, healing and leadership in a new life. In only one passage did I find him presenting Jesus as partner in creation and providence (*De prin.* I,2,4). As might be expected from a teacher, he emphasized the teaching of Jesus.

Origen challenged the philosopher Celsus to produce another teacher like Jesus, whose "system of doctrines and opinions" were so "beneficial to human life," converting men from the practice of wickedness. The doctrines given by Christ have the power to "elevate the soul and understanding of man" (*Contra Celsum* II,8; II,5).[38] Such teaching, from a person of humble origins and no formal training, is available

---

36. In II,7,1 it is clear the Marcion and Valentinus are the opponents of this argument. See also the *Homilies on Luke*, tr. J. Lienhard, Fathers of the Church #94 (Washington, DC: 1996) XVI, 4-5 for a similar argument invoking the works of Simeon in Lk. 2:34 concerning both the fall and rise of many in Israel.

37. *On Prayer* 6.4; *De prin.* I,8,4.

38. English citations from *Contra Celsum* are from the ET of Crombie in ANL, with some corrections for contemporary English usage; Greek citations are from the edition of Borret, SC ##132,136,147,150.

both to the uneducated and to the distinguished, though the latter could discern the higher, hidden meanings (I,29). Origen compared Jesus' capability as a teacher to the arrival of a master physician in a city racked by plague, in which the other physicians had exhausted their abilities and training (*Hom. Luke* XIII,2).

Through Christ's teaching, one comes to know the mind of God (*On Prayer* intro). By entering into a life guided by his teachings, one is elevated to "friendship with God." Then by "communion with the divine," one can rise to the level of divine life (*Cont.Cel.* III,28). In the great mass of his teaching, Origen seems obsessed with intellectual pursuits as the primary means of achieving these goals, which means that gifted or privileged individuals are fated to be better Christians, as we will show in section 7.3.e below. There is, however, clear reflection of the revised paradigm in Origen's presentation of Jesus' living example.

In Jesus, one encountered divine life in human flesh, but accommodation to humanity was an essential part of his power. Citing Paul's famous passage about "emptying" (*kenōsis*) in Philippians 2:7, Origen commented: "by that same power by which he humbled himself, he grows. He had appeared as weak, because he had assumed a weak body ... The Son of God 'had emptied himself' and for that reason, again he is filled with wisdom" (*Hom.Luke* XIX,2). Twice Origen cited Jesus' description of himself as "one who serves" (Luke 22:27). In *Cont.Cel.* II,7, he appropriately connected the passage with the washing of the disciples' feet in John 13 and the adjectives "meek and humble" (*praus ... kai tapeinos*) in Matt 11:29. That complex may clarify the other citation (*Hom. Luke* fragment #210), where he could seem to see Jesus as the servant of the Father, but not necessarily of the needy.

If there were any doubt as to the core of Jesus' "living pattern," Origen taught that the nature of Jesus' death on behalf of others demonstrated the characteristic attitude for Christians to follow (*Cont. Cel.* II,16; II,38). His "voluntary death for the common good" (I,31) showed his desire "to confer benefits on all humanity" (II,33).

In reference to Christ, Origen then saw Jesus as living a life in which teaching, humility of behavior and voluntary sacrifice contributed to a powerful force for good in the transforming of human life. This agenda he handed over to humble and untrained disciples (III,39). To those disciples we now turn.

Gratitude and Humility in the Disciples

Origen wrote of an appropriate response to the favor and gifts bestowed by the Benefactors. What he considered important and not important are both significant. In an unexceptional manner, Origen indicated that those who were favored should respond in praise both in hymns[39] and in prayers (*Hom. Luke* VI,10; Prayer 13,3). In addition, gratitude for gifts given may take the form of service given to God (*Cont. Cel.* VIII,8), though it is not clear that this service moves beyond the gathering times of worship and instruction. Finally, honor and gratitude should be given in the form of the righteous life which is brought about by the teachings of Christ and the church (III,34). By righteous life, Origen meant adherence to fairly basic moral codes. He did not speak clearly of the areas of compassion or the transforming of social values.

When Origen spoke of the abandonment of the pursuit of wealth or pleasure, he did not hint that one should do this in order to devote such means to others, but only that it is a spiritual problem.[40] It keeps you away from God and makes you liable to judgment. He did not see that to live in such a manner contradicts the purposes of God for addressing the needs of humanity. So gratitude does not mean practical imitation or replication of the values of God, in the manner so clear in Clement.

With reference to seeking and granting of public honor, Origen was clear in a limited fashion. He showed no embarrassment at Celsus' attack on the humble status of Christians (*Cont.Cel.* II,46; III,44), but considered it a compliment that Christians are so recognized, for the message of the Christians is aimed at all classes (III,48–49). In these matters, Christians were the direct recipients of both the message and example of Christ. Citing Matt 6:5ff. and John 5:44, Origen wrote strongly against the search for public recognition, approval or praise (*On Prayer* 19.2; *Hom. Ex.* XII). In other words, *philotimia* as a motive for public action is forbidden. Of course, one could act appropriately

---

39. *Homily on Exodus* VI,1. The Homilies on Genesis and Exodus are cited from the translation of Heine.

40. *Hom.Luke* 111; *Hom.Gen.* X,1; *Hom.Ex.* III,3; VI,3; VII,2; XII,2; *Commentary on Matthew* XIII,21. This last is cited from ANF vol. 9.

but still be "defiled with the desire of human glory ... or filthy with ... jealousy and malice."[41]

As one might expect, humility was then a prime virtue for Christians. Origen rooted this

virtue in Jesus' words "I am gentle and humble in heart" (Matt 11:29), and defined it by the Latin term *humilitatem*, and two Greek terms: *atuphia, metriotēsHom. Luke* VIII,4–5). He saw humility as a prime element in the new way of life, and an essential prerequisite to receiving the grace of the Holy Spirit (*Hom.Levit.* VI,2,5). So the working of God in this world requires the gentle and peaceful spirit.

Humility is necessary both to the leader and the led in the community of Christians. "For the leaders of the people ought to be the kind of men who not only are not proud, but who hate pride." Origen cited Moses as an example of a leader who delegated authority and accepted counsel from several others who might not be considered to be "on his level" in respect or honor (*Hom.Exod.* XI,6). In another place, he argued that a simple style of address was quite appropriate to the nature of the target audience for Christ, Paul and subsequent spokespersons for Christianity (*Cont.Cel.* VI,2). Finally, no position or gift within the community was considered inherently higher than others, though Origen spoke in conflicting ways on this issue.[42]

Origen clearly saw a problem developing in his own day and addressed it in his last work (*Com.Matt.* XI,15). He identified leaders at several levels in the church as working with the hope of praise and both expecting and responding to flattery. He apologized for digressing; I think he never spoke more appropriately to current issues.

Shaping the Community of Benefaction

Origen insisted on great breadth in the mission of this new community. Not only did he delight in the fact that this group were to be found throughout the world (*Cont.Cel.* I,67), but the benefits which were brought effect new moral habits, heal mental and physical disorders and created a gentle and humane attitude in converts. Christians are to consider themselves under obligation to all races and social classes

41. Origen *Homilies on Leviticus 1-16*, tr. G. Barkley. I,5,2. See also *Hom.Luke* II,7.
42. For both sides of the issue, see the discussion of Verbrugge, "Origen's Ecclesiology," 276–94.

(III,54). Origen wrote quite clearly that those who represented Christ are to bring benefit to the "greatest possible number and, so far as they can, to win over... through their love for humanity every one without exception -- intelligent as well as simple" (VI,1). It is not difficult to see why Celsus would be so upset that many ordinary folks were speaking to members of elite households and successfully enlisting them for the new movement (III, 55). His complaint indicates that some Christians of the lower class were considering themselves viable instruments to speak the message in their place of work.

It is in the homilies that Origen spoke clearly that Christians in general are to be "lights of the world" through the light of Christ which had been given (*Hom.Gen.* I,5). That light moves through several levels:[43] Christ, leaders, disciples within the church, then those in darkness. Similarly, Christians both individually and as a group are to regard themselves as a field which produces fruit copiously (*Hom. Gen.*I,3).[44]

Origen expected Christians to produce in the area of benevolence. Eloquently expounding the story of the good Samaritan, he encouraged Christians to imitate the hero of the story by involving themselves in redressing the misfortunes of others, for Jesus also gave such an example (*Hom. Luke* XXXIV,9). Further, the fact that the Samaritan had the provisions for benevolence with him when he encountered the beaten man showed, in Origen's mind, that Christians should think ahead and be prepared to meet need (XXXIV,6). Yet his thought seems curiously restricted.[45]

In a homily on Leviticus (IV,9,1), Origen stated that "... mercy toward the poor pours oil on the sacrifice of God, but the ministry which is rendered to the saints adds the sweetness of incense." It is clear that he favored the latter. In another spot in the same homily (IV,3,1), he cited the sayings of Jesus about imitating the Father who is merciful and perfect (Luke 6:36; Matt.5:48) and encouraged his listeners to take them seriously, but the goal is not to benefit others, but to preserve the

---

43. These levels of mediation are especially apparent in his *Commentary on John* I,24.

44. Origen mentioned miracles as still present among Christian communities, but gave few examples (*Cont. Cel.* II,8).

45. Twice Origen quoted the words of Jesus: "I was hungry and you gave me something to eat" (Matt 25:34–35); *Hom. Gen.* X,3; *De prin.* III,1,6). In both cases, however, the citation had nothing to do with the practice of compassion, but is a support for another point.

image of God by doing the right things. Finally, Origen clearly tried to motivate his listeners to practice almsgiving as one of three ways to achieve remission of sin: baptism, martyrdom and alms (*Hom.Lev.* II,4,5ff). In short, well-doing had quite a different focus and motive in Origen than in the revised paradigm, where gratitude and generosity flow from a new attitude and vision, initiated by God.

Disjunctions to the Revised Paradigm in Origen

Origen did not treat the matter of universal honor in the human community nor even of the reversal of honor within the Christian community, which Paul expounded in 1 Corinthians 12. The reason can be found in the fact that Origen supported a variety of honor distinctions in humanity and in the Christian community as well. His patterns of speech reveal a major failure to hear, teach or practice this part of the revised paradigm.

Origen reflected the developing pattern of separating catechumens from believers. They must prove themselves in a variety of ways to be worthy of the advanced status: penance, learning and good works. They are definitely second class citizens, though addressed warmly.[46] Women were considered to be lesser citizens of this community, since the man has the rational sense and the intellectual spirit (*Hom. Exod.* II,1). Further, the fact that Simeon preceded Anna in the infancy narratives of Jesus (Luke 2) showed that women too (!) can be saved and used of God: "how beautiful the order is! The woman did not come before the man" (*Hom.Luke* XVII,9).

Though Origen did in one passage (*Com.Matt.*XIII,26) show that he understood the meaning of "little ones" (*nēpios*) to refer to humility or lack of status, he also simply stated that they are the immature in mind and faith. This is in keeping with his bias for intellectual gifts.[47] Rather frequently, Origen spoke of classes of Christians, only one of which was gifted by God for the understanding of higher or secret meanings, those "who know how to draw water from the depth of the well." Others were simply untrained and inexperienced (*Hom. Gen.* X,2). He supported his

---

46. *Hom. Luke* XXI,4; XXII,8; VII,7-8. *Cont.Cel.* III,51.

47. In replying to Celsus (*Cont. Cel.* I,9), Origen states a clear preference for those who have both the ability and means for intellectual pursuits. One could not build the Christian community out of those who were not so inclined.

contention with the saying of Jesus that those outside get parables and those inside get explanations (*Hom. Luke* fragment 114). The Gerasene demoniac was sent home because he "did not have the capacity for more" (fragment 124). While Jesus and his immediate disciples gave certain necessary doctrines to the masses of people, the "grounds of their statements they left to be investigated by such as should merit the higher gifts of the Spirit ... the graces of language, wisdom and knowledge" (*De Prin*. I,preface,3). Thus in a variety of ways, Origen set up a rather large distinction in the community and exalted an elite teaching group, of which he was the foremost, above the mass of Christians.

Conclusions

Within the limits of his project, Sextus enunciated the goodness and impartiality of God, while teaching that the same values belong to those called children of God. A seriously different orientation toward the seeking of honor and collecting possessions was clearly encouraged, while giving both generalized honor to all and specific donations of goods to the needy. What is missing are specific religious themes concerning Jesus as the Savior and the reward to be given in the final judgment, as well as gratitude as a primary motivation for action toward God and others.

Clement provides the fullest exposition of the revised paradigm in this second and third century period. His treatment is ubiquitous and interrelated. It follows the balance of New Testament material, being lightest with regard to reward and heaviest with regard to the dynamics of transformed patterns of behavior. Further, Clement sets the material in the context of the purpose of the career of Jesus and the purpose of the new community.

Origen gives evidence of having been taught the elements of the revised paradigm, but was obviously not really interested in it. He mentions the first order benefaction of God and Jesus, but with rarity and often simply in passing. He repeats some of the matters of response, but does not seem to see the power of gratitude as a primary dynamic motive. He sees the power of impartiality and humility in the work of God through Jesus, but does not see how that is to continue in the community. He simply does not reflect the change in honor values at all, but reinforces a range of social distinctions in and out of the new community. Even benevolence is simply presented as a moral growth phenomenon in which the primary matter is the personal development of each person, not the shaping of a community. One should not seek public praise, but that is a matter of interior spiritual development, not important with regard to the effects on social relationships and the purposes of God. Further, there is a profound elitism of intellectual gifts and places in the community throughout his writings. This is reflected in the panegyric in his honor composed by his student Gregory Thaumaturgos, exceptional for its specific purpose and for the lack of Christian values.

A final word about the actions of two bishops of Alexandria may conclude this chapter. The resentment of bishop Demetrius toward the ordination of Origen and the attempt to "own" him for Alexandria exhibited an understanding that the bishop' dignity was to be preserved at all costs. He objected to Origen's preaching: "It has never been heard of and it never happens now that laymen preach homilies in the presence of bishops" (Eusebius, *H.E.* VI,8,5; VI,19,17). Those bishops who had given Origen the opportunity and later ordained him responded to Demetrius by pointing out several examples of what he had just denied. This interchange illustrates a diversity of opinion about the relative privileges of clergy and laity, from leaders in southern Palestine.

When juxtaposed with the letters of Dionysius a bit later in the century, where Dionysius clearly wrote as a "great man" to other great men,[48] it would seem that the office of the bishop had gathered a dignity and power over the community. This is a development that we have seen particularly in Rome and Syria in church order documents. Though perhaps a Dionysius of Alexandria would handle the power quite differently than Stephen of Rome or Paul of Samosata, the gathering of honor and power was identical.

---

48. he speaks of the "blessed papa Heraclas" (*tou makariou papa Hērakla*, Eusebius, *H.E.* VII,7.4) and after giving a list of "presidents" (*hoi proestōtes*), he noted that he had given only the "more eminent bishops" (*tous . . . periphanesterous tōn episkopōn*, VII,5). Still, one must note that he confronted a heresy in Arsinoë by dialogue rather than by his authority as a "papa" (VII,24,4fff.).

9

The Christian Communities of North Africa

AS IS THE CASE REGARDING THE CHURCH IN ALEXANDRIA, THE ORIGINS of the North African Christian community are obscure. How did the revised paradigm fare in an area so closely tied to Rome in language, economy and culture? Tension in this area between a more rigorous style and a more accommodating one, though more obvious in the schisms of the fourth and fifth centuries, can be seen in writings of the third century as well. Before we compare the writings of Tertullian and of Cyprian, we can glimpse the people through the windows of two martyrdom documents: that of the confessors at Scilli, and the justly famous account of Perpetua and her companions.

Early Martyr Documents

On July 17, 180, a group of twelve Christians were examined and executed in Carthage. From Scilli, whose location is uncertain, the accused found a spokesperson in Speratus. Two aspects of the examination transcript, and it seems little more than that, are significant. First, Speratus answered the initial challenge of the proconsul by saying that Christians show respect for "their own emperor" (*imperatorem nostrum obseruamos*) by not doing evil, not giving themselves to unfairness (*iniquitati*), not speaking evil but giving thanks when abused.[1] Second, Speratus referred to the Christian way as the "mystery of simplicity," and the anonymous editor confirmed that description by applying no rhetorical or honorific language in the composition of the narrative obviously connected to the record. Very simple answers by both female

---

1. *Acts of the Scillitan Martyrs* 2. All citations from this document, as well as the martyrdom documents of Perpetua and Cyprian, are from Musurillo, *Acts*.

and male figures confirmed that understanding amid the issues which they faced in the interrogation.

In contrast to the short and simple transcript of the martyrs of Scilli, the *Martyrdom of Perpetua and Felicitas* is longer and more beautifully crafted, composed of narrative, visions and public testimony. It reflects a local persecution in Carthage during the reign of Septimius Severus, and tells the story of the incarceration, trial and execution of a group of catechumens, with primary interest in the two women whose names head the documents.

The editor declared the purpose of such literature to be the celebration of God's favor (*gratiam*), while granting honor to God and comfort to community members (1.1). Perpetua, a young woman of high social rank (*honeste nata, liberaliter instituta*, 2.1), was the primary figure in the events and in the account, much of which came from her own pen (*conscriptum manu sua*, 2.3). In view of her prominent place, the opening words of the editor are particularly notable. He quoted the prophecy of Joel 2:28–29, about the Spirit of God empowering both sexes with prophecies and visions, and it is Perpetua who especially fulfilled that prophecy in this narrative. The editor also asserted that this expectation was in some eclipse in the Christian community in general, but not the one in Carthage. "Let those then who would restrict the power of the one Spirit to times and seasons look to this: the more recent events should be considered the greater ... and this is a consequence of the extraordinary graces promised for the last stage of time ... So too we hold in honor and knowledge not only new prophecies but new visions as well, according to the promise" (1.3; 1.5).

Perpetua then proceeded to function as the leader of the group, interpreting their experiences through her visions and writing. Her father and the visiting proconsul appealed to her on the basis of the honor code of the Roman family, expecting her to change her commitment for the sake of her father's shame and the needs of her infant (ch.4ff.). She refused, though the story is candid about her pain.

Saturus, another Carthaginian leader who had been instrumental in the training of these imprisoned catechumens, also contributed a vision to the document. It presented Perpetua as the one person able to mediate problems between the higher clergy of the community (chap. 11).[2] Her slave Felicitas was called the "fine friend" (*bonam sociam*, 15.3)

---

2. This Saturus was first a visitor, then was arrested and became a companion of those soon to be executed.

of the rest of the martyrs. The two women died together, both highly regarded by the Christian community.

Honorific language was used to exalt these martyrs in the final section of the document and occasionally during the document as well (1.6; 16.1; 18.4). No exalted language was used with regard to other clergy or members. The relationship between Perpetua's secular rank and her leadership role in that Christian community is not clear, but she does not seem to have been highlighted because of her rank, but because of her gifts and wisdom.

These martyrdom documents reveal an interest in simplicity and honor for all, as well as the full participation of women and men in leading the Christian community.

Tertullian: Influential Radical

Both enigmatic and highly influential, the leader and writer Tertullian flourished in the community at Carthage during a forty year period which closed the second century and opened the third.[3] He represented a significant portion of that Christian community, in spite of his stringent criticism of those who did not hold the rigor he favored in ethics and ascetic practice. Further, he rejected some of his contemporaries for not respecting the work of the Holy Spirit as he did, in what seems to have been a Montanist view. Yet he did not, to our knowledge, ever have to leave the community either of his own will or by the demand of others, as the Montanists of Asia Minor were forced to do. Indeed, his reputation seems solid in the ancient period until Gelasius ordered him declared a heretic in the fifth century. For the purposes of this project it is not necessary to engage in questions of his background, position in the church or the vexed question of his "orthodox" and "Montanist" periods. His views are remarkably consistent in the areas that are germane to this investigation. I will use a cross section of his writings and state from the beginning that some of his positions are thin because

---

3. Discussion of the background of this striking person has ranged from the facile conclusion of Eusebius (*H.E.* II,2,3), that he was a famous jurist of the same name, to the often stated assumption that he was a presbyter in the community at Carthage, to the nearly complete and rigorous skepticism of Timothy Barnes (*Tertullian*). Let us simply say that the characteristics of his literary corpus point rather in the direction of an advocate, not a teacher. Barnes is right, however, that little is securely established or can be.

he was always the controversialist, even when writing instructional pamphlets.

God and Christ as First-Order Benefactors

Tertullian argued much more from history than from nature, but he did identify God as the maker and sustainer of all nature (*Chaplet* 5.4; *Apology* 17.1),[4] the One who provided the "vast fabric" of the habitable world (*magno ... habitaculum*) as a matter of divine generosity. This reality he argued against Marcion extensively, ending with these words in the *Adversus Marcionem*: "Learn then the goodness of our God among these things and up to this point; learn it from his excellent works, from his kindly blessings, from his indulgent bounties, from his gracious providences" (*Marc.* II,4). Though Tertullian considered the natural order a lower level gift of God, it was clearly one that he saw as critical.

Much more material is available to show Tertullian's understanding of the benevolence of God in historical matters. The mercy of God toward all is argued extensively in his tract *On Penitence*. Gifts given to the chosen Hebrew nation loom large: "therefore He gathered together His people and favored them with a profusion of bountiful gifts" (*multis bonitatis suae largitionibus favit*, chap. 2). Further, God promised great favor for later days, in which he intended to illumine the whole world. Seeing that promise fulfilled in the life of Jesus, Tertullian argued the goodness of God at length from Jesus' teachings.

Jesus' parable of the great supper (Luke 14:16ff.) revealed the character of a God who makes "abundant provision of eternal life," and who extended that abundance to "strangers and persons unconnected by ties of relationship" (*Marc.* IV,31). In Tertullian's view, the God portrayed in this parable contradicted the standard social pattern of honoring with dinner those already considered worthy by prior bonds. Jesus reveals his Father as a passionate person, not an "unmoved Mover," a notion which Tertullian accused Marcion of adopting from Stoic philosophy. "Then He was moved; (He did well to be moved, for since Marcion denies emotion to his god, he must be my God!); and commanded them to invite guests from the streets and lanes of the city. After that, as there

---

4. Parenthetical documentation will refer to the first few letters of the first noun in the title, with sections indicated.

was still plenty of room, he ordered them to be gathered in from the highways and hedges" (*Marc.* IV, 31). Of course, such a God would also have great compassion for those who had no protector, and Tertullian saw just such care both in the Hebrew Scriptures (Isaiah 58:7) and in the ministry of Jesus who God had sent: "for God always and everywhere enjoined that the poor and orphan and widow should be protected, assisted, refreshed" (*Marc.* IV,16).

Finally, Tertullian strongly asserted the benevolence of God in spiritual matters, granting forgiveness (*Pen*.3) and restoring people to their proper function and strength. God "favors you with what you need for the restoration of that which you lost; be grateful for His repeated, na rather for His increased beneficence. For to give back is greater than to give ..." (*Pen.* 7). Even the judicial acts of God, so attacked by Marcion, demonstrate an impartial goodness in the working of discipline and punishment (*Marc.* II,13), for "in the meantime, He treats all humanity equally, both in concession and in warning" (*aequalis est interim super omne hominum genus et indulgens et encrepans, Apol.* 41,3).

Much of what Tertullian had to say about Christ was pointed in the direction of fighting heretics in their various forms. He often argued in ways that do not touch on our project. However, some of what he said about Christ is relevant.

With reference to Jesus' ministry, one hears a profusion of titles. Jesus is the "moderator (*arbiter*) and teacher of grace and discipline, illuminator and guide (*deductor*) for the human race" (*Apol.* 21,7). Many benefits were listed from these various roles, mostly having to do with healing and teaching. The teaching was addressed to "all humanity equally" (*Prescription* 10) and all actions should be public, in the light of day and from the housetops. This, for Tertullian, reflected the character and plan of the Hebrew God who sent Jesus.

In a sustained polemic, Tertullian argued the essential unity of the agenda of Jesus and of the God of Abraham, in intending and accomplishing good for humanity (*Marc.* IV,4). He worked specifically from the Sermon on the Mount (Matthew 5–7), providing an extensive catalog of Hebrew Scripture that correlated with the Sermon. Jesus' own identity was clarified with reference to the prophecies of Isa 61:1ff., which spoke of the good done to the needy and oppressed. These themes were further extended with regard to abandoning the honor of the world and attending to the humble (IV,15) and also to the practices of compassion, first to the neighbor and then to strangers (IV,16).

Tertullian emphasized Sabbath controversies as linking the Hebrew practice to its proper employment, "to do good, to save life and not to destroy it" (*Marc.* IV,12). The radical commandment to love one's enemies demonstrated a "primary and perfect goodness, shed voluntarily upon strangers without any obligation of friendship, begun in the first covenant and expanded in scope in the second (I,23).

Interestingly, the greatest gift of all from a Christian perspective is not prominent in the major works of Tertullian. Christ "suffered the penalty in our presence and surrendered his life, laying it down for our sakes" (*Marc.* IV,14).[5] The relative silence with regard to the Passion is curious, at least.

Along with the gifts of Jesus and his Father, Tertullian emphasized the ongoing work of the Spirit of God, continuing and finishing what has begun. God's Spirit is the "vicar of Christ," leading the community into a fuller understanding and practice of the truth (*Praescr.* XXVIII), the continuing favor of God (*gratia dei, Virg.*, I,5). The members of this community require perfecting, for their "human mediocrity" could not grasp everything at once (*paraclitum miserit dominum, ut quoniam humana mediocritas omnia semel capere not poterat, Virg.* I,6). So the work of the Spirit, as well as that of Christ, is understood to be a continuation, as well as an expansion or fulfillment, of the interests and plans of a most benevolent God, the god of the Hebrew Scriptures.

Gratitude and Humility in the Members

It was the responsibility of those who are the greatest recipients of God's favor to be specifically grateful for that favor. One's speech and actions alike should provide a response to "His vast liberality ... [giving] the due return of his graciousness" (*Marc.*IV,17; *Apol.* 42,2). Christians should follow the example of their leader, who clearly honored God "in his own beneficent acts and miracles" (*Apol.* IV,18), and acknowledged the glory of God in public and in his own prayer (John 17). "God should be blessed in all places and at all times, because it is everyone's duty

---

5. When he mentioned the Crucifixion in the *Apology* (21.19ff.), his interest is the miraculous signs which were reported to accompany it. Of course, propitiation is not a prime topic for an apology.

to be mindful of his benefits" (*Prayer* 3.2). Throughout his works, he gave evidence of the rich devotional practices of the vigorous African church, but the eminently practical Tertullian had much more in mind as an appropriate response to God. Honor is not just internal, but very public (*Pen.* 5). Tertullian insisted that the public honor values of "the world" give way to a new pattern and motivation.

Preeminent in the definition of this community was a renunciation of the world and its "pomps." Like Clement, Tertullian knew a good deal about the ways of this world. In rejecting the wearing of crowns, he listed them as part of "the pomps of the Devil and his angels." In several writings, he referred to a great variety of honors, dress, behavior and accoutrement that the elite used to define their position in the world, insisting that others recognize them as such.[6]

This complex of material goods and social ceremony was explicitly renounced as part of the baptismal rite: "When we step into the water and profess the Christian faith in the terms prescribed by its law, we bear public witness that we have renounced the devil and his pomps and his angels" (*Spect.* 4; *Chaplet* 3.2). The teaching of Tertullian defined this public confession further by speaking of "the sustained desire (*concupiscentia*) of the world, which ... has its roots in pride, avarice, ambition ..." (*Wife* 4). One must rather "despise the world" (*Pat.* 7.2). "For how can you fulfill the precept of humility which we profess as Christians if you do not keep in check the use of wealth and finery which so encourage the pursuit of glory" (*Apparel* 9.5). Though he spoke more sharply than his contemporary Clement about the matter, they agreed that wealth was not to be simply abandoned. Rather, Tertullian taught his readers to be detached first from the practice of spending in luxurious or ostentatious ways, then to find the appropriate orientation: simplicity and generosity. If then it were to go or be taken away, one was prepared for the simpler life which was exemplified in Jesus (*Pat.* 7.2).

Jesus was the clear example of simplicity and humility, which was tied into an appropriate treatment of other humble people: "He did not force one who was unwilling to stay close to him; he scorned no one's table or dwelling; in fact he ministered personally to His disciples by washing their feet. He did not despise sinners or publicans ... he healed the ungrateful" (*Pat.* 3.5-6). Such gentle humility Tertullian connected with the teaching of Jesus about public displays or religion, avoiding

---

6. *Chaplet* 13.3 & 7; *Spect.* 7,2 & 12.6; *Wife* II,8 ; *Apparel* 9.1 & 4.

attention either by the manner of behavior or by the stentorian voice (*Prayer* 1.4; 17.1ff.). One should pray quietly or in secret.

With regard to possessions, simplicity was the key: "those things only which meet the necessities of human life by providing plain service, real assistance and honorable comfort are fit for ... sacred history or for Christ himself" (*Chaplet* 8.5). This stark utilitarianism was supported as well by the words of Jesus about the "bread of the day" and about conquering anxiety about basic needs (*Prayer* 6.4; Matt 6:11, 25). Tertullian also saw the community of goods, rooted in Acts 4:32, as standard practice for Christians of his own day (*Apol.* 39,11).

Shaping the Community of Benefaction

Benevolence is central to this new community and its members, who fulfill the promises and programme of the God who sent their leader. Rarely stated in specific terms, this understanding permeates Tertullian's though and argumentation.

Community vitality was clearly rooted in the Hebrew tradition. Isaiah's prophecy about turning "swords into plowshares" (2:1fff.) was interpreted to mean that the minds of Christians would be changed from cruel to kind, productive of good fruit (*Marc.* IV,1). The process of Christian discipline developed further a benevolence inherent to the Torah, but which had only been expressed in part (IV,17). In what form would it be expressed?

Tertullian mentioned a "community chest," to which each member made contributions voluntarily (*Apol.* 39,5). These "reverent trust funds" (*deposita pietatis*) were used to "feed the poor and bury them, [to provide] for boys and girls who lack property and parents, and then for slaves grown old and shipwrecked mariners; and any who may be in the mines" (39,6). Further, along with its communal focus, the common meal of the community was intended to meet the needs of the poor (39,16). As we have seen in other places, the clergy no doubt controlled the benevolence connected with such community structures. That did not, however, exhaust the actions of the Christians.

In discussing problems that could occur if a wife was Christian with a non-Christian spouse, Tertullian commented: "if a fast is to be observed, her husband will prepare a feast that very day; if it is necessary to go out on an errand of Christian charity, never are duties at home more urgent! Who indeed, would permit his wife to go about the streets to the houses of strangers, calling at every hovel in town in order to visit the brethren?" (*Wife.* II,4). Allowing for rhetorical overstatement, clearly he expected women to fulfill acts of Christian charity in public. In a complementary passage, where he responded to the criticism that the Christian religion was impoverishing the traditional temples, Tertullian asserted that "our compassion spends more street by street than your religion temple by temple" (*Apol.* 42.6). Benevolence was not then confined to a particular person or place.

Citing Isa 58:7, Tertullian taught that both gifts and loans should be given to those who are in need, not only without demanding repayment, but specifically given to those who obviously could not repay (*Marc.* IV,17, 31; Luke 6:35). This action honors God and brings God's blessing on all concerned; for the Christian would "give out of pity, not out of fear . . ." (*Flight* 13.1). To not practice benevolence is to dishonor the God who planned and initiated such a community. One who refuses to practice beneficence "repudiates the Giver when he abandons the gift; he rejects the Benefactor when he dishonors the benefaction... not only willfully disobedient to the Lord, but . . . ungrateful to Him also" (*Paen.* 5).

Finally, Tertullian reinforced the idea that one does not expect honor or reward for benevolence done, for Christ "forbids the recompense to be expected now . . . this is the very plan of the Creator, who dislikes those who love gifts and follow after reward" (*Marc.* IV,31). In the end, God initiates, approves and rewards all benefaction (*Quorum . . . auctor et defensor sit, necesse est proinde et acceptator; si acceptator etiam remunerator, Paen.* 2).

Honor and Rank in the Community

With regard to "outsiders," Tertullian did not teach a universal honor for all humanity, but he seems to assume it in teaching that all are to be treated the same. Note in the following that this is explicitly connected to the character and actions of God.

> . . . the loyalty (*fides*) owed to emperors [if from] that type of character which God as truly requires of us . . . toward the emperor . . . as he requires it in the case of all men. For it is not to emperors alone that we owe these works of a good heart. No ex-

ception of persons is allowed in any good action we discharge...
not that we plan to get any return in praise or recompense from
man but from God who requires and rewards a benevolence
that makes no distinction between persons ... (*Apol.* 37.2–3)

Every time Tertullian spoke of the emperor as great or even as the greatest of humanity, that statement is qualified by a phrase or clause such as "through God." His Apology is distinctive precisely in lacking the florid eulogy to the emperors which opens most second century apologies.

Within the community, all Christians were "servants of God" and "priests of peace." Very little time was spent in his writings emphasizing differences between members, in the churches he considered orthodox. With regard to the churches of heretics, however, he complained that catechumens had the same privileges as believers (*Prescription* 41). This would seem to indicate a difference in status and privilege for those in "membership training."

In the same work, an early one, Tertullian complained that women were involved in tasks which should belong to the clergy: teaching, baptizing, healing and exorcizing (*Presc.* 41). In another, he recommended the veiling of women as a sign of their inherent lowliness (*Chaplet* 14.1). Here the distinction between phases of his life may be striking, for later in life he spoke warmly of women in shared ministry, when speaking to his wife as well as to sisters generally.[7] In addition, he clearly considered the Montanist Prisca a prophetess of the Lord (*Exhort.* 10). Women were expected to participate both in worship services, in the interactive manner advocated by St. Paul in I Corinthians 14, and to take initiative in acts of mercy. Whether their leadership could extend beyond moments in which they were divinely inspired, into the structure of the clergy, is not clear with regard to his later conceptions.

Tertullian is remarkable for his restraint in speaking of Christian leaders. He rarely mentioned the ranks of clergy and did not laud them in particular. He affirmed their authority and position, speaking of the "thrones of the apostles," still "preeminent in their places" (*Praesc.* 22), on which I would assume their successors sat. Yet he spoke strongly of the difference of the public presentation of Christian leaders: "no crown ever rested on the head of a patriarch or prophet, Levite, priest or ruler

---

7. "Dearest companion in the service of the Lord" (*Wife* 1); "dearest fellow-servant" (8); "handmaidens of the Lord, my fellow servants and sisters ... since we are all temples of God because the Holy Spirit has entered into us ... (*Apparel* 1.1).

... nor in the new dispensation, do we read of an apostle, a preacher of the gospel or bishop who wore a crown" (*Chaplet* 9.1). When he spoke of leaders, he tended to emphasize their character (*probati; honorem istum non pretio, sed testimonio adepti Apol.* 39,4), and the nature of the relationships within the community ("title of brotherhood and bond of hospitality," *Praesc.* 20).

One group was singled out for special honor above the rest of the members, namely celibates. Widows were also especially honored by God, not just as the objects of solicitude, but as those who have become more favored by their celibacy (*Wife* 4.8). In his later ascetic writings, Tertullian exalted the single and celibate lifestyle in a manner similar to Methodius in the Aegean circle and Tatian in Syria.

To summarize the evidence from Tertullian, one first notes that the dominance of controversy rather than instruction has apparently minimized the presentation of God and Christ as first order benefactors, though the thought is not absent. The argument advanced against Marcion, however, has provided us with a rich understanding of the continuity of Hebrew and Christian practice specifically focused on "doing good," and the Apology reinforced that presentation. The treatment of gratitude is slim, but clear.

Dynamics of honor and humility were strongly and clearly presented, in continuity with the revised paradigm. Universal honor was expected toward all humanity, including the "outsider," although within the community catechumens and married women seem to have had a limited position.

The most extensive evidence found detailed Tertullian's rejection of the *cursus honorum* and the substitution of a disciplined simplicity for the purposes of benevolence, broadly received and broadly extended to others.

Cyprian: The Bishop as a Great Man

Our picture of Cyprian is quite different from that of Tertullian. Though the corpus of works is much smaller, we can see Cyprian in a variety of roles and moods. We know that he was of the elite classes (an *insignis personae*, *Letters* 8.1.1), that he became a cleric rather too quickly and served during one of the most difficult periods for the Christian community, marked by the persecutions of first Decius and then of Valerian.

He was both revered and vilified from within the community, and has left for us a marvelous treasure in a collection of letters. This corpus contained not only copies of the letters which he sent to other leaders, but letters from others which can sometimes be correlated with his answers. He considered himself, as the bishop of Carthage, in authority over three areas: Africa Proconsularis, Numidia and Mauretania. How did Jesus revision of the patronage paradigm fare with a man whose position both before and after his conversion would clearly have been exceptional?[8]

God and Christ as First Order Benefactors

Though he did not speak of it frequently, Cyprian clearly regarded God as the first-order benefactor in both natural and spiritual spheres. It is not surprising that he was explicit particularly in his work on alms: "For whatever belongs to God, belongs to all by our appropriation of it, nor is anyone kept from His benefit and gift, nor does anything prevent the whole human race from equally enjoying God's goodness and generosity. Thus the day illuminates equally; the sun radiates, the rain moistens" (*Opere* 25). In discussing the patience of God, he tied together a similar presentation of cosmic goodness and religious gifts (*Patience* 4). He spent more time, of course, exploring the latter. "Many and great, most beloved brethren, are the divine blessings by which the abundant and copious clemency of God the Father and of Christ has both worked and is always working" (*Opere* 1). There is no moderation or measure, said Cyprian, to the "divine munificence" of God, pouring out bountifully and without boundaries by the Spirit (*Don.* 5–6). Further, this generosity by the Maker of all is extended to all, without regard to status, age or position, for He "shows himself a Father equally to all, being evenhanded in the distribution of His heavenly graces" (*Letters* 64). So Cyprian showed an appropriate conception of God for the revised paradigm, in both the extent of benevolence and the impartiality of its distribution.

The cosmic benefactions were understood to flow from the Father; no extensive role in that sphere was assigned to Christ. Jesus' work lay in

---

8. With the exception of the letters, cited by the English title with number and section, the writings of Cyprian will be cited parenthetically by the first 3 or 4 letters of the first significant word in the Latin title, then chapter and section. See the bibliography for editions used.

the religious sphere, and on that theme Cyprian waxed eloquent. Light had come to the nations and a "saving splendor had shown forth for the preservation of humanity" (*Eccl.* 3). In various ways the needs of humanity for insight, healing and restoration had been provided by the work of Christ. From the time of his coming, he has given constant guidance for those who had wandered in darkness, and has helped them to walk in a new way of light (*Domin.* 1), "teaching and preparing and strengthening" (*Mort.* 2). Cyprian both assumed and spoke directly of the benefits of the redemptive death on the Cross, further releasing a variety of good effects in human life (*Dem.* 26; *Domin.* 30; *Opere* 1).

In addition, Jesus left a profound and consistent example of the way which he brought and continued in the lives of his disciples: "humility in conversation, steadfastness in faith, modesty in words, justice in deeds, discipline in morals, not to know how to do an injury and to be able to bear one done ..." (*Domin.* 16). Like Tertullian, Cyprian found both a foundation and an example in the person of Jesus for the continuing life of his followers.

Gratitude, Imitation, and Humility

It is not surprising that a pastoral figure writing for the church would emphasize praise and gratitude to God. Cyprian spoke of thanking God always, even in times of persecution: "For it is not possible even for an enemy to prevent us, who love God with our whole heart and soul and power, from proclaiming His blessings and praises always and everywhere with glory" (*Laps.* 1). More unusual was the way he explicitly united the themes of gratitude and imitation at the end of his treatise on prayer: "let us who by the indulgence of God have been recreated spiritually and reborn imitate what we are destined to be ... let us who are destined to pray always and to give thanks to God, not cease here to pray and to give thanks" (*Domin.* 36). One could see the above as referring only to being a person of praise, but Cyprian expands the concept elsewhere, commenting on the description of Acts 4:32, the striking re-reorientation with regard to the use of possessions: "This is truly to become a son of God by spiritual birth; this is to imitate the equity of God by the heavenly law ... with this example of equality [referring to Matt 5:45], the possessor on the earth who shares his returns and fruits, while he is fair and just with his gratuitous bounties, is an imitator of

God the Father" (*Opere* 25).⁹ As we have seen in the quote above about the example of Jesus, however, this imitation of God's generosity was to be combined with a life of humility and simplicity.

When one considers Cyprian's apparent social status in conjunction with his extensive discussion of the patron/client paradigm in *Ad Donatus* 10ff., it is clear that Cyprian well understood both the benefits and shortcomings of the traditional paradigm. He strongly emphasized its shortcomings and recognized that he did so (*Don.* 11). He insisted that even at its best, though profitable both financially and socially, it was based on abuse and contempt and granted no peace at any point in the process. Many ruined themselves by their pursuit of honor, only to be abandoned by the public and those who had been their clients (11). Others simply became recluses, refusing to be involved with anyone any more (10). The passion of Cyprian is that of the new convert, for the treatise to Donatus is his earliest.

Cyprian had done what all Christians had done at his baptism, renouncing the world and all its "riches and pomps" (*Letters* 13.5.3; *Domin.* 13). He abandoned his estates and gave them to the church, reserving only his residence and a garden. Apparently they were returned to him as bishop, for he seems to have had enormous resources available for that office. Other had not made the initial sacrifice, however, from his perspective.

When trying to cope with the aftermath of the Decian persecution, Cyprian saw the reason for this persecution in laxness on the part of Christians: "this persecution has come upon us for our sins; we have not been keeping to the way of the Lord … instead, property and profit we strive for (*patrimonio et lucro studentes*), pride we pursue, our time we devote to rivalry and dissension (*aemulatio et dissensioni vacantes*), innocence and faith we neglect, the world we renounce with words only, not deeds" (*Letters* 11.1.2). A large portion of "the lapsed" (those who did deny their faith and sacrificed to the Roman gods) abandoned their commitments rather quickly, before being challenged or put on trial (*Laps.*7–8).¹⁰ Cyprian attributed this to the "cowardice of a luxury-lov-

---

9. Note also the principle enunciated in the following: "one imitates the gods whom he venerates" (*Don.* 8) and "we ought to act as sons of God … let us live as temples of God, that it may be clear that the Lord dwells in us. Let not our acts depart from the Spirit" (*Domin.* 11).

10. Cyprian rather fully defined this notion by listing the activities of such laity (increasing property and devoted to luxury), the neglect of ministry by clergy and the

ing mind" (*Mort.* 1). Both the desire to increase one's estate and to enjoy its privileges were such strong attachments that denying their faith was rather easily done.[11] For him, their refusal to discipline their lives and resources had already denied the heart of the way.

Commitment to the way of the Christians included at its core a vision of higher things, which brought perspective and discipline to the believer. In the early *Ad Donatus* he said: "when does he learn thrift, who has become accustomed to lavish banquets and extravagant feasts? ... He who has been delighted by the fasces and public honors cannot become an inglorious citizen. He who has been attended by crowds of clients, or has been honored by a crowded assemblage of an officious throng thinks it a punishment to be alone" (*Don.* 3). But when one has encountered the glory of God?

> Nothing can he now seek from the world, desire from the world, who is greater than the world ... As the sun radiates of its own accord ... so the heavenly spirit infuses itself. When the soul gazing upon heaven recognizes its Author, higher than the sun and more sublime than all this earthly power—it begins to be what it believes itself to be ... [the decorated villa] will seem to be of no account when you realize that you ... are to be adorned ... in this house where the Holy Spirit begins to live. Let us embellish this house with the colors of innocence; let us illuminate it with the light of justice ... this abides in a beauty perpetually vivid, in complete honor, in everlasting splendor. (Catena from *Don.* 14–15)

The vision was accompanied by a self denial focused particularly upon luxury and display, which impeded both growth and practice of the new way (*Letters* 11). Cyprian was worried by the resistance he encountered to this discipline.

His contemporaries objected that God had given them this wealth for their enjoyment (*Hab.* 7; 11). Cyprian responded by insisting that we should "walk even as He [Jesus] walked," and that we should avoid the desire of the eye and flesh, and the boastful pride

---

absence of discipline and compassion for the needy (*Laps.* 5).

11. *Laps.* 10ff. Later (chap. 30) Cyprian will note that some wanting to be restored to the church were still claiming to be in mourning for their sin, but actually were still caught in the trap of luxury, and had no time or money for the needy. In *Opere* 12, he said that some of his people deserved the title "Pharisee," because they loved money as the Pharisees did, mocking the teaching of Jesus (Luke 16:14).

of possessions. Both references are from I John (2:6, 15–16). Wealth given by God should rather be used for the known purposes of God, that is, it should be given to those who are in need. To do so is to "feed Christ" (*Hab.* 11; *Opere* 11).

Another objection of his contemporaries was that they would use up their estates and become one of the poor themselves (*Opere* 9ff.). In the turbulent and inflationary third century, one can see the force of such an objection. Our teacher's response was that one must trust God to supply; he argued that it is God's business, supporting his position with a quote from the Hebrew Bible, "he who gives to the poor will never want" (Prov 28:27), "unless you think that he who feeds Christ is not himself fed by Christ, or that earthly things will be lacking for those upon whom heavenly and divine things are bestowed, whence this unbelieving thinking" (*Opere* 11). Without going into the details as Clement and Tertullian did, Cyprian supported the same simplicity of life.

Humility was part of this way. Cyprian denied a place for boasting, for all that is appropriate for those who have received so much is gratitude (*Don.* 4). Further, all public eloquence should be avoided as drawing attention to the speaker rather than the message, whereas when one spoke of God, the simple truth should suffice (2). To accuse one's opponents of a lack of humility was serious, for arrogance put one out of favor with God (*Letters* 59.3.1–2). When a leading layperson Florentianus wished to challenge Cyprian's election and behavior under persecution, he also accused him of lacking humility. The bishop responded that his humility was "perfectly well-known and appreciated by the brethren, even by the pagans themselves" (*Letters* 66.3.1). At least they agreed that humility was important.

In any event, glory and honor would not be lacking at the end of the way, for God rewards those who follow it. There will be the honor of sharing in the joys of salvation not only along the way, but God "promises to those who glorify Him a reward in their turn" (*Letters* 58; *Zelo* 15–16).

Shaping the Community of Benefaction

Cyprian had a great deal to say about benefaction and of alms in particular, devoting an entire treatise to the matter. The most basic matters of spiritual life were explicitly connected to public mercy. Prayer or fasting were fruitless without mercy, while the good works strengthened their power (*Domin.* 32). As we have already seen, the openhanded orientation towards possessions was a primary expression of faith in God and Christ, who promised both supply and future reward (*Opere* 8). Citing the example of the widow's mite (Mark 12:43), Cyprian both shamed the rich and challenged the poor to do all that they could see to do (15). He interpreted the parable of the Pearl of Great Price as meaning that one should "buy the kingdom" by dispersing one's goods to the poor (7). After quoting Matt 25:31-46, he drew two very important conclusions: (1) if giving to the poor is giving to Christ, one could *not* decline, and (2) that response to Christ should stimulate eve those not inclined to be compassionate (23). Taking the example of Acts 4:34, he aimed to shame the rich.

> But with us unanimity has been so diminished that even the liberality of our good works has been lessened. *Then* they sold their homes and estates, and laying up treasures for themselves in heaven, they offered to the apostles the proceeds to be distributed for use among the poor. But now we do not even give a tenth of our patrimony and although the Lord orders us to sell, we rather buy and increase. So has the vigor of faith withered in us. (*Eccl.* 26)[12]

Cyprian had a word for this decline in faith, vigor and compassion: *sterilitas*. He warned, based on the prophecy of John the Baptizer (Matt 3:10) about unfruitful trees, that "sterile men" would be cast into the fire, for "the merciful are called to the kingdom" (*Opere* 8). He asked his readers how they could defend their "sacrilegious sterilities," not "repaying Christ even in small measure" (23). They are immersed in laziness and the darkness of avarice (22). Cyprian piled on the shame, then reinforced his point with the words of Christ to the church at Laodicea (Revelation 3) and the parable of the rich fool (Luke 12).

Cyprian made explicit and prominent a notion that had been in earlier literature only hinted or mentioned in passing: redemptive alms.

---

12. Cyprian built his case from Scripture, citing repeatedly Prov 19:17; Isa 58:6ff. (though he limited its application to the household of faith), Tobit 4:5ff.; 12:8; 14:10ff.; 1 John 2:15ff.; 3:17; 1 Cor 7:30–31; the examples of Cornelius the centurion in Acts 10 and the widow of Zarephath in 1 Kings 17, Jesus' commands in the Sermon on the Mount, as well as Matt 19:21 and Luke 12:33. See *Opere* 7, 8, 15, 17, 20, 25; *Eccl.* 26; *Domin.* 17, 26.

He approached the matter in two ways. First, alms atone for or make up for previous sins. The giving of one's resources made "reparation for the guilt of sin" (*laps.* 35), and atoned for one's faults rather than increased them (*Hab.*11). Sins were "washed away" or "purged" (*Opere* 1, 5; *Laps.* 5). He interpreted the sequence of thought in Isaiah 58 in terms of this notion: first sin, then compassion, then mercy from God.[13] Some of the time, he was speaking of post-baptismal sin and of the sin of lapsing in particular, speaking perhaps of a cleansing discipline, rather than atonement.

Second, Cyprian spoke of redemptive alms in terms of merit that created obligation on God's part. He thought the assurances given to Cornelius (Acts 10) meant that the "merits of our works" force God to deal with our prayers at least quicker (*Opere* 33). Our mercy *merits* God's mercy and makes God accessible to us (5 and 14). God becomes our debtor; God *owes* us (*Opere* 16; *Hab.* 11; *Laps.* 35).

To the extent that Cyprian seems to see these matters as more legal than personal, he is not in the center of Christian thinking. In neither the traditional patronage model nor in the revised one could one repay the debt. This thinking comes from another direction entirely. Countryman argues that Cyprian's motive was to access the wealth of the elite to refill the community chest.[14] I would argue that it is simply traditional Roman religion.

Cyprian and His People

It remains to pursue the matter of honor exchanged between Cyprian and the people of his congregations. Significant distance is discernible between his rank and that of the people, which is at least one of the reasons he was chosen to be bishop when he could not have been ready for

---

13. In *Opere* 2, he makes a distinction between past sin, cleansed by Christ's sacrifice, and current ones, cleansed by alms and faith. He quoted Sirach 3:30: "as water quenches fire, so alms quench sin." Elsewhere he spoke of liberating souls by alms and delivering from death (*Opere* 5; *Laps.* 35). Some of these expressions do not necessarily imply atonement, but when combined with others, a strong complex of thought was created.

14. *Rich Christians*, 195–97. I am not ready to concede this point. Cyprian did not emphasize giving to the community chest (though that might be understood), but giving to the poor.

that role.[15] Yet Cyprian never spoke in demeaning manner of or to the people. They were the receivers of God's Holy Spirit in great abundance, without regard to age, sex or position (*Letters* 69.14.1). On a number of occasions, Cyprian referred to the function of the assembly of the people (*plebi universae*), who approved clerical advancements, participated in judgments being made and policies being formulated.[16] In theory at least, their power included the selection and rejection of bishops. They could and should separate themselves from an evil bishop, "especially as they have in their own hands the power both to select bishops who are worthy and to reject those who are unworthy" (*Letters* 67.3.2). He assured the people, who also are "beloved brothers and sisters," that the disciplining of those who had fallen would be decided "in your presence and with the help of your judgments" (17.1.1-2). Considerable respect was thus shown to the people in general.

Cyprian did, however, clearly identify higher levels of honor. Like many others, he saw dedication to virginity as a more exalted state, sacred in a special sense. He worried that they might lose that honor while being incarcerated for their faith (*Letters* 62.2.3). Citing Revelation 14:4, he stated that "their glory is the more exalted. They are the flower of the tree that is the church, the beauty and adornment of spiritual grace ... the more illustrious part of Christ's flock" (*Hab.* 3). Thus he set apart that group as having extraordinary glory.

Another group to be highlighted was the confessors. Here Cyprian used both elite and military language to set them apart as having greater glory. They were noble, glorious and heroic, "illustrious for acts of bravery" (*Letters* 39.1). Numidicus, a confessor left for dead in the street by a mob, was "radiant with the brilliant light of his confession and ennobled by the dignity won by his courage and faith ..." (40.1.1). Such examples could be multiplied.[17] Suffice to say, they were the "most holy martyrs" (36.2.3). They hold an honored rank, which Cyprian compared to that of

---

15. Decidedly different rank is shown in the writing styles of letters from others in Carthage and Numidia, and in different treatments for Cyprian (*relegatio*, not *exsilium*) and for the people, who were beaten and chained for the mines. See Clarke's notes on letter # 46 (*Letters* IV, p. 278).

16. *Letters* 15.3-4; 34.4.1; 44.2.1; 49.2.3; 64.1.1. See Clarke's note 80, on letter 59 in *Letters*, vol. III, p. 261.

17. This theme is scattered throughout his letters, since he had to deal with their special place in both persecutions. This section only samples the attention paid to them. See also *Letters* 10; 13.4.1; 18; 28; 37.1-2; 39.2-3; 60; 68.5.1; and *Laps.* 2-3.

a patrician in the world (30.4; 39.2.3). True, the great body of believers who did not deny have a glory almost equal, but that was a passing note, while the ennobling vocabulary for the martyr/confessor was frequent. Thus there were two classes of Christians with superior honor. Neither, however, came close to that of the clergy.

From the time of his withdrawal from the scene in the early phases of Decius' persecution to his martyrdom in 258, Cyprian's letters reveal a growing concept of the dignity and authority of the clergy and of bishops in particular. We see it first in his concern that those who fell during the persecution were being forgiven and restored to the church rather too quickly and not by the clergy but by the confessors, who were regarded by everyone as having special status with God. Cyprian's pastoral concern was clear, for the public denials of those who had fallen should be handled carefully, to test the sincerity of the repenting. However, he strongly denied the right of the confessors to forgive at all. Their forgiveness was null and void, a subtle evil. They had neither the position to make a sacrifice, nor the authority to impose their hands in forgiveness (*Laps.* 15; *Letters* 15), though they could if Cyprian gave his permission (*Letters* 18)!

The other ranks of clergy are mentioned as having significant honor and authority. The confessors Celerinus and Aurelius were elevated to the rank of reader, their proper place being the tribunal, an "elevated position ... befitting the brilliance of his honor" (39.4.1). Numidicus will "take his seat with us among our clergy," evidence of distinct seating arrangements in the assembly. Numidicus could look forward to a "more exalted ecclesiastical station" when Cyprian returned to his chair (40.1.3). In both these letters, Cyprian alluded to the increase of the "lustre of our clergy." With reference to both presbyters and bishops, Cyprian spoke of the honor of the divine priesthood (*divino sacerdotio honorati*, 1.1.1), citing Hebrew scriptures to warn those who did not pay them due regard (Sir 7:1; Deut 17:12). Even the presbyters, however, needed to be careful not to give "insult to the episcopal dignity" (16.2.1), truly in a class by itself.

Cyprian repeatedly spoke of the dignity and honor of the episcopal position or chair.[18]

---

18. *Letters* 3; 33.1.1; 36.3.3; 67.8.1. See also 13.1, where he stated that the glory of the church is the glory of the leader and in a larger share.

This dignity must be protected from upstart confessors, from presumptuous elders or deacons, and against any who would presume to set up an alternative line of authority. The church over which they preside has its own "solemn majesty and dignity," but since the bishops "hold as a possession the one church in all its entirety" (*Letters* 68.2.2; 73.2.2), all the powers and gifts of the church were episcopal property. A properly conducted episcopal election was a divine office, unassailable except by manifest moral failure. It is clear that Cyprian's mode of office, in spite of his insistence on modesty and humility, was that of the paternal Roman magistrate.

Like a magistrate, Christian leaders are "men of gravity," who give their strength to the community (55.3.1).[19] He complimented Stephen of Rome for his gravity and wisdom, for it complimented appropriate episcopal authority (72; also 68.5.1). Like the magistrate, they decided people's fate, for the moment and sometimes for eternity. Let the people have respect!

Cyprian himself often acted much as a great man would. He controlled matters, asked for service from others and required his letters to be carried only by a cleric (29.1.1). After all, he had reached the highest point of the priesthood (*sacerdotii sublime fastigium*), like his brother Cornelius of Rome (55.8.2). He had been a significant person, as he reminded his readers several times, and he continued to be one. It is not an accident that the Roman clergy, without a bishop for a while, addressed him as "honored papa Cyprian" (*Letters* 8; 30; 31; 36). *His* clergy received their monthly allotments from him and he could interrupt them at any point (34; 39).[20] In all these ways, Cyprian shaped the church of North Africa in a very traditional Roman way, with himself as the patron. He encouraged all the rest of the bishops to see themselves similarly. It was no wonder that the bishop's position was a constant source of envy (*Zelo* 2), nor that others were trying to take his place.

---

19. See Letter 4, where Christ is compared to a Roman husband who will be most *angry* if his virgins are sullied, for they are his property and his honor is tied to their purity (3.2). Here Cyprian revealed that his understanding of Christ and of Christian leaders was that of protecting a supreme honor, not of granting it to others.

20. Clarke summarized these themes by referring to Cyprian as a *grand seigneur* (*Letters* II, p. 15). See also the 1988 Yale dissertation of Charles Bobertz, "Cyprian as Patron," for a comprehensive discussion of these matters.

Conclusions

When one looks at the early martyrdom documents and Tertullian, there is a sense of shared identity that centered upon fairness and goodness. Women shared in a substantial way in the actions and honor of this community, though Tertullian does not ever seem to escape a patriarchal framework. Women are not visible in leadership in an official way, though very little was said about leaders.

Tertullian never wrote the kind of piece that would push him to think systematically. Yet most of the elements of the revised paradigm were present and rooted firmly in the Hebrew tradition and Jesus' teaching. He clearly saw God and Christ as the Patrons. Praise was due. He refused the *dignitas* and *gravitas* of the great man, with respect for both God and others. The *Cursus honorum* was undermined; in its place he put humility, simplicity and benevolence. Honor and fairness were for all, yet he accepted a second-class role for catechumens and women. Finally, he simply does not seem to have shown it all connected in a flow of purpose and gratitude takes a distant second place to obligation.

Cyprian saw many of the issues very clearly. Certainly he believed that in the new way of the Christians, the primary Benefactors were God and God's Son. Gratitude was mentioned and humility of life was emphasized heavily. Benevolence was expected and taught strongly, sometimes in ways that clearly reflect the new paradigm. Often his understanding of the motives for such alms was directed to the search for forgiveness, for "leveraging" God. This notion takes legitimate ideas from Hebrew and Christian tradition, that one actions toward others have impact on one's relationship with God, and reinterpreted them into a legalistic framework quite foreign to the original context and vision.

Cyprian did not speak of universal honor nor of the inversion of honor values within the new community. He did not see great activity or dignity among the laity, except in the area of alms. He rarely speaks of women at all, except among two of the three exalted groups: virgins and confessors, who with the clergy have greater honor than other Christians.

More serious still is the way in which Cyprian condemned the *cursus honorum*, yet in his language about the episcopal office and in his manner of dealing with subordinates, he reinstated it in practical terms. The bishops owned the church and all its benefits, drawing allegiance and honor from the dispensing of goods and spiritual benefits. The people performed essentially the same functions in this community as they did in the general Roman community. They were his clients and his clients' clients.

When Cyprian was gone, the African church continued with great tensions between those who wished to follow the revised paradigm and those who saw Cyprian's reinstatement of the tradition one as the true model. It was a critical time when Cyprian, a man not steeped in the new paradigm, was forced to deal with the pressures of persecution, apostasy and opposition. He simply was not thoroughly prepared, so he returned to the default position, the traditional paradigm of greatness and leadership. His answers shaped the center of the African church and because of his influence, many other leaders and writers.

10

Conclusion

An Overview of the Patristic Project

PATRONAGE WAS A VERY WELL ESTABLISHED PRACTICE AND ONE THAT had enormous influence on the shape of Roman society. Jesus and his followers critiqued that practice and challenged it with an alternative, a revised paradigm of greatness and benefaction. In its main lines, this revision placed God and Christ in the place of the class of "great men" who functioned as patrons. As the supreme patrons, they gave gifts to all and required two primary responses in gratitude, accompanying praise give verbally to them.

First, honor and dignity were to be granted to all humanity, regardless of their station, resources or gifts. Within the community of disciples, honor was to be granted first most strongly to those who normally would not receive it at all. The leaders of this community were to be called by titles drawn from the workplace and servile labor, and were to be focused on serving rather than being served. Second, all members of whatever social position were to consider their resources as given in trust from God, to be used generously and kindly for the benefit of anyone in need. No honor or glory should be expected or demanded for such benefaction, for all credit belonged to the supreme Benefactors, who regarded all benefits done to the needy as a gift back to them. In short, honor giving changed from a paradigm that sent honor from many to few to the paradigm in which it was given freely from many to many. Similarly, benefaction changed from a paradigm in which sent benefits from the few to the many to one in which benefits were given by many to many. The character and purposes of the supreme Benefactors anchored the entire process.

Such a profound revision of patronage produced a community of strong social and moral energy, but its stark contradiction to traditional practice demanded consistent practice and constant reinforcement. It proved to be difficult for even the earliest of Jesus' followers to practice what they had been taught and shown. It is then understandable that considerable difficulty would be experienced by subsequent generations in changing times and places. So we have seen, and now we seek to see their history together.

The Revised Paradigm in the "Best of Times": 95–175 CE

It was a vigorous time for all concerned. The period of the "good emperors" was a time in which Christianity flourished along the northern edge of the Mediterranean, at least. We suspect, but cannot prove, that Egypt, North Africa and Osrhoene were also making good beginnings. Our meager evidence comes from Rome, the Aegean, and Syria.

Clement of Rome enunciated a rather complete reflection of the revised paradigm, integrated into an argument for humility and respect, though he did not emphasize the inversion of honor. He wrote not as a bishop nor to a bishop, but as representative of local elders. His defense of the order of leaders, based on analogy from the Roman military and from the function of the Hebrew priesthood, is striking because it did not emerge from Christian roots. His letter was very influential in the future, alongside the writings which would become the New Testament, and his arguments for the authority of leaders would be used repeatedly.

Church order documents from the period (the Pastoral Epistles, the *Didache*, and the *Epistle of Barnabas*) reveal a vital community and reflect elements of the revised paradigm. However, they show slight attention to God or Christ, the essential anchors of the revision and do not teach the inversion of honor values. As guides to discipleship and leadership, they were struggling with possible abuses of power and of the generosity of the community. They show a tendency to gather honor around the leaders: 1 Timothy directed double honor for teachers and the *Didache* referred to prophets in the community as "your high priests." This is the beginning of a process of investing those carefully chosen leadership terms, from the work and servile world, with a kind of honor they were not intended to bear.

Two pastors related by circumstance stand out in the early second century, Ignatius and Polycarp. Polycarp is difficult to evaluate from one letter, though in it he does emphasize humility and kindness. Ignatius, from a larger set of letters, demonstrated an uncritical acceptance of the traditional paradigm of patronage in his language, his carefully orchestrated martyr's journey, and his emphasis on the bishop with his clergy as the center of the community. The bishop should be in complete control, and the almost complete lack of the revised paradigm is not due only to the type of literature or the situation, but to Ignatius' own understandings, startlingly contrary to the revised paradigm. Ignatius deeply influenced Syrian Christianity, which is apparent in the use of his language and ideas in the later *Didascalia*.

We have two windows into the community in Rome in the period 130–155 CE. Hermas, in his dark apocalyptic work, reveals to us a community in tension. On the one hand, he assumes the operation of the revised paradigm in his writing, not least as the basis for his critique of leaders and members who continued the traditional one in and out of the church. Groups with different perspectives were competing for the allegiance and resources of members of several congregations, cultivating the wealthy and neglecting the poor as well as the inversion of honor. Meanwhile, Justin's *Apology* presented the best and ideal in the community, seeing all members as a "high priestly race." Marcion would have agreed, as he arrived with a radical sense of the new paradigm, unfortunately accompanying that conviction with a rejection of its Hebrew roots, alienating enough of the Roman Christian network to be asked to leave. It is at least seriously arguable that the enduring strength of Marcion's movement was due to its continuing practice of a radical and revised paradigm.

Meanwhile, apologists for the Christian community were writing their defenses; in the ones that survived, we have the clearest expressions of the revised paradigm. Though it is clear that they were enunciating the ideal, they at the very least give testimony to an enduring vision of a community in which greatness and benevolence were practiced in a profoundly new manner and the relations between gift and response. Not everyone had all the elements we have outlined, but none were missing much. It should be noted that none appear to have been clergy with the possible exception of Tatian.

From the very end of this period, we hear the testimony of Polycrates that great spiritual leaders had led the churches of western Asia Minor. A common thread in their leadership was the power of the Holy Spirit, animating the effective leadership of John the Seer, the four daughters of Philip, and Melito of Sardis. Like Justin, Melito emphasized the character of the entire people of God as a holy priesthood. Bordering that vigorous area was Phrygia, where the Montanist movement insisted on the active work of God's spirit in their people and in women in particular. No opposition is recorded from the churches of the lower Aegean shores, but was strong in eastern Anatolia, Antioch and the western shores of the Black Sea. Serious disagreement is apparent over the freedom of all members to practice God's gifts in public.

Finally, we must note that honorific language ("most honored"; "noble"; "greatest") was used prominently with regard to martyrs and Polycarp in particular, whose public persona in Smyrna may have also developed as a "great man," if the story of his martyrdom is trusted with regard to the manner in which official authorities treated him in his arrest. Eventually both confessors and clergy will be described with many of the terms used of the martyrs in the martyrologies, but not yet. We must also note that individuals of high imperial position were connected to the church and its leaders, such as Apollonius in Rome and the friend of Polycarp who was of the imperial household. They had not, however, been enlisted as leaders.

In this period, then, the revised paradigm is well attested, though not without struggle, especially in Rome. Ignatius was clearly out of step with the Christian communities in general, but his writings were preserved and revered due to his martyrdom and explicit rejection of "Gnosticism." Leaders were gathering honor and power in a gradual process, but the vigor of the community balanced it. The strongest and most balanced presentation of the continuing revision was in the apologetic writings and weakest in church order documents.

The Revised Paradigm during Times of Upheaval: 175–220 CE

Toward the end of the second century, the Empire entered a phase of turmoil. Commodus proved to be manifestly incompetent, and the Severans emerged from an embarrassing struggle which followed his death. Though the Severans did establish a measure of stability, it was tenuous. During this period, we have the creation of large bodies of literature within the Christian community, but from fewer individuals. More individuals from higher classes were involved; vigorous but localized persecutions broke out in areas previously quiet.

Irenaeus of Lyons spent most of his time and writings on the intricacies of the heretics, especially those later called Gnostics, but he did enunciate the revised paradigm of patronage, in part as a basis for his critique. He saw the heretics as pursuing members for advantage, pursuing an elite position themselves and ignoring important parts of the agenda of Jesus. In his own instruction, he taught that God gave gifts to all members for the performance of good works. He emphasized the work of the Holy Spirit, seeing a balance between the work of leaders and people. Two things should be remembered. First , he was the first bishop to give such a full exposition. Second, he was rooted in the dynamic Christian communities of western Asia Minor.

In Rome, the darker fears of Hermas seem to have come true, though some of the revised paradigm can be seen in the apologist Minucius Felix, linked both to North Africa and Rome. Zephirinus and Callistus seem to have returned to the traditional paradigm, thinly disguised in religious garb. For them, a bishop functioned as a religious patron of the wealthy of both sexes, trading religious favors more secular ones. This can be maintained even if we believe that the testimony of Hippolytus is overstated.

In Syria, there is somewhat better news. Bishop Theophilus shows a clear grasp of most of the elements of the revised paradigm in his apology to Autolycus. Though we have no pastoral documents from which to evaluate his actions, no affinity with the elitism of Ignatius. Meanwhile, the Odes of Solomon show that the people were singing songs which affirmed the gifts of God and their own role in handing on divine life and light to others.

Church order documents show a different focus. The Teaching of the Twelve Apostles and the Doctrine of Addai gave a great deal of attention to the clergy and almost none to the people, which is a telling omission. Emphasis on humility and benevolence contrasts strongly with the heavy focus on leaders and a correlative neglect of both the work and honor of the people. We cannot conclude that the new community dynamics were absent, but a neglect of the elements of the revised paradigm, in documents composed by clergy for clergy guidance, is certainly unfortunate.

The teachers of Alexandria, Sextus and Clement, put significant emphasis on most of the elements of the new paradigm throughout their works. Sextus concentrated on behavior patterns, and implicitly showed how the new paradigm was in agreement with prior philosophical criticism, though he does extend those critiques. Clement was a recognized teacher with a strong apologetic emphasis and provides the most complete and integrated exposition of the new paradigm since the New Testament. His achievement is the more significant since he clearly was concerned to reach and retain members of the elite classes. He addressed the ideal to them in very detailed fashion. Like Sextus, he was interested in showing agreement with what he saw as the best of prior philosophical thought, but I do not see him as excessively dependent on that tradition. One final observation: Clement was not a member of the formal clergy, but held a position closer to that of Justin in the Roman community, a teacher and apologist.

In North Africa, another group of communities began to come into view in two martyr documents which reveal women acknowledged as leaders and peers, receiving honor both before and after their death. Tertullian, in a long and challenging career, reveals a strong interest in the revised paradigm. His presentation of a community led by a divine Benefactor and continuing that benefaction in multiple ways is quite extensive. Certainly, a disciplined refusal of the *cursus honorum*, with all that is implied, was presented in some depth. Because of the size of his corpus of writing and his espousal of Montanism, we cannot always understand how completely he understood and taught the inversion of honor values. His attitudes toward women were conflicting, sometimes restricting and sometimes encouraging their active participation. To complicate matters, he barely spoke of the clergy at all, though rare references pointed in the direction of clerical status and privilege. For him, that would have been balanced across his career by an emphasis on the work of the Holy Spirit in cross section of community members of all ranks and both genders.

In this period, we see the martyrdom documents becoming more elaborate and using stronger honorific language, regarding the martyrs as a new nobility and as victors in a spiritual war. We can just begin to see that same honor devolving upon still living confessors, and an assumption by writers and their readers, that these confessors have a special power with God. They *deserve* more honor.

Finally, it is clear from the problems in Rome and the extensive strictures of both Clement and Tertullian that in increasing percentage of the Christian community were from the elite classes. Yet they were not taking the leadership positions. Vettius Epagathus and Attalus in Lyons both stood up as significant citizens to defend the Christians, and both paid the price. Neither were members of the clergy and were not especially feted for their sacrifice. Clement may have been from the elite, but was not clergy. Nearly all the writings of the period saw wealth as a challenge, but a challenge successfully met in terms of the revised paradigm, expect in Rome. All this will change in the next period.

The Revised Paradigm in a World of Confusion: 220–290 CE

As the Severan dynasty struggled and fell, the empire entered a period with much political turmoil, economic decline and environmental difficulties such as plague and crop failure. Christian communities flourished in this period, however, in part because their benevolence made many friends. As it grew and garnered approval, the church became more visible and a more attractive place for a career. Origen complained about a growing ambition for offices within the community. That is indeed the major story of this period.

In Rome, the unfortunate competition between the two "papas" Callistus and Hippolytus continued and was replicated in the next generation, between Novatian and Cornelius. Though complicated by new issues during and after the Decian persecution, ambition continued to play a role. Some reasons can be seen the Apostolic Tradition, a Roman church order document attributed to Hippolytus. In it a full hierarchy of church officers is apparent, and the workplace terms which once downplayed position now have distinct levels of honor and privilege. The people have once again become clients of a great man, the bishop. Benevolence continues, but it is clearly in the mold of the traditional patronage paradigm.

Yet there is evidence that the discipline and broad-scale benevolence of this community continued in Egypt and North Africa. We have no evidence that the flourishing of Christian community in Provence and the Aegean circle is following this return to Roman tradition, while the continuing flourishing of Montanism in central Anatolia militates against it. All of these areas were strongest in support of the revised paradigm.

Ignatius' heritage continued to shape Syria and neighboring Cappadocia. The composition of the *Didascalia Apostolorum* articulates a model of the community quite similar to that of the Apostolic Tradition of Rome, but even more strongly worded with Ignatian language. Exhortations of humility addresssed to the clergy stand in powerful contrast to the obeisance expected of the people. Activities of the people were to be severely restricted and any honor to be given to them is absent.

Meanwhile, the two major figures of Cappadocia and Pontus, Firmilian and Gregory Thaumaturgos, were of aristocratic families and continued to be aristocratic in their episcopal offices. Gregory's writings show no real comprehension of the revised paradigm, after years of study with Origen, but Origen had no apparent passion for it either. When the qualifications for a bishop in Pontus included a choice from "those who appeared to be outstanding in eloquence and family,"[1] that then would not have been a surprise. These developments make the case of Paul of Samosata quite understandable.

Paul simply took to its logical conclusion what had become the standard model among urban clergy: he *was* a "great man." That was now standard for bishops, especially in a major urban center like Antioch. As for becoming a procurator ducenarius by the patronage of the Palmyrene dynasty—why not? Other Christians held high imperial positions,[2] why not combine two great positions: bishop of Antioch and procurator of Syria? He was a bit ahead of his time, but not as far as might be thought. "Eminent bishops" gathered in council to discipline him, and the case eventually reached the ears of Emperor Aurelian.

When I read the encomium of Gregory Thaumaturgos for Origen, I was struck by the lack of Christian ideas. In view of the time he had studied with Origen, regularly in his own day and often since consid-

---

1. *Life of Gregory Thaumaturgos*, 9,63 (Slusser trans.).

2. Marinus, of high rank in the army (Eusebius *H.E.* VII,13); public educators Anatolius and Eusebius of Alexandria (VII,32); Senator Astyrius (VII,16); Philoromus, a public official in Alexandria (VII,9,7). For other figures in the late third century and early fourth century, see *H.E.* VIII, chaps. 5,6,11,12,14.

ered one of the greatest Christian teachers. After reading Origen, I understood. He quite thoroughly bypassed the heart of Christian ideals, transmuting them into abstract ideas and personal spiritualities. Origen did not contradict the revised paradigm as much as simply neglecting it consistently. When one is as revered and influential as Origen, that is decisive. A new intellectual elitism was enunciated which had extensive consequences.

All of this third-century development demonstrates that the common understanding of the community and its leaders had moved, in the major centers of the empire, back toward the traditional Roman paradigm. No one illustrates this movement better than Cyprian of Carthage. From the Roman aristocracy and deeply moral, Cyprian taught many of the values of the revised paradigm: gratitude, humility, a simplified lifestyle, benevolence broadly conceived and practiced. However, many of his actions and understandings of his place within the church belied the teachings and moved his influential community decisively into a traditional patron/client model of operation. If the bishops are proprietors of salvation, rather than servants among servants, their acts will be shaped by a very different logic. So they were, and since Cyprian was deeply influential in the West, many adopted his theology and the behavior which it engendered.

The movement of "significant people" into episcopal positions in this period, in addition to the gathering of power and honor around the same led to increasing numbers of members from those classes. The same language which those classes would expect to be used of them in civil positions became normal for ecclesiastical positions as well. Those honorifics were not rooted in anything specifically Christian, so the motive and dynamic to expect anything specifically Christian in the use of resources was consistently undercut. Now not just martyrs and ascetics, but any officeholder, should be described as noble and exceptional. If honor were also to apply to the rest of the members, it would mean nothing to the officials, so it is not applied to the laity.

Conclusion

Jesus and his earliest followers posed a profound challenge to the practice of traditional patron/client relations, connected so deeply to honor and ambition. For the changes implied by that challenge to have succeeded would have required constant reaffirmation and thorough practice. That simply did not happen in the early Christian communities.

Universal honor for all humanity was the first to go. Maintaining a rejection of the traditional *cursus honorum* was quickly a struggle in Rome and Antioch, and it was in those two centers of imperial power that the clearest erosion of the inversion of honor also occurred. The practice of benevolence began to be concentrated in the "community chests" by the mid-second century, increasing the power and respect of the clergy. Both Alexandria and Carthage maintained more of this challenging inversion until about the middle of the third century, and we may postulate even slower change for southern Palestine and the Aegean littoral. Finally the weight of the great urban centers prevailed over the great bulk of Christians. Cyprian enunciated the rights and privileges of the clergy in ways which became the norm for leaders and people.

One can summarize in a helpful was the whole process in the history of the designation "priest." Jesus did not use the term, but it emerged in 1 Peter and Revelation as a designation for the people of God as a whole, "royal priesthood." Rooted in Exod 19:6, to be a priest was not to hold an exclusive office with extra honor relative to the rest of the people. Rather, one functioned within a large privileged group whose borders were open to all humanity. This language was explicitly echoed by Justin, Melito and Tertullian; the idea underlay much of the vision of the revised paradigm. So when Cyprian crystallized much of what had happened in the third century by speaking of "the honor of the priesthood," he spoke in Roman, not Christian terms. Elite members of the community held position and honor beyond and over the typical member.

By the year 290, the paradigm of patronage which operated in the churches was largely a religious form of the traditional Roman one. By claiming ownership of the gifts of God *and* of his people, the clergy operated as patrons of spiritual benefits, as well as material. By concentrating spiritual benefits in their positions and material resources in institutional chests, they restricted or eliminated individual initiative in doing good. Broad-scale benevolence, gratitude and honor became phenomena of the past. In an important sense, the community ceased to be Christian.

Appendix 1

Semantic Field Sketch (Latin)

Terms of Reciprocity

beneficium = a kindness, benefit, favor, service, privilege
colere / observare = cultivate, show respect
fides = trust, confidence, reliance, faith
Transferred: faithfulness, conscientiousness, promise, word of honor, safe-conduct
gratia = favor, esteem, regard, popularity (used in conjuction with *debere, reddere, referre, pendere, persolvere*)

—favor done, service, kindness
—indulgence regarding an offence
—thankfulness, thanks
—that which is pleasing, attraction

favor (faveo) to favor, show goodwill toward
hospitium = hospitality, reception
meritum = a (just) desert, merit, a good action, benefit, service
munus = public duty, office
necessitas = intimate connection, friendship, relationship
obstringere = to bind, obligate
officium = dutiful or respectful action, ceremonial action, duty, sense of duty, respect, courtesy, deference, submission, allegiance
patrocinium = patronage, protection, defence, service, sponsoring
praesidium = protection, help, aid, defense
salutatio = usually by client to patron, could work the other way → commendation
suffragatio = public recommendation for office

testificatio = vouch for, attest

Terms of the Giving of Honor

benemerenti = well-deserving

Terms of the Giving of Honor

benemerenti = well-deserving
clarissimus = illustrious, distinguished
egregius = excellent (often to procurators)
eminentissimus = most renowned
honos, dignitas = honor, glory
nobilitas = of high family, especially consular
patronus = protector, sponsor, patron
perfectissimus = most accomplished
primores viri = city father, higher decuriones

Terms of Defined Place Relative to a Patron

amicus = friend
ambactus = vassal
cliens = client
plebs = common people
servus = slave, servant
libertus = freedman
indigentes = destitute, desperately poor
pauperes = poor, with no resources

Terms Descriptive of the Patron/Client Bond

benignitas = kindness, mildness, liberality, generosity
dignitas = worth, worthiness
gloriae adpetens, contentio honorum = struggle for glory or honor
infamia = disgrace
liberalitas = generosity
studiosus, fervidus = eager, intent

Appendix 2

Semantic Field Sketch—Greek

Terms of Reciprocity

didonai heautous = to give oneself to
euergesia = good work, benefit
eupoieō = do good
leitourgia = service, obligation, responsibility, worship
marturion = testimony, attestation
martureō = witness to, verify, attest
opheileō = to be indebted
opheiletēs = one who is indebted
pistis = trust, faith, conviction
pistos = faithful, trustworthy, reliable
philonexia = hospitality
philanthrōpia = both the benefitting of others *and* its answer
charis = favor, grace, thanks, credit
charitoō = favor someone
charisdzomai = give gifts to (graciously)
charisma = gift of favor
chorēgeo = to be a supplier

Terms of the Giving of Honor

anēr agathos = good man, recognized as such
axios = worthy (many cognates and compounds)
aretē = excellence
doxa = glory (many cognates)

epiphanēs = illustrious, distinguished
eugeneia = noble, of high family, well-born
euergetēs = benefactor
kalokagathia = nobility of character
philagathon = loving the good
kratiste = excellent, most excellent
prepontōs = conspicuously, appropriately
presbeia = representative
presbus = elder in standing
prostatēs = patron, protector
proxenos = patron, protector, representative
(ta) proteia = the leading citizens
Sōtēr = Savior (word family can denote many kinds of help)
timē = honor (many cognates)

Terms of Giving Place Relative to a Patron

diakonos = servant
kolax = flatterer, "hanger on," (aspiring client?)
pelatēs = client
penētai = poor, without resources
penēs, penichros
ptōchos = desperately poor, indigent
philos = friend
hetairos = friend, companion

Terms of Motivation and Attitude in Benefaction

hagneia, amemptos = blameless, without reproach
authairetos = of one's own accord
dōrean = without charge, as a gift
eilikrinēs = sincere
eleutheriotēs = generosity, free-acting
epieikeia = kindness
eunoia = good will
kata dunamin = according to ability, as much as possible
metriotēti = measured, modest
pronoia = forethought

phrontidzō = giving thought, concern
spoudaiōs = eagerly
ektenōs = intently, strenuously
tupos, hupodeigma = pattern, example for others
philotimia = love of honor
philodoxia = love of recognition
chrēstos = kind, helpful

Bibliography

Primary Sources: Greco-Roman Background

Dio Chrysostom. *Discourses* Vol.5. Translated by H. Lamar Crosby. LCL. Cambridge: Harvard University Press, 1964.
Juvenal. *Satires*. Translated by Rolf Humphries. Bloomington: Indiana University Press, 1958.
Pliny the Younger. *The Letters of the Younger Pliny*. Translated by Betty Radice. Baltimore: Penguin, 1967.
Plutarch. "Precepts of Statecraft." In *Moralia*, vol. 10. Translated by H. N. Fowler. LCL. Cambridge: Harvard University Press, 1960.
Seneca. *Moral Essays*. Vol. 3. Translated by J. W. Basore. LCL. Cambridge: Harvard University Press, 1964.

Secondary Sources: Graeco-Roman Background

Brilliant, Richard. *Gesture and Rank in Roman Art*. Memoirs of the Connecticut Academy of Arts and Sciences, Vol. XIV. New Haven: The Academy, 1963.
Brunt, P.A. "*Amicitia* in the Later Roman Republic." In *The Crisis of the Roman Republic*, edited by Robin Seager, 199–218. Proceedings of the Cambridge Philological Society. Cambridge: Cambridge University Press, 1969.
Carcopino, Jerome. *Daily Life in Ancient Rome*. Translated by E. Lorimer. New Haven: Yale, 1940.
Cotton, Hannah. *Documentary Letters of Recommendation in Latin from the Roman Empire*. Beiträge zur Klassischen Philologie 132. Koenigstein: Hain, 1981.
Danker, Frederick. *Benefactor: An Epigraphic Study of a Graeco-Roman and New Testament Semantic Field*. St. Louis: Clayton, 1982.
Edlund, Ingrid. "Invisible Bonds: Clients and Patrons through the Eyes of Polybius." *Klio* 59 (1977) 129–41.
Erskine, Andrew. "The Romans as Common Benefactors." *Historia* 43 (1994) 70–87.
Friedländer, Ludwig. *Roman Life and Manners under the Early Empire*. 4 vols. Translated by Leonard A. Magnus. 1913. Reprinted, London: Routledge & Kegan Paul, 1965.
Garnsey, Peter. *Social Status and Legal Privilege in the Roman Empire*. Oxford: Oxford University Press, 1970.
Garnsey, Peter, and Richard Saller. *The Roman Empire: Economy, Society and Culture*. Berkeley: University of California Press, 1987.

Gelzer, Matthias. *The Roman Nobility*. Translated by Robin Seager. Oxford: Oxford University Press, 1969.
Gold, Barbara, ed. *Literary and Artistic Patronage in Ancient Rome*. Austin: University of Texas Press, 1982.
Hands, Arthur Robinson *Charities and Social Aid in Greece and Rome*. London: Thames & Hudson, 1968.
Harmand, Louis. *Un aspect social et politique du monde romain: le patronat sur les collectivities des origines au Bas Empire*. Paris: Presses universitaires de France, 1957.
Hopkins, M. Keith. "Social Mobility in the Later Roman Empire." *Classical Quarterly* 11 (1961) 239–49.
Levick, Barbara. "Imperial Control of the Elections under the Early Empire: commendatio, suffragatio and 'nominatio.'" *Historia* 16 (1967) 207–30.
Lewis, Naphtali, and Meyer Reinhold. *Roman Civilization*. 2 vols. Records of Civilization: Sources and Studies. 1955. Reprinted, New York: Harper Torchbook, 1966.
May, James. "The Rhetoric of Advocacy and Patron-Client Identification: Variations on a Theme." *American Journal of Philology* 102 (1981) 308–15.
Millar, Fergus. *The Roman Near East*. Cambridge: Harvard University Press, 1993.
Mott, Stephen "The Power of Giving and Receiving: Reciprocity in Hellenistic Benevolence." In *Current Issues in Biblical and Patristic Interpretation*, edited by Gerald Hawthorne, 60–72. Grand Rapids: Eerdmans, 1975.
Nicols, John. "Pliny and the Patronage of Communities." *Hermes* 108 (1980) 365–85.
Saller, Richard P. *Personal Patronage under the Early Empire*. Cambridge: Cambridge University Press, 1982.
Syme, Ronald. *The Roman Revolution*. Oxford: Oxford University Press, 1966.
Szemler, G. J. "Priesthoods and Priestly Careers in Ancient Rome." In *Aufstieg und Niedergang der Römischen Welt* II.16.3. Edited by H. Temporini and W. Haase, 2315–31. Berlin: de Gruyter, 1979.
Veyne, Paul. *Bread and Circuses: Historical Sociology and Political Pluralism*. Translated by Brian Pierce. London: Lane, 1990.
Wallace-Hadrill, Andrew, editor. *Patronage in Ancient Society*. London: Routledge, 1992.

Primary Sources: New Testament

New American Standard Bible Anaheim: Foundation Press, 1973.
The Greek New Testament. 3rd edition. Edited by Kurt Aland et al. Stuttgart: United Bible Societies, 1983.

Secondary Sources: New Testament

Bartchy, S. Scott. *"Call No Man Father": The Apostle Paul's Vision of a Society of Siblings*. Forthcoming.

———. "Community of Goods in Acts: Idealization or Social Reality?" In *The Future of Early Christianity: Essays in Honor of Helmut Koester*, edited by Birger Pearson, 309–18. Minneapolis: Fortress, 1991.

———. "The Credibility Factor: How Christian Practice Affected the Persuasiveness of Early Christian Preaching." In *Faith in Practice: Studies in the Book of Acts*, edited by D. A. Fiensy and W. D. Howden, 151–81. Joplin, MO: College Press, 1995.

———. "Slave, Slavery." In *Dictionary of the Later New Testament and Its Developments*. Edited by Ralph Martin and Peter Davids. Downers Grove, IL: InterVarsity Press, 1997.

———. "Table Fellowship." In *Dictionary of Jesus and the Gospels*, edited by Joel B. Green et al., 796–98. Downers Grove, IL: InterVarsity Press, 1992.

Beavis, M. A. "Ancient Slavery as an Interpretive Context for the N.T. Servant Parables with Special Reference to the Unjust Steward." *JBL* 111 (1992) 37–54.

Burkert, Walter. "Craft versus Sect: The Problem of Orphics and Pythagoreans." In *Jewish and Christian Self-Definition*, vol. 3, edited by Ben Meyer and E. P. Sanders, 1–22. Philadelphia: Westminster, 1982.

Capper, Brian. "The Palestinian Cultural Context of the Earliest Christian Community of Goods." In *The Book of Acts in Its Palestinian Setting*, edited by Richard Bauckham, 323–56. Grand Rapids: Eerdmans, 1995.

Chow, J. K. *Patronage and Power: A Study of Social Networks in Corinth*. JSNTSupp 75. Sheffield, UK: Sheffield University Press, 1992.

Conzelmann, Hans. "*chairō, ktl.*" In *TDNT* 9 (1974) 373–415.

Davids, Peter H. *The Epistle of James: A Commentary on the Greek Text*. New International Greek Testament Commentary. Grand Rapids: Eerdmans, 1982.

Dibelius, Martin, and Heinrich Greeven. *James: A Commentary on the Epistle of James*. Translated by Michael A. Williams. Hermeneia. Philadelphia: Fortress, 1976.

Dunn, James D. G. *Romans 9–16*. Word Biblical Commentary 38A. Dallas: Word, 1988.

Elliot, John H. *The Elect and The Holy: An Exegetical Examination of I Peter 2:4–10 and the Phrase "Basileion Ierateuma."* 1966. Reprinted, Eugene, OR: Wipf & Stock, 2006.

———. "Patronage and Clientism in Early Christian Society: A Short Reading Guide." *Forum* 3.4 (1987) 39–48.

Grant, Robert M. *Early Christianity and Society: Seven Studies*. San Francisco: Harper & Row, 1977.

Hanson, K. C. "'How Honorable!' 'How Shameful!' A Cultural Analysis of Matthew's Makarisms and Reproaches." *Semeia* 68 (1996) 81–111.

Hauck, F. "*makarios, ktl.*" In *TDNT* 4 (1967) 362–70.

Johnson, Luke Timothy. *The Letter of James: A New Translation with Introduction and Commentary*. Anchor Bible 37A. New York: Doubleday, 1995.

Kloppenborg, John S. "*Philadelphia, Theodidaktos* and the Dioscuri: Rhetorical Engagement in I Thess. 4:9–12." *New Testament Studies* 39 (1993) 265–89.

Lull, David. "The Servant-Benefactor as a Model of Greatness." *NovT* 28 (1986) 289–310.

Malina, Bruce J. "Patron and Client: The Analogy behind Synoptic Theology." *Forum* 4 (1988) 2–32.

Malina, Bruce J., and Jerome H. Neyrey. *Calling Jesus Names: The Social Value of Labels in Matthew*. Social Facets. Sonoma, CA: Polebridge, 1988.

———. "Conflict in Luke-Acts." In *The Social World of Luke-Acts: Models for Interpretation*, edited by Jerome H. Neyrey, 97–122. Peabody, MA: Hendrickson, 1991.

Malina, Bruce J., and Richard L. Rohrbaugh. *A Social Science Commentary on the Synoptic Gospels*. 2nd ed. Minneapolis: Fortress, 2003.

Marshall, Peter. *Enmity in Corinth: Social Conventions in Paul's Relations with the Corinthians*. WUNT 2/23. Tübingen: Mohr/Siebeck, 1987.

Mitchell, A.C. "The Social Function of Friendship in Acts 2:44–47 and 4:32–37." *JBL* 111 (1992) 255–72.

Moxnes, Halvor. "Patron-Client Relations and the New Community in Luke-Acts." In *The Social World of Luke-Acts: Models for Interpreters*, edited by Jerome H. Neyrey, 241–68. Peabody, MA: Hendrickson, 1991.

Neyrey, Jerome H., editor. *The Social World of Luke-Acts: Models for Interpretation*. Peabody, MA: Hendrickson, 1991.

Reicke, Bo. *The Epistles of James, Peter and Jude*. Anchor Bible 37. Garden City, NY: Doubleday, 1964.

Rengstorff, Karl Heinrich. "*apostellō, ktl.*" In *TDNT* 1 (1964) 398–447.

Reumann, John. "Contributions of the Philippian Community to Paul and to Earliest Christianity." *NTS* 39 (1993) 438–57.

Saldarini, Anthony "Delegitimation of Leaders in Matthew 23." *Catholic Biblical Quarterly* 54 (1992) 659–80.

Sampley, J. Paul. *Pauline Partnership in Christ: Christian Community and Commitment in Light of Roman Law*. Minneapolis: Fortress, 1980.

Winter, Bruce. *Seek the Welfare of the City: Christians as Benefactors and Citizens*. First-Century Christians in the Graeco-Roman World. Grand Rapids: Eerdmans, 1994.

Primary Sources Early Patristic Christianity

The Acts of the Christian Martyrs. Edited and translated by Herbert Musurillo. OECT. Oxford: Oxford University Press, 1972.

Apostolic Fathers, The. 2 vols. Edited and Translated by Kirsopp Lake. LCL. Cambridge: Harvard University Press, 1977.

Aristides and Athenagoras. Apologeten, Die ältesten. Edited by Edgar Goodspeed. Göttingen: Vandenhoeck & Ruprecht, 1915.

Athenagoras. *Embassy for the Christians*. Translated and annotated by J. H. Crehan. ACW 23. New York: Newman, 1956.

Clement of Rome. *Clément de Rome: Épitre aux Corinthiens*. Edited and translated by Annie Jaubert. SC 167. Paris: Cerf, 1971.

———. *First Epistle of Clement to the Corinthians*. Edited by W. K. Lowther Clarke. Translations of Early Documents. London: SPCK, 1937.

Clement of Alexandria. *The Exhortation to the Greeks; The Rich Man's Salvation; To the Newly Baptized*. Translated by G.W. Butterworth. LCL 92. Cambridge: Harvard University Press, 1979.

———. *Christ the Educator*. Translated by Simon Wood. FOC 23. New York: Catholic University of America, 1954.

———. *Clément d' Alexandrie: Le Pédagogue*. Livre I . SC 70. Edited by H. I. Marrou. Paris: Cerf, 1960; Livre II. SC 108. Edited by C. Mondésert. Paris: Cerf, 1965; Livre III. SC 158. Edited by C. Mondésert. Paris: Cerf, 1970.

———. *Miscellanies*. ANF 2. Translated by W. Wilson. New York: Scribners, 1885.

———. *Clemens Alexandrinus: Stromata Buch I-VI*. Edited by Otto Stählin. GCS 15/17. Leipzig: 1936/1909.

———. *Stromateis I–III*. Translated by John Ferguson. FOC 85. New York: Catholic University of America, 1991.

Cyprian of Carthage. *The Lapsed / The Unity of the Catholic Church*. Translated and annotated by M. Bénevot. ACW 25. New York: Newman, 1956.

———. *The Letters of Cyprian*. Translated and annotated by G. W. Clarke. 4 vols. ACW. New York: Newman. Vol. 1-2, ACW 43-44, 1984; vol. 3, ACW 46, 1986; vol. 4, ACW 47, 1989.

———. *Saint Cyprian: Treatises* (To Donatus, To Demetrian, On the Unity of the Church, The Lapsed, The Dress of Virgins, Mortality, The Good of Patience, The Lord's Prayer, Works and Almsgiving, Jealousy and Envy, Exhortation to Martyrdom, That Idols Are Not Gods). Translated and edited by Roy Deferrari et al. FOC 36. New York: Catholic University of America, 1958.

———. *S. Thasci Caecili Cypriani: Opera Omnia*. Edited by W. Hartel. CSEL III. 1871. Reprinted, New York: Johnson Reprint, 1965.

The Didache (with the Epistle of Barnabas, Epistles and Martyrdom of St. Polycarp, Fragments of Papias and the Epistle to Diognetus). Translated by James Kleist. ACW 6. Westminster, MD: Newman, 1948.

Didascalia Apostolorum in Syriac, The. Vol. 1. Translated by Arthur Vööbus. CSCO 402. Louvain: Peeters, 1979.

Didascalia Apostolorum: The Syriac Version Translated and Accompanied by the Latin Verona Fragments. Translated by R. H. Connolly. 1929. Reprint, Ancient Texts and Translations. Eugene, OR: Wipf & Stock, 2010.

Doctrine of Addai. ANF 8. Translated by B. P. Pratten. New York: Scribners, 1903.

Early Christian Biographies. Edited by Roy Deferrari. FOC 15. New York: Catholic University of America, 1952.

Eusebius of Caesarea. *The Ecclesiastical History*. 2 vols. Edited and translated by K. Lake, J. E. L. Oulton and H. J. Lawlor. Cambridge: Harvard University Press, 1975.

Hermas. *Hermas: Le Pasteur*. Introduced, edited, and translated by Robert Joly. SC 53. Paris: Cerf, 1968.

Hippolytus of Rome. *Hippolyte de Rome: La Tradition Apostolique* second edition. Edited and translated by Bernard Botte. SC 11. Paris: Cerf, 1968.

———. *The Apostolic Tradition of Hippolytus*. Translated with introduction and notes by Burton S. Easton. 1924. Reprinted, New York: Archon, 1962.

———. *The Refutation of All Heresies*. Translated by J. H. MacMahon. ANF 5. New York: Scribners, 1899.

———. *Refutatio Omnium Haeresium*. Edited by Miroslav Marcovich. Patristische Texte und Studien 25. Berlin: de Gruyter, 1986.

Irenaeus of Lyons. *Against Heresies*. Translated by A. Roberts and W. Rambaut. ANF 1. New York: Scribners, 1899.

———. *Contre Les Hérésies*. Introduction, notes, critical edition, and translation by Adelin Rousseau, Louis Doutreleau et al. Livre I, SC 263–64, 1979; Livre II, SC 293–94, 1982; Livre III, SC 210–11, 1974; Livre IV, SC 100, 1965; Livre V, SC 152–53, 1969.

Justin Martyr. *The Apologies of Justin Martyr and the Epistle to Diognetus*. Edited with notes by Basil Gildersleeve. Douglass Series of Christian Greek and Latin Authors 5. New York: Harper, 1877.

———. *Justin Martyr: The Dialogue with Trypho*. Translated with introduction and notes by A. Lukyn Williams. London: SPCK, 1930.

———. *Writings of Saint Justin Martyr*. Translated by Thomas Falls. FOC 6. New York: Christian Heritage, 1948.

Melito of Sardis. *Melito of Sardis: On the Pascha and Fragments*. Edited by Stuart G. Hall. OECT. Oxford: Oxford University Press, 1979.

———. "A New English Translation of Melito's Paschal Homily." Translated by Gerald Hawthorne. In *Current Issues in Biblical and Patristic Interpretation: Studies in Honor of Merrill C. Tenney Presented by His Former Students*, edited by Gerald Hawthorne, 147–75. Grand Rapids: Eerdmans, 1975.

Methodius of Olympus. *The Banquet of the Ten Virgins*. Translated by W. R. Clark. ANF 6. New York: Scribners, 1899.

Methodius. Edited by G. N. Bonwetsch. GCS 27. Leipzig: Hinrichs, 1897.

Minucius Felix. *Octavius: Lateinisch und Deutsch*. Edited by Bernhard Kytzler. Bibliotheca Scriptorum Graecorum et Romanorum Teubneriana. Leipzig: Teubner, 1982.

———. *Octavius / Uitgegeven in van Commentaar Voorzien*. Edited with notes by Gilles Quispel. Grieksche in Latijnsche Schrijvers 61. Leiden: Brill, 1949.

Montanist Oracles and Testimonia. Edited by Ronald Heine. Patristic Monograph Series 14. Macon, GA: Mercer University Press, 1989.

Montanist Inscriptions and Testimonia. Edited by W. Tabbernee. Patristic Monograph Series 16. Macon, GA: Mercer University Press, 1997.

Musurillo, Herbert. *The Acts of the Christian Martyrs: Introduction, Texts and Translations*. OECT. Oxford: Oxford University Press, 1972.

The Odes of Solomon. Edited and translated by James H. Charlesworth. SBL Texts and Translations 13. Chico, CA: Scholars, 1977.

Origen of Alexandria. *Against Celsus*. 2 vols. Translated by Frederick Crombie. ANL. Edinburgh: T. & T. Clark, 1872.

———. *Commentaire sur Saint Jean*. Tome 1. Edited and translated by Cécile Blanc. SC 120. Paris: Cerf, 1966.

———. *Commentary on John*. Translated by Allan Menzies. ANF 9. New York: Scribners, 1903.

———. *Commentary on Matthew*. Translated by John Patrick. ANF 9. New York: Scribners, 1903.

———. *Homilies on Genesis and Exodus*. Translated by Ronald Heine. FOC 71. Washington, DC: Catholic University of America, 1981.

———. *Homilies on Leviticus 1–16*. Translated by Gary W. Barkley. FOC 83. New York: Catholic University of America, 1990.

———. *Homilies on Luke*. Translated by Joseph Lienhard. FOC 94. Washington, DC: Catholic University of America, 1996.

———. *Homélies sur S. Luc*. Introduction, translation and notes by H. Crouzel, F. Fournier and P. Périchon. SC 87. Paris: Cerf, 1962.
———. *Homélies sur les Nombres*. Edited by Louis Doutreleau. SC 415. Paris: Cerf, 1996.
———. *On First Principles*. Translated by G.W. Butterworth. London: SPCK, 1936.
———. *Prayer, Exhortation to Martyrdom*. Translated and annotated by John O'Meara. ACW 19. New York: Newman, 1954.
Tatian. *Oratio ad Graecos and Fragments*. Edited and translated by Molly Whittaker. OECT Oxford: Oxford University Press, 1982.
Teaching of the Apostles (Syriac). Translated by B. P. Pratten. ANF 8. New York: Scribners, 1903.
Tertullian of Carthage. *Adversus Marcionem*. 2 vols. Edited and translated by Ernest Evans. OECT. Oxford: Oxford University Press, 1972.
———. *Apology and De Spectaculis* and Minucius Felix *Octavius*. Translated by T. R. Glover (Tertullian) and G.H. Rendall (Minucius). LCL 250. Cambridge: Harvard University Press, 1977.
———. *Contre Marcion*. 2 Vols. Edited by René Braun. SC 365, 368. Paris: Cerf, 1990–1991.
———. *Disciplinary, Moral and Ascetical Works*. Translated by Rudolph Arbesman et al. FOC 40. New York: Fathers of the Church, 1959.
———. *Exhortation to Chastity*. Translated by S. Thelwall. ANF IV, 50–58.
———. *Prescription against Heretics*. Translated by Peter Holmes. ANF III, 243–68.
———. *Tertullianus: Opera*. 2 Vols. I:*Opera Catholica; Adversus Marcionem*; II: *Opera Montanistica*. Edited by E. Dekkers et al. CCSL I–II. Turnhout: Brepols, 1954.
———. *Treatises on Marriage and Remarriage: To His Wife, An Exhortation to Chastity, On Monogamy*. Translated and annotated by W. P. Le Saint. ACW 13. New York: Newman, 1951.
———. *Treatises on Penance: On Penitence and On Purity*. Translated and annotated by W. P. Le Saint. ACW 28. New York: Newman, 1959.
Theophilus of Antioch. *Ad Autolycum*. Edited and translated by R.M. Grant. OECT. Oxford: Oxford University Press, 1970.

Secondary Sources for Pre-Constantinian Christianity

Bardy, Gustave. *Paul de Samosate*. 2nd ed. Specilegium Sacrum Lovaniense 4. Paris: Champion, 1923.
Barnes, Timothy. *Tertullian: A Historical and Literary Study*. Oxford: Oxford University Press,1971.
Bauer, Walter. *Orthodoxy and Heresy in Earliest Christianity*. 2nd ed. Edited by Robert Kraft and Gerhard Krodel. Philadelphia: Fortress, 1971.
Blackman, E. C. *Marcion and His Influence*. New York: AMS, 1978.
Bobertz, Charles. "Cyprian of Carthage: A Social Historical Study of the role of Bishop in the Ancient Christian Community of North Africa." PhD diss. Yale University, 1988.
Bowe, Barbara E. *A Church in Crisis: Ecclesiology and Paraenesis in Clement of Rome*. Harvard Dissertations in Religion 23. Minneapolis: Fortress, 1988.

Brown, Raymond E., and John P. Meier. *Antioch and Rome: New Testament Cradles of Catholic Christianity*. New York: Paulist, 1983.

Brown, Richard. "The Meaning of *epitugchano* in the Epistles of St. Ignatius of Antioch." *VC* 28 (1974) 1–14.

Bridge, Steven. "To Give or Not to Give: Deciphering the Saying of *Didache* 1.6." *JECS* 5 (1997) 555–68.

Burkitt, E.C. *Early Eastern Christianity*. London: Murray, 1904.

Burns, J. Patout. "On Rebaptism: Social Organization in the Third Century." *JECS* 1 (1993) 367–407.

Burrus, Virginia. "Rhetorical Stereotypes and the Portrait of Paul of Samosata." *VC* 43 (1989) 215–25.

Countryman, L. William. *The Rich Christian in the Church of the Early Empire: Contradictions and Accomodations*. Texts and Studies in Religion 7. New York: Mellen, 1980.

Crouzel, Henri. *Origen: The Life and Thought of the First Great Theologian*. San Francisco: Harper & Row, 1989.

Davies, Stevan L. "The Predicament of Ignatius of Antioch." *VC* 30 (1976) 175–80.

Donovan, Mary A. "Irenaeus in Recent Scholarship." *SC* 4 (1984) 219–41.

Drijvers, Han J. W. *East of Antioch: Studies in Early Syriac Christianity*. London: Variorum, 1984.

Faivre, Alexandre. *The Emergence of the Laity in the Early Church*. Translated by David Smith. New York: Paulist, 1990.

Frend, W. H. C. *The Early Church*. Philadelphia: Fortress, 1982.

Garrison, Roman. *Redemptive Almsgiving in Early Christianity*. JSNTSup 77. Sheffield, UK: JSOT Press, 1993.

Grant, Robert M. *Greek Apologists of the Second Century*. Philadelphia: Westminster, 1988.

Griffith, Sidney. "Asceticism in the Church of Syria: The Hermeneutics of Early Syrian Monasticism." In *Asceticism*, edited by Vincent Wimbush and Richard Valantasis, 220–45. Oxford: Oxford University Press, 1995.

Hawthorne, Gerald, ed. *Current Issues in Biblical and Patristic Interpretation*. Grand Rapids: Eerdmans, 1975.

Hagner, Donald A. *The Use of the Old and New Testaments in Clement of Rome*. NovTSup 34. Leiden: Brill, 1973.

Harnack, A. von. *Entstehung und Entwickelung der Kirchenverfassung des Kirchenrechts in den zwei ersten Jahrhunderten*. Urchristentum und Katholismus. Leipzig: Hinrichs, 1910.

———. *Marcion: The Gospel of the Alien God*. Translated by J. Seely and L. Bierma. Durham, NC: Labyrinth, 1990.

Hinson, E. G. *The Evangelization of the Roman Empire: Identity and Adaptability*. Macon, GA: Mercer University Press, 1981.

Horsley, G.H.R. et al., editors. *New Documents Illustrating Early Christianity: A Review of the Greek Inscriptions and Papyri*. 9 vols. North Ryde, NSW: Macquarie University Press, 1981–2002.

Hoffman, R. Joseph. *Marcion: On the Restitution of Christianity. An Essay on the Development of Radical Paulinist Theology in the Second Century*. AAR Academy Series 46. Chico, CA: Scholars, 1984.

Kannengiesser, Charles, and William Peterson, editors. *Origen of Alexandria: His World and His Legacy.* Notre Dame: University of Notre Dame Press, 1988.

Kinder, Donald. "Clement of Alexandria: Conflicting Views on Women." *SC* 7 (1989-90) 213-20.

Klawiter, F. C. "The Role of Martyrdom and Persecution in Developing the Priestly Authority of Women in Early Christianity: A Case Study of Montanism." *Church History* 49 (1980) 251-61.

Klijn, A. "Christianity in Edessa and the Gospel of Thomas." *NovT* 14 (1972) 70-77.

Livingstone, Elizabeth, ed. *Studia Patristica.* Vol. 17. Oxford: Pergamon, 1982.

———. *Studia Patristica.* Vols. 19-23. Leuven: Peeters, 1989.

Maier, Harry. "Purity and Danger in Polycarp's Epistle: The Sin of Valens in Social Perspective." *JECS* 1 (1993) 229247.

———. *The Social Setting of the Ministry as Reflected in the Writings of Hermas, Clement and Ignatius.* Dissertations SR 1. Waterloo, ON: Wilfred Laurier University Press, 1991.

Methuen, Charlotte. "Widows, Bishops and the Struggle for Authority in the Didascalia Apostolorum." *Journal of Ecclesiastical History* 46 (1995) 197-213.

Millar, Fergus. "Paul of Samosata, Zenobia and Aurelian: The Church, Local Culture and Political Allegiance in Third Century Syria." *Journal of Roman Studies* 61 (1971) 1-17.

Mühlenberg, Ekkehard. "Marcion's Jealous God." In *Disciplina Nostra: Essays in Memory of Robert P. Evans,* edited by Donald F. Winslow, 93-113. PMS 6. Cambridge, MA: Philadelphia Patristic Foundation, 1977.

Norris, Frederick. "Paul of Samosata: Procurator Ducenarius." *Journal of Theological Studies* 35 (1984) 50-70.

Osborn, Eric. "Clement of Alexandria: A Review of Research 1958-1982." *Second Century* 3 (1893) 219-44.

Osiek, Carolyn. Rich *and Poor in the Shepherd of Hermas: An Exegetical-Social Investigation.* Catholic Biblical Quarterly Monograph 15. Washington, DC: Catholic Biblical Association, 1983.

Pernveden, Lage. *The Concept of the Church in the Shepherd of Hermas.* Studia theologica Lundensia 27. Lund: Gleerup, 1966.

Petterson, A. "Perpetua—Prisoner of Conscience." *VC* 41 (1987) 139-53.

Powell, Douglas. "Tertullianists and Cataphrygians." *VC* 29 (1975) 33-54.

Reiling, J. *Hermas and Christian Prophecy: A Study of the Eleventh Mandate.* NovTSup 37. Leiden: Brill, 1973.

Schoedel, William R. *Ignatius of Antioch: A Commentary on the Letters of Ignatius of Antioch.* Hermeneia. Philadelphia: Fortress, 1985.

Scourfield, J. H. "The *De mortalite* of Cyprian." *VC* 50 (1996) 12-41.

Segal, J. B. *Edessa: "The Blessed City."* Oxford: Oxford University Press, 1970.

Sevenster, J. N. *Paul and Seneca.* NovTSup 4. Leiden: Brill, 1961.

Sider, Robert. "Approaches to Tertullian: A Study of Recent Scholarship." *SC* 2 (1982) 228-60.

Trevett, Christine. *Montanism: Gender, Authority and the New Prophecy.* Cambridge: Cambridge University Press, 1996.

———. "Prophecy and Anti-Episcopal Activity: A Third Error Combatted by Ignatius." *Journal of Ecclesiastical History* 34 (1983) 1-18.

Wilken, Robert, editor. *Aspects of Wisdom in Judaism and Early Christianity*. University of Notre Dame Center for the Study of Judaism and Christianity in Antiquity 1. Notre Dame: University of Notre Dame Press, 1975.

Wilson, J. Christian. *Toward a Reassessment of the Shepherd of Hermas: Its Date and Pneumatology*. Lewiston, NY: Mellen Biblical Press, 1993.

www.ingramcontent.com/pod-product-compliance
Lightning Source LLC
Chambersburg PA
CBHW060609230426
43670CB00011B/2033